Teach Me about God

Teach Me about God

The Meaning and Significance of the Name of God

WALTER ORENSTEIN

JASON ARONSON
Lanham • Boulder • New York • Toronto • Oxford

Published in the United States of America
by Jason Aronson
An imprint of Rowman & Littlefield Publishers, Inc.
A wholly owned subsidiary of
The Rowman & Littlefield Publishing Group, Inc.
4501 Forbes Boulevard, Suite 200, Lanham, Maryland 20706
www.rowmanlittlefield.com

P.O. Box 317, Oxford OX2 9RU, UK

Copyright © 2005 by Walter Orenstein

All rights reserved. No part of this publication may be reproduced, stored in a retrieval system, or transmitted in any form or by any means, electronic, mechanical, photocopying, recording, or otherwise, without the prior permission of the publisher.

British Library Cataloguing in Publication Information Available

Library of Congress Cataloging-in-Publication Data
Orenstein, Walter.
  Teach me about God / Walter Orenstein.
    p.   cm.
  Includes bibliographical references and index.
  ISBN 0-7657-6188-2 (alk. paper) — ISBN 0-7657-0011-5 (pbk. : alk. paper)
    1. God (Judaism) I. Title.
BM610 .O74 2005
296.3'11—dc21

00-052184

Printed in the United States of America

∞™ The paper used in this publication meets the minimum requirements of American National Standard for Information Sciences—Permanence of Paper for Printed Library Materials, ANSI/NISO Z39.48-1992.

CONTENTS

Preface	vii
Acknowledgments	ix
Introduction	xi
1. The Significance of the Names of God	1
2. The Thirteen Divine Attributes	23
3. The God of Adam and Noah	39
4. The God of the Patriarchs	55
5. The God of Moses	113
6. The Meaning and Significance of Providence	185
7. When God Relates to Man	217
8. When Man Relates to God	235
Index	257

PREFACE

As children we were told that there is a God in Heaven, that He created the world and its inhabitants, that He looks down from His Heavenly abode and keeps an eye on His children below. Most of us pictured God as an old man with a long white beard and a flowing white robe perched on a white cloud in the Heavens above. As we matured, we slowly but surely began to lose confidence in the image of God we had conjured up in our minds, so that by the time we were teenagers we totally rejected it as childish anthropomorphism. Alas, for most of us there was no image to take its place. God's essence was simply unimaginable.

I was a sixteen-year-old yeshiva student when I began to delve into the fundamentals of Jewish philosophy. Very much concerned with the concept of God and His relationship to the world, I questioned my teachers, but I met with little success. These matters were considered off-limits in the yeshiva. That God exists and is concerned with the world is a "given" never to be questioned or even probed by the young, and rightly so. God has revealed the Torah to the Jewish people, and they are obligated to study it by day and by night in order to master its tenets and learn how to observe the laws properly. This, too, is a given. There were no differences of opinion among the faculty, and as such there was no need for discussion on these matters. As students, we were to concern ourselves with the study of the Torah, the Talmud, and the Codes of Jewish law, a task with which we were occupied for most of the day. In point of fact, there was simply no time to delve into the esoteric. Those of us who were persistent were referred by our Rebbe (teacher) to the philosophic works of Saadya Gaon,[1] Judah HaLevi,[2] and Maimonides[3] and left to fend for ourselves.

Needless to say, with no training in philosophy the ideas put forth in these works were extremely difficult to follow. The fact that some of the references had been translated into English did not help matters very much. Some of us who undertook the challenge and spent long hours working through the philosophical texts, namely, proofs for the existence of God, the meaning of providence, reward, and punishment, and the like, met with some success; others who were not as bright simply lost patience and gave up the pursuit. Attributing their failure to immaturity, the "lost ones" vowed to pick up their philosophical inquiries later in life, hoping that as adults they would be better equipped to handle them. After all, the Talmud teaches us: "Do not inquire into things that are too difficult for you, do not search what is hidden from you; study what you are allowed to study and do not occupy yourself with mysteries."[4]

This volume is an attempt to present some ideas about God and the way He relates to the world. It is written in layman's language that can be understood even by those who have a limited background in Jewish philosophy. The material is based entirely on traditional Jewish sources: the Bible, the Talmud, the Midrash, and both the medieval and the modern Jewish philosophers. With the exception of direct quotes where the names of God have been translated for literary considerations, the Hebrew names of the Supreme Being have been transliterated.

---

1. Saadia ben Joseph, *The Book of Beliefs and Opinions*.
2. Judah Halevy, *The Kuzari*.
3. Moses Maimonides, *The Guide of the Perplexed*.
4. *Hagigah* 13a.

ACKNOWLEDGMENTS

I wish to express my appreciation and thanks to my wife, Nellie, for editing the manuscript and offering some important creative suggestions for its improvement. Most of all, I wish to thank her for the constant encouragement she has given me in all my literary efforts.

INTRODUCTION

One would be hard pressed to find a more formidable challenge to man's intelligence, his imagination, and his ability to reason than that which is posed by the Bible, the record of the "encounter" between God and man. Some have dared to ask; others, not so bold, have merely contemplated: Is the record credible? Does God exist? If God does exist, what is the nature of His essence? Finally, given that God exists, how does He relate to the world at large and man in particular?

Philosophers and theologians have pondered the meaning and significance of God and man's place in the universe from earliest times. Some have focused their efforts on metaphysics; others have concentrated on man, suggesting ideas on the purpose of man's existence in this world and the obligations that are incumbent upon him in that regard; still others have concerned themselves exclusively with the nature of providence. Be that as it may, one can say with relative certainty that every human being at one time or another has pondered the matter of God's existence and the way in which He relates to the world. Indeed, it was the great sage Moses Maimonides who opened his *magnum opus* the *Mishneh Torah* with the words: "The basic principle of all basic principles and the pillar of all wisdom is to know that there is a First Being who brought every existing thing into being."[1]

To the traditional Jew, of course, God's existence is not a matter open

---

1. M. Maimonides, *Mishneh Torah*, trans. M. Hyamson (Jerusalem: Boys Town Jerusalem, 1965), chap. 1:1.

Introduction

to question or investigation; it is a given. Nonetheless, we shall present some of the arguments commonly referred to as "proofs for the existence of God," if for no other reason than to strengthen the conviction of those who need the support of reason. Not so, the nature of the Divine essence. Despite the vast knowledge that man has acquired through the centuries, notwithstanding the monumental advances he has made in science and technology and his ever-increasing understanding of the scheme of things in the universe, he is no closer to knowing the essence of God than were his ancestors. The truth of the matter is that man simply lacks the intellectual capacity to comprehend the essence of God.

Providence, i.e., God's concern with the universe and His regard for man in particular, is another matter. Providence is clearly evident from the Bible. Literally hundreds of biblical verses speak directly to this issue. From among them, we have selected those that are most revealing of the Divine attributes, and we have expounded upon them. We have shown how the names of God as interpreted by our sages from ancient to modern times are symbolic of these Divine attributes. We have also demonstrated the relevance of the names to the issue or issues spoken of in the text. We have discussed the meaning of Divine providence and given illustrations from the books of the Prophets and the Writings as interpreted by our sages. Lastly, we have shown how God relates to man through the medium of prophecy and how man relates to God through prayer and *mitzvot*.

Before we begin this treatise, however, we must focus on two important issues: the relationship between revelation and reason, and the proofs for the existence of God.

REVELATION AND REASON

In Genesis 1:26 we read: "And God created man in His image; in the image of God He created him." According to Maimonides and others, what is meant by the "image of God" is man's intellectual capacity and

Introduction

his ability to reason.[2] No other creature has been so generously endowed. It is man's ability to reason that has enabled him to probe the workings of the universe, to examine the nature of reality, and to discover thereby God's hand in all existing things. In Psalm 19:2 we read: "The heavens declare the glory of God, the sky proclaims His handiwork." What does this mean? The unbiased pursuit of reason in studying the universe will ultimately lead to the discovery of God's hand. The discovery of God's hand in nature leads to an appreciation of the wonders of nature. The fact that God has given us the opportunity to live in the world and to derive benefit from these wonders leads to the love of God and the insatiable desire to praise Him for His beneficence.

Be that as it may, there is another way to come to know God; it is through revelation. It is one thing to conceptualize a First Cause; it is quite another to perceive the Supreme Being in a personal encounter. The fruits of reason are the result of an initiative taken by man; the fruits of revelation are the result of an initiative taken by God. There are limitations to what man is capable of discovering about God through reason. What God chooses to reveal to man about the nature of reality, man's designated place in the world, and the significance and the ramifications of providence is potentially unlimited.

There are those who suggest that the only conclusion that one can derive about God from reason is that He is unknowable. They further contend that as such the only reliable knowledge of God derives from revelation, namely, the encounter between God and the prophets and the one-time encounter between God and the nation of Israel when the Torah was revealed at Sinai.[3] Others add that the knowledge of God and His rule imparted by revelation would have taken the philosophers and theologians of the world centuries to discover on their own had they had to rely on the process of reason alone. Comparing reason to revelation, Isidore Epstein comments most succinctly, "Revelation is a short and more direct route to truth."[4] Of course, there is an additional advantage of revelation over reason: it provides the masses with truths that they

---

2. Cf. M. Maimonides, *Guide of the Perplexed* (New York: Hebrew Publishing Company), Part I, chap. i, p. 32, and D. Kimhi, commentary on Genesis 1:26.

3. Cf. I. Epstein, *The Faith of Judaism* (London: Soncino Press, 1954), p. 81.

4. Ibid., p. 84.

could never discover on their own, either because they lack the intellectual capacity to do so or because they simply lack the time.

Jewish tradition avers that in the final analysis revelation must override reason. The patriarch Abraham already set the precedent for this principle in the biblical narrative of the "Binding of Isaac."[5] Instructed by God to bring his son Isaac as an offering, Abraham was confronted with the most difficult decision of his life. Should he follow his heart and spare his son or should he comply with the Divine charge? Reason would dictate the former. Had God not promised him, "It is through Isaac that offspring shall be continued for you?"[6] Besides, human sacrifice is clearly an act of murder; Jewish law forbids it.[7] But for Abraham to choose not to comply with the Divine charge would have been an incomparable expression of hubris. It would have been a declaration of the infallibility of human reason, and it would have established the precedent that in the final analysis man's will should prevail over the will of God. By choosing to comply with the Divine charge, Abraham demonstrated the limitations of human understanding and the superiority of revelation over reason.

As we have pointed out, reason can best establish that there is a First Cause. Some might go so far as to posit that it could establish that there is a "guide" or "controlling force" in the universe.[8] But reason alone cannot lead to religion. Religion is founded on the premise that God and man can relate to one another. Reason cannot engender such a relationship. Religion can only be established by revelation. Note the incisive remark by I. Epstein in this regard:

> The essential nature of the religious belief that marks it off sharply from the mere theism arrived at by philosophy is the assumption of a personal relationship between man and God. "Thou shalt call and the Lord will answer; thou shalt cry and He will say, 'Here I am' "

---

5. Genesis Chapter 22.
6. Genesis 20:12.
7. Cf. *Yoma* 28b. Although it might be argued that the Torah had not yet been revealed to Israel, Abraham fulfilled the commandments on a voluntary basis. Besides, the prohibition of murder is one of the Noahide commands, which apply to all people.
8. Cf. J. Halevi, *Kuzari* (New York: Pardes, 1946), part IV, no. 15.

Introduction

(Isaiah 48:9). This close relationship which religion with varying force and clearness has ever sought to affirm is . . . the true secret of religion's overwhelming hold over the human heart in all ages.[9]

THE PROOFS FOR THE EXISTENCE OF GOD

To speak of Divine attributes is to assume that God exists, and although some philosophers have challenged the validity of this assumption, others, both Jewish and non-Jewish, have offered proofs to confirm God's existence. Brief mention of some of the arguments for the existence of God is certainly in order.

The more frustrating the quest to explain the mysteries of life becomes, the more evident it is that man's perception of reality is limited both in depth and in scope. The more perplexing is the enigma of man's survival in a world that seems bent on self-destruction, the more convincing is the contention that there exists a Supreme Being whose will ultimately prevails and whose providential hand plays a major role in the determination of man's destiny. The words of Robert Browning ring loud and clear:

> The year's at the spring and the day's at the morn;
> Morning's at seven; the hillside dew pearled;
> The lark's on the wing; the snail's on the thorn;
> God's in His Heaven—all's right with the world.[10]

Much to the dismay of every decent human being, man has not chosen to use his intelligence and his freedom of will, the sublime gifts with which he has been endowed by his Creator, to attain the greatest good for the greatest number of people. Alas, left to man alone, in all likelihood society would not have survived to the twenty-first century. It is the inscrutable will of God that has preserved the human species. As we move further into the twenty-first century, these words become

---

9. I. Epstein, op. cit., pp. 99–100.
10. R. Browning, *Pippa Passes*, Part I.

more and more evident. Perhaps this in itself is the best argument for God's existence.

There are three well-known proofs for the existence of God. They are commonly referred to by the philosophers as: the cosmological argument, the teleological argument, and the ontological argument.

The Cosmological Argument

The cosmological argument asserts the following: We know from experience that everything in the world is the result of the process of causation, namely, all existing things are caused by or dependent upon other existing things. For example, we walk along the beach and notice seashells in the sand. How did they get there? The waters swept them onto the shore. What caused the waters to do this? It was the ebb and flow of the tides. But the tides do not operate independently. They are caused by the attraction of the moon and the sun, which itself has a cause. Take the daily newspaper. It was printed (caused) by sophisticated printing presses. These presses were constructed (caused) and operated by man. To the query, "Who caused man?" one might answer, "His parents," and so on. To put it simply, *Everything has a cause*! But how did this process of cause and effect begin? There had to have been an original or "first cause," what some call a "Prime Mover," whose existence is independent of any cause. This Prime Mover we call "God." Parenthetically, one must recognize that this argument only contends that there is a Prime Mover. It does not suggest that this Prime Mover has any attributes nor does it suggest that it has any special relationship to the universe in general or to man in particular other than being the Prime Mover.

The Teleological Argument

The teleological argument for the existence of God focuses on the implication of design in the universe. For example, would anyone contend that a clock is merely a conglomeration of different parts that operate independently and tell time merely by chance? Would an observer of a towering skyscraper insist that its parts came together spontaneously? Who would contend that the music of an opera or a symphony is simply a random series of notes? It is obvious to every rational person that these are all works designed and constructed by man. *Design implies a designer!* The teleological argument or the argument by design, as it is commonly referred to, asserts the following: We know from experience that there is design in the universe. The revolution of the planets around the sun, the incessant pattern of the seasons and the coordinated systems of plant, animal, and human life all imply that there is a purposive mind who designed the universe, whose "watchful eye" sees to it that this design in nature does not cease. This purposive mind is called "God."

The Ontological Argument

The ontological argument for the existence of God is addressed to anyone who uses the term "God." Based on the principle that the more numerous the attributes of a particular creature or being the greater is its perfection, the argument asserts the following: The name "God" means "the Being greater than which nothing can be conceived." Given this definition, God must exist. For if God does not exist, one can conceive of a Being greater or more perfect than God, namely, a God who exists.

It is interesting to note that the medieval Jewish philosophers focused on the cosmological argument for the existence of God. It is found in the works of Saadya Gaon,[11] Maimonides,[12] Bahya Ibn Pekudah,[13] Hisdai Crescas,[14] and Joseph Albo.[15] The teleological

---

11. Cf. Saadya Gaon, *Beliefs and Opinions*, trans. by S. Rosenblatt, vol. 1 (New Haven: Yale University Press, 1948), p. 46.
12. M. Maimonides, *Mishneh Torah*, op. cit., Part II, Introduction and chap. i.
13. Bahya Ibn Pekudah, *Duties of the Heart*, trans. by M. Hyamson (New York: Feldheim Publishers, 1970), *Shaar HaYihud*, chap. v.
14. H. Crescas, *Light of the Lord* (Vienna, 1856), Book II Part 3, chap. ii, pp. 40b–41a.

argument was given by some to reinforce the cosmological argument or as evidence of providence, but it seems that it was never relied on to prove God's existence.[16] The ontological argument is not found at all in Jewish sources.

There are three other arguments for the existence of God, and it behooves us to mention them as well. They are: the argument from morality, the argument from religious experience, and the argument from tradition.[17]

The Argument from Morality

The concept of right and wrong exists in every society. While the standard by which these terms are defined may differ from one group to another, every society recognizes the need to define and enforce proper behavior, for without enforceable laws society could not long endure. In point of fact, every human being knows in his heart that some things are intrinsically right while others are intrinsically wrong. But from where does this sense of morality derive? An act that society designates as "proper" is not always a pleasant experience. It may be difficult to perform as well. Conversely, an act designated as "improper" may be quite pleasurable and easy to perform. Clearly, the "ought" or sense of duty that motivates an individual to act or refrain from acting in a particular way is not predicated on how difficult or how pleasant that act may be. What then is it that motivates man to be moral or ethical in his behavior? One must conclude that man's sense of "right" derives from an outside force. This outside force that has implanted morality in man is the Supreme Being of the universe.

---

15. J. Albo, *Sefer HaIkarim* (Philadelphia: Jewish Publication Society, 1946), Book II, chaps. iv and v.

16. Cf. H. A. Wolfson, "Notes on Proofs for the Existence of God in Jewish Philosophy," H.U.C. Annual, vol. I, 1924, pp. 573–583.

17. Cf. L. Jacobs, *Principles of the Jewish Faith* (New York: Basic Books, 1964), pp. 46–49.

Introduction

The Argument from Religious Experience

Of major import in this argument is the fact that testimony as to the authenticity of the religious experience derives from written statements by the prophets of Israel. From their writings, it is quite evident that the prophets of Israel were men of great intellect and unimpeachable moral integrity. They prophesied what they claimed was revealed to them by God. Often putting their lives on the line, they brought ominous messages from God to the kings of Israel. Were the prophets trustworthy? Was their religious experience an authentic one? Is their testimony to the existence of God reliable? The most logical answer would have to be "yes." For if men of such caliber cannot be trusted and are suspect of being charlatans or of having themselves been deceived by their zealousness and their vivid imagination, the meaning of trust and the ability of man to discover the nature of reality is seriously brought into question.

The Argument from Tradition

The argument from tradition pivots on the credibility of a tradition that has been transmitted from father to son and from teacher to student for thousands of years. This tradition posits that God revealed the Torah to Moses on Mount Sinai in the sight of the entire nation of Israel. The people of Israel accepted the Torah and committed themselves and their children as well as all future generations to observe the 613 commandments of the Torah as a way of life. Is this tradition credible? Needless to say, credibility in this regard would simultaneously establish the existence of God. Let us look at it from a historical perspective. Jews the world over have maintained a commitment to this tradition through the generations. They have made the Torah their way of life. Despite the persecution, suffering, and humiliation they had to endure in many of the countries of their dispersion, knowing full well that were they to renounce Judaism and convert to another religion they could live in peace, they remained loyal to the religion of their forefathers. Had this

Introduction

tradition been merely a myth, it could never have inspired such loyalty among the brilliant and insightful leaders of the Jewish people nor among the masses.

THE SURVIVAL OF ISRAEL

Lastly, we must consider the matter of the survival of the nation of Israel. Through the course of history, great nations have faded into memory, vast empires have fallen, and whole civilizations have vanished. One nation alone has defied this unwritten rule of history—the nation of Israel. Clearly the smallest of nations, to the student of history this phenomenon is truly an enigma. Israel is a nation that was born out of slavery. It spent the first forty years of its history without a homeland, wandering aimlessly in the wilderness waiting for the time to arrive when it would inherit the Promised Land of Canaan. In about the twelfth century B.C.E. Israel became a people with a land of their own, but they were not destined to abide there for very long. In 586 B.C.E. the holy Temple in Jerusalem was destroyed and the Jews were exiled to Babylonia. Seventy years later, they were permitted to return. They settled the land and rebuilt the Temple, but in 70 C.E. an invading Roman enemy destroyed the Temple and the Judean kingdom fell once again. For close to 2,000 years the Jewish people have lived with the dream of returning to the land of Israel, their God-given homeland. Not until our day was this dream fulfilled.

What held the Jews together during this 2,000-year exile? How has Israel been able to survive through the centuries when nations far greater in number could not escape the hand of destiny and have perished? Many historians have sought a rationale for this enigma, but they have all come up empty-handed. Only the believer, the person of faith, can offer a plausible explanation. It was the Divinely ordained destiny of the nation of Israel that enabled it to survive through the centuries. It was in order to fulfill its mission to be a kingdom of priests and a holy nation that it was given Divine protection. It was to set the example of morality in the world that God preserved them. Note the words of God to Moses in Exodus 19:3–5:

Introduction

> Thus shall you say to the house of Jacob and declare to the children of Israel. You have seen what I did to the Egyptians, how I bore you on eagles' wings and brought you to Me. Now then, if you will obey Me and keep My covenant, you shall be My treasured possession among all the peoples. Indeed, all the Earth is Mine, but you shall be to Me a kingdom of priests and a holy nation . . . All the people answered as one saying, "All that the Lord has spoken we will do."

The example that was to be set by the Jewish people through the generations was intended as a lesson for all of mankind. Defining the mission of the Jew, Rabbi Samson Raphael Hirsch explains that the relationship of the Jewish people to God is as His exclusive treasure. The obligation to become completely and exclusively God's possession in every phase of one's being is the obligation that all human beings should and will eventually take upon themselves. For all of the world belongs to God and the time will come when each and every nation will recognize this truth and will commit itself to God and to be educated by God's law.[18]

Indeed, the survival of the Jewish people is no enigma. They have survived because it is God's will that they survive. The Jewish nation lives! Perhaps this reality is the best argument of all for the existence of God.

Despite the fact that the proofs and the arguments for the existence of God that we have presented are logical, and to some even convincing, none of them is perfect. One may be stronger than another, but they all have weaknesses. Were one to discover a perfect, unimpeachable proof for the existence of God, there would no longer be any room for doubt. The existence of God would not be a matter of belief; it would be a fact. Only a total fool would reject that which can be proved absolutely. Nevertheless, these and other such proofs and arguments have rendered the matter of God's existence reasonable. Ultimately, one must rely on faith. Perhaps it is better that way. To have faith that God exists

---

18. S. R. Hirsch, Commentary on the Torah (London: Isaac Levy, 1956), Exodus 19:5.

and to commit oneself to live in strict accordance with that faith takes a great deal of courage and self-sacrifice. It is testimony to man's nobility, a badge of honor to be worn proudly by the faithful.

Given that God exists, that He created the world, and that He is concerned with that which He has created, how does this effect one's life? Knowing God leads to love of God, and love of God engenders a strong commitment to obey God's word. Let us explain this process.

In Deuteronomy 6:5 we are enjoined: "You must love the Lord your God with all your heart and with all your soul and with all your might." Maimonides comments:

> And what is the way that will lead to love of Him . . . When a person contemplates His great and wondrous works and creatures and from them obtains a glimpse of His wisdom, which is incomparable and infinite, he will immediately love Him, praise Him, glorify Him and long with exceeding longing to know His great name; as David said, "My soul thirsts for God, for the living God" (Psalm 42:3) . . . Even as our sages have remarked in connection with the love of God, "Observe the universe and hence, you will realize Him who spoke and the world was."[19]

According to Maimonides, contemplation of the Divine wisdom made manifest in the universe leads to love of God. The overwhelming experience of the wonders of nature and the knowledge that comes from an understanding of the multiplicity of systems that work together harmoniously in nature to benefit and preserve the universe engenders within man a feeling of awe and this leads to an all-encompassing love of God. Even more, writes Maimonides,

> One only loves God with the knowledge with which one knows Him. According to the knowledge will be the love. If the former be little or much so will the latter be little or much. A person ought therefore devote himself to the understanding and comprehension

---

19. M. Maimonides, *Mishneh Torah*, op. cit., Book of Knowledge 2:1, 2.

Introduction

of those sciences and studies which will inform him concerning his Master, as far as it lies in human faculties to understand and comprehend.[20]

Love in turn inspires man to praise God for His wondrous works, and engenders the desire to know Him in as many ways as He can be known by the human mind. The more knowledgeable man becomes in the processes that are operative in nature the more sophisticated is his understanding of the universe and the greater is his awe and love of God.[21]

It is important to recognize that belief in the existence of God does not in and of itself lead to religion. Unless God is concerned with man there can be no religion. For the pillar of religion, indeed, its most fundamental principle is "relating." God relates to man and man relates to God. If God exists, but He is not at all concerned with man, what practical difference would it make whether man believes that He exists or not? If there was no such thing as providence, God's existence would be totally irrelevant to man. It would certainly be of no practical concern to him. In light of this, we must pose the question, "What evidence is there that God is truly concerned with man?"

There is no doubt that the most impressive evidence of God's concern is the Torah. The Torah is a code of absolute ethics and morality that speaks to every aspect of interpersonal relations and has been demonstrated to be relevant to all situations in the past as well as the present. The fact that God has revealed the Torah to the nation of Israel is significant evidence that He is concerned with the human species, not only with its survival but with its happiness as well. In point of fact, not only does the study of nature lead to the love of God, the study of Torah does as well. Maimonides himself writes: "Love is the result of the truths taught in the Torah, including the knowledge of the existence of God."[22] Aharon HaLevi also makes the point:

---

20. Ibid., 10:6.
21. Cf. Ovadia ben David, commentary entitled *"Perush"* on *Mishneh Torah: Foundations of the Torah 2:1*.
22. M. Maimonides, *Guide of the Perplexed*, op. cit., Part III, chap. lii, p. 296.

> We were commanded to love God as it is written, "You shall love the Lord your God etc." This means to contemplate on His works and decrees thus maximizing our potential to comprehend Him, deriving thereby the utmost spiritual pleasure. This is our love obligation. The *Sifre* writes: It is written: "And you shall love," but how does one love [God]? What follows is "And these words shall be upon your heart." In this way you will recognize Him who spoke and the world came into existence. In other words, study of the Torah will implant within your heart the love [of God]. Our sages say that this love will motivate one to influence others to love God as well.[23]

Once love of God has been attained, whether through contemplation of the universe or the study of Torah, a new approach to Torah study emerges. Again, Maimonides writes:

> Whoever serves God out of love, occupies himself with the study of the Torah and the fulfillment of the commandments and walks in the paths of wisdom, impelled by no external motive whatsoever, moved neither by fear of calamity nor by the desire to obtain material benefits; such a man does what is truly right because it is truly right, and, ultimately happiness comes to him as a result of his conduct. This standard is, indeed, a very high one; not every sage attained to it . . . When one loves God with the right love, he will immediately observe all the commandments out of love.[24]

The highest level of serving the Supreme Being is out of love. To love God means to fulfill the *mitzvot* simply because He has commanded them. It is to obey God without ulterior motives or preconceived notions regarding the benefits, material or otherwise, that may incur by fulfilling the *mitzvot*. Understandably, obedience of this kind is a noble goal perhaps potentially attainable by all, yet attained by very few. Maimonides further explains:

---

23. Aharon HaLevi, *Sefer HaHinukh: Mitzvah 418*.
24. M. Maimonides, *Mishneh Torah: Laws of Repentance*, 10:3.

Introduction

> One should pursue the powers of the soul to the utmost of his intellectual ability . . . with one goal, i.e., to perceive God as fully as is humanly possible and direct all his efforts when in motion or at rest to that goal. His eating, drinking, sleeping, etc., should all be oriented toward attaining a healthy body. The purpose of attaining a healthy body should be to provide the best means for the soul to attain the greatest wisdom. As such he will not pursue bodily pleasure as a goal but rather as a means. This is what God asks of us and is implied in His words, "You shall love the Lord your God etc . . ." Our sages implied this principle to its fullest capacity in their brief but concise statement: "And all your deeds shall be for the sake of Heaven" (Ethics of the Fathers 2:12).[25]

We refer to God as our Father who is in Heaven (*Avinu she-ba-Shamayim*). The love of a child for his father inspires obedience to his word. In a similar manner the love of God, whether it is brought on by contemplation of God's works or the study of the Torah, inspires obedience to His word. To the Jew, obedience means commitment to the 613 *mitzvot* and fulfillment of as many of them as are applicable in a particular age. To the non-Jew, obedience means commitment to the seven Noahide commandments.[26]

To love God is to walk in His ways. The child/father analogy applies here as well. Just as a child who admires his father learns from his ways and mimics him so, too, should man learn from the ways of God and pattern his behavior accordingly. In Deuteronomy 13:5 we read: "After the Lord your God shall you walk, and revere none but Him; observe His commandments alone, and heed only His orders; worship none but Him, and hold fast none to Him." On this verse the Talmud teaches the following lesson.

> "After the Lord your God shall you walk." What does the text mean? Is it then possible for a human being to walk after the Presence [of God]; for has it not been said, "For the Lord your God

---

25. M. Maimonides, Introduction to *Ethics of the Fathers*, chap. v.
26. See Chapter IV for a list of these commandments.

is a devouring fire"?[27] But [the meaning is] to walk after the attributes of the Holy One, blessed be He. As He clothes the naked, for it is written, "And the Lord God made for Adam and his wife garments of skin and clothed them,"[28] so should you clothe the naked. The Holy One, blessed be He visited the sick, for it is written, "And the Lord appeared to him by the oaks of Mamre,"[29] so should you also visit the sick.[30]

Divine compassion manifests itself more than casually in the life of every human being. We have only to sensitize ourselves to recognize it. The Talmud makes the point that the ways of God are compassionate; they serve as a lesson to man. Man must learn from the example set by the Supreme Being of the universe. He must be concerned with his fellow man with no regard for race or creed. He must offer to help in time of need and always treat his fellow man with compassion. To do so is to actualize one's moral potential as a human being created in God's image. More importantly, it is to contribute to the perfection of society, for concern and compassion are infectious. By assimilating Divine qualities, man becomes a partner with God in Creation.

There is an interesting interpretation of a Talmudic statement on the thirteen Divine attributes. In Exodus 34:6 we read: "The Lord passed before him [Moses] and proclaimed: The Lord the Lord! A God compassionate and gracious, slow to anger, rich in steadfast kindness . . ." On this verse the Talmud teaches the following:

> R. Johanan said: "Were it not written in the text it would be impossible for us to say such a thing; this verse teaches us that the Holy One blessed be He drew His robe round Him like the reader of a congregation and showed Moses the order of prayer. He said to him: 'Whenever Israel sin let them carry out this service before Me and I will forgive them . . .'" R. Judah said: "A covenant has

---

27. Deuteronomy 4:24.
28. Genesis 3:21.
29. Genesis 18. Since the preceding verses deal with Abraham's circumcision, the sages deduced that God's visit took place when Abraham was recovering.
30. *Sotah* 14a.

been made with the thirteen attributes that they will never be turned away empty handed."[31]

It would not at all be presumptuous to ask: "Is it not true that there have been many people throughout the generations who have recited these words but were not successful in obtaining atonement?" Could this be due to a misinterpretation of the God's words to Moses? The text does not say "read" (*imru*) this service but "do" (*asu*) this service. One must incorporate the Divine attributes into one's personality and treat one's fellow man accordingly. Then, and only then, does one merit Divine forgiveness for one's sins.[32]

Let us now proceed to the matter of the names of God and their significance.

---

31. *Rosh Hashanah* 17b.
32. *Etz Yosef* commentary ad loc.

1

THE SIGNIFICANCE OF THE NAMES OF GOD

When speaking of names, the first thing that comes to mind is the familiar words of William Shakespeare: "What's in a name? That which we call a rose by any other name would smell as sweet."[1] Upon reflection, one wonders to what extent if at all this statement of the bard is true. Perhaps it needs clarification or qualification. It is certainly true that for all intents and purposes a person's character is not affected by the name he is given at birth. It is equally true that the characteristics of an animal or the qualities of an object are in no way affected by the name they bear, for names are merely descriptive. Nevertheless, names do make a difference.

There are names that classify or indicate definitive characteristics that are common to all that bear such names. For example, by definition, *all* mammals have milk-secreting glands to suckle their young. A creature that lacks such glands is simply not a mammal. To call

---

1. William Shakespeare, *Romeo and Juliet*, Act II Scene II, line 43.

it a mammal would be a misnomer. By definition, *all* vertebrates have spinal columns. A creature that lacks a spinal column is not a vertebrate. To call it a vertebrate would be a misnomer. The classification of metal as fourteen-karat gold differentiates it from other metals and designates its value. The name *human being* distinguishes man from all other creatures by virtue of his ability to speak and to reason abstractly.

NAMING A CHILD

There are many things that we can learn about people and their culture from the names they give to their children at birth. Fifty years ago, Jewish children born in the United States who were of European ancestry were given names after deceased members of their family. This was the Ashkenazic tradition. Some were given Yiddish names that were translations of the original Hebrew such as *Hersh* from *Tzvi* or *Roiza* from *Shoshana*. In the Sephardic tradition, children were usually named after the living as a gesture of honor. In both traditions, children born in the United States were given English names to complement their Hebrew or Yiddish names. For all intents and purposes, the friends and relatives of these children knew them by their English names. This was fifty years ago.

Although there is a segment of the Jewish population where things have not changed, there are communities where the common practice in the United States has changed substantially. Although Jewish children are given English names in those communities, they are known to their friends and family by their given Hebrew or Yiddish names. Quite often these names are simply transliterated and used as English names such as *Moshe*, *Rahel*, *Rivka*, and *Dovid*. These practices can be explained in sociological terms. If one were to do a sociological study of what has happened in the United States in the past fifty years with regard to human rights and freedom of expression and how this has affected the self-pride of American Jews, the reasons for today's practices would become self-evident. We must, therefore, take issue with the sweeping statement of the bard. There is a great deal in a name. Yes, a rose by any other name would smell as sweet, but its name would be a misnomer.

The Significance of the Names of God

THE DIVINE NAMES

The names of God are of ultimate significance to man for they represent the Divine attributes, i.e., the way God relates to the world. They are meant to help man in his never-ending quest to know God and to perceive the wisdom of His ways. To demonstrate this, we shall focus on ten such Divine names: *E-l, E-lohim, Havayah, Adney, Ehyeh, Sha-dai, Kadosh, Tsur, Av,* and *Melekh*.[2] According to one opinion, all these names, with the exception of *Havayah,* are appellations denoting Divine attributes.[3] In a very general sense, the Midrash teaches us the meaning of several of the Divine names. On the name *Ehyeh Asher Ehyeh*[4] the Midrash comments:

> At that time, Moses requested of the Holy One blessed be He that He reveal His great name, and God said to Moses: When I judge mankind I am called "God"; when I make war with the wicked, I am called "[Lord of] Hosts"; when I suspend the sins of man, I am called "God Almighty"; and when I have compassion for My world, I am called "Lord."[5]

Let us begin with some general rules.[6] When the Supreme Being is referred to in the Bible as the "Master" of the universe, the "Being" who has brought all things into existence, a manifestation of compassion of the highest order, He is called "Lord." When He is referred to in His creative capacity, He is called "God." This name designates the fact that He created all things, and He designed them with inherent qualities that enable them to function in a specified limited capacity. It is a manifestation of the Divine law that operates in nature. He is called "Lord" when He judges man with compassion, and He is called "God" when He judges man with strict justice. When both names appear in the

---

2. Cf. *Soferim* chapter IV, for a listing of the seven holy names and the laws that concern these names.
3. Maimonides, *Guide of the Perplexed*, trans. M. Friedlander (New York: Hebrew Publishing Company), chap. lxiv, p. 240.
4. Exodus 3:14.
5. Exodus Rabbah 3:6.
6. Cf. M. Malbim, commentary on Leviticus 18:2.

biblical text it is usually a manifestation of Divine justice tempered with compassion. The name "God" adjoined to the name "Israel" as in "the God of Israel" (*E-lohe Yisrael*) implies the highest level of providence, a blessing afforded to Israel alone from among the nations of the world. It is important to make mention of the fact that there are times when the meanings that our sages have given to these names overlap somewhat, but they are few in number. Note the following: *It is of the utmost importance to recognize that the multiplicity of names designates a multiplicity of attributes and not a multiplicity of deities. Such a notion would be sacrilege. Monotheism is perhaps the greatest contribution the Jewish people have made to society.* As the Midrash teaches: "The Holy One blessed be He said to Israel: 'Everything that I have created, I have created in pairs: Heaven and Earth are pairs; the sun and the moon are pairs; Adam and Eve are pairs; this world and the hereafter are pairs. But I am unique in the universe.'"[7] Let us now focus on the names of God.

E-l

The term *el* already appears in Genesis 31:29 where we read: "It lies within the power [*el*] of my hand to do you harm; but the God of your father said to me last night, 'Beware of attempting anything with Jacob good or bad.'" Appropriately, our sages commented: "Whenever *E-l* appears as a Divine name it signifies strength and abundance of power, namely, omnipotence.[8] The first time the Supreme Being is referred to as *E-l* (usually rendered "God") is in Genesis 14:18, 20 where we read:

> And Malchizedek, king of Salem, brought bread and wine; he was priest of God [*E-l*] Most High. He blessed him saying, "Blessed be Abraham of God [*E-l*] Most High, creator of Heaven and Earth. And blessed be God [*E-l*] Most High who has delivered your foes into your hand."

---

7. Deuteronomy Rabbah 2:22.
8. Rashi, commentary on Genesis 31:29.

Nahmanides provides the background for the name and suggests: "Since there were among the nations, priests serving the angels *elim* ("the mighty ones") . . . the Holy One blessed be He is called *E-l Elyon* ("God Most High"), the purport thereof being "the Mighty One who is Supreme over all . . ." Others suggest that the name symbolizes the attribute of loving-kindness. Until the time of Abraham, the world was not worthy of existence and would have been destroyed had it not been for God's loving-kindness. This is implied in Psalms 52:3 where we read: "The loving kindness of God [*E-l*] endures constantly."[9] The name is also connected with salvation. In Isaiah 12:2 we read: "Behold God [*E-l*] is my salvation." Divine salvation is not the result of or in any way dependent upon man's merit or his future behavior. It is simply a manifestation of Divine loving-kindness.[10] In Numbers 23:22 we find the following: "God [*E-l*] who freed them from Egypt is for them like the horn of the wild ox." Here the name is clearly a manifestation of great strength. One might suggest that in this instance the name *E-l* implies that it was Divine loving-kindness rather than the merit of the Israelites that was responsible for their redemption from Egypt.[11]

E-lohim

E-lohim is the first Divine name to appear in the Bible. It is rendered "God" in most English translations. In Genesis 1:1 we read: "In the beginning God created the Heavens and the Earth." The Midrash explains that this name represents the Divine attribute of strict justice and depicts God as He who created the law of nature, and as He who is the Judge of the world.[12] Rashi (an acronym for Rabbi Solomon

---

9. Cf. M. Alshikh, commentary on Genesis 14:19.
10. M. Malbim, commentary on Isaiah 12:2.
11. In Deuteronomy 9:5 we find: "It is not because of your virtues and your rectitude that you will be able to occupy their country, but because of the wickedness of those nations the Lord your God is dispossessing them before you, and in order to fulfill the oath the Lord made to your fathers Abraham, Isaac, and Jacob."
12. Cf. Genesis Rabbah 12:15. In Exodus Rabbah 3:6, God informs Moses: "When I judge mankind, I am called *E-lohim*."

Its'haki, the renowned French Bible commentator of the eleventh century) contends that whenever the term *E-lohim* appears in the Bible it signifies Divine authority. As such the name designates God as the Supreme Authority of the universe.[13] Others contend that the name *E-lohim* derives from the term *el* and signifies Divine omnipotence.[14]

The name *E-lohim* intimates that since God is the Creator and Master of the universe, all existing things must serve Him.[15] He created the laws that govern each and every one of His creations and He gave them the ability to survive in the world, albeit for a limited period of time. Known to us as the law of nature, God has given it permanence. The Talmud states quite clearly: "The world pursues its natural course."[16] Accordingly, we would suggest that *E-lohim* is the name through which God's glory is revealed to the world. As we read in Psalm 19:1, "The Heavens recount the glory of God; the sky proclaims His handiwork." Finally, *E-lohim* signifies eternity. God is the Eternal Supreme Being of the universe.[17]

What is most striking about the name *E-lohim* is the fact that it is plural in number (the singular is *E-loha*). Is it not strange that Judaism, the religion that that has brought monotheism to the world, would use a plural form for one of the names of God? Several explanations have been offered for this phenomenon, the simplest of which is that the name *E-lohim* is the *pluralis majestatis*, a form commonly used when

---

13. Rashi, commentary on Genesis 6:2.
14. M. Nahmanides, commentary on Genesis 1:1.
15. Cf. M. Maimonides, op. cit., Part II, chap. ii, p. 158, who writes: "The Creator is called the God of the Heavens and the God of the universe on account of the relations between Him and the Heavens; He governs, and they are governed. The word "*E-lohim*" does not signify "master" in the sense of "owner"; it expresses the relation between His position in the totality of existing beings, and the position of the Heavens or the universe; He is God, not they."
16. *Avodah Zarah* 54b. Miracles pose a serious problem in this regard. Is a miracle contrary to the law of nature? If so, would it not conflict with this statement in the Talmud? For a full discussion of this problem, the reader is referred to Jacob Breuer, *Fundamentals of Judaism* (New York: Philip Feldheim, 1948), pp. 252–257.
17. O. Seforno, commentary on Genesis 1:1. As we shall see in our discussion, most commentators associate eternity with the *Tetragrammaton*.

addressing a king or monarch, as a sign of respect.[18] Others suggest that the name is derived from the word *eileh* ("these") to indicate God's concern for the multiplicity of things that He has created. For were God to relinquish His concern for his creations for even a single moment the world would return to its original "void and unformed" condition.[19]

It has also been suggested that while the name *E-lohim* signifies a multiplicity of things, there is a unifying quality about it. Accordingly, the Divine name *E-loha* could designate "the One whose might and will encompasses all these objects together in unity . . . the One who is ruler, director, law giver, and judge of the world."[20] By referring to God as *E-lohim*, Judaism means to imply that the multiplicity of phenomena that exist in the universe and the power behind them have not only been created by God but that they are continuously under His exclusive rule. Additionally, the plural number signifies that the Supreme Being is the God of all people. True, He is at present referred to as the God of Israel, but this is because the rest of humanity has not yet come to accept the validity of the Torah.[21]

Finally, let us note that the Torah also employs the name *elohim* when referring to strange gods, i.e., images that people worship as gods. Thus in Exodus 20:3 we read: "You shall have no other gods [*elohim*] beside Me," and in Exodus 34:17 we read: "You shall not make molten gods [*elohe*] for yourselves."

Havayah

The most sacred of Divine names is known as *Shem Hameforash* ("the explicit name")[22] and as *Shem HaMeyuhad* ("the singular name").[23] It

---

18. Cf. M. Ibn Ezra, commentary on Genesis 1:1.
19. Cf. J. Mecklenburg, *HaKetav V'ha-Kabbalah* (New York: Ohm Publishers, 1946), Genesis 1:1.
20. S. R. Hirsch, commentary on Genesis 1:1.
21. Y. L. of Gur, *Sefat Emet* commentary on the Torah (Jerusalem: Yahdut, 1970), comments on *Shavuot*.
22. Cf. *Mishnah Yoma* 6:2.
23. *Sifre:* Numbers 143.

consists of the four Hebrew letters *yud, he, vav, he,* and is commonly referred to as *Havayah*[24] or the Tetragrammaton. It is rendered "Lord" in most English translations, and it appears initially in Genesis 2:4 where we read: "Such is the story of Heaven and Earth when the Lord God made Earth and Heaven." As we have noted, Maimonides opines that this name refers to God's essence, and it is applied exclusively to Him. All other names are appellations, i.e., derive from actions.[25] The name and its pronunciation convey the meaning of "absolute existence," says Maimonides.[26] Perhaps this is the reason for the trepidation regarding the pronunciation of this name. For as we know, the name *Havayah* (purposely mispronounced) was only to be pronounced correctly by the appointed priests in the Temple when they recited the threefold priestly blessing[27] and by the High Priest in the Holy of Holies during the Temple service of Yom Kippur.[28]

In contradistinction from *E-lohim*, which focuses more on Divine transcendence, the name *Havayah* denotes Divine immanence, the personal character of God made evident by revelation to the individual prophet and to the masses of Israel.[29] This interpretation is in line with the notion that *E-lohim* represents the attribute of strict justice and *Havayah* that of compassion.[30] As such "Lord," the most common

---

24. This expression is substituted for the real name in order to avoid pronunciation of the sacred name in vain.

25. M. Maimonides, op. cit., Part I, chap. lxi, p. 226.

26. Cf. Numbers 6:27 and *Sotah* 38a where the Tetragrammaton is designated as God's exclusive name. Cf. also Maimonides, op. cit., Part I, chap. lxii, p. 231 concerning the pronunciation and meaning of the name. He writes: "It was not known to everyone how the name was to be pronounced, what vowels to be given to each consonant . . . Wise men successively transmitted the pronunciation of the name; it was only communicated to a distinguished disciple once in seven years. I must, however, add that the statement 'The wise men communicated the Tetragrammaton to their children and their disciples once in seven years,' does not only refer to the pronunciation but to its meaning."

27. Numbers 6:24–26.

28. *Sotah* 38a.

29. J. Halevi, *The Kuzari* (New York: Pardes, 1946), Part IV, no. 15.

30. Cf. Genesis Rabbah 12:15; also D. Z. Hoffmann, commentary on Genesis 2:4, who adds that the many aspects of mercy included in the name *Havayah* are manifestation of the love of the Supreme Being for His creations.

The Significance of the Names of God

English rendering for *Havayah*, is accurate for it means "master," and as the Midrash indicates, mastery over the universe is one of the aspects of Divinity indicative of the name.[31] There is no need for Divine mercy in the natural world; it operates in strict accordance with the law. Inanimate objects as well as plant and animal life lack freedom of will; they are all programmed, so to speak, to operate in strict accordance with the will of God. As such the name *E-lohim* is employed exclusively in the first chapter of Genesis. Man, on the other hand, has been endowed with freedom of will; he is able to choose between obedience and disobedience to God's law. In the second chapter of Genesis, man becomes the central figure of the narrative. The name *Havayah* is juxtaposed to the name *Elohim* to indicate that for the sake of man's survival compassion has now entered the world.[32]

Many scholars contend that the name *Havayah* derives from the Hebrew words *hayah, hoveh, v'yihyeh*, the three tenses of the verb "to be," and as such denotes eternity. Accordingly, the name could be rendered "The Eternal One." Others reject this rendering; they claim that the grammatical form of *Havayah* indicates that it means the one who causes existence and "who is always ready to give new existence, and that is, in its full depth, the attribute of mercy."[33]

The Torah states that the name *Havayah* was not known to the Patriarchs. It is important that we understand the meaning of this statement. In Exodus 6:3 God said to Moses: "I appeared to Abraham, Isaac, and Jacob as God Almighty, but I did not make Myself known to them by My name Lord [*Havayah*]." Rashi explains: "I was not recog-

---

31. Genesis Rabbah 17:5.
32. Cf. S. R. Hirsch, commentary on Genesis 2:4. Note the words of Rashi on Genesis 1:1: "It does not state 'the Lord [*Havayah*] created' because at first God intended to create it [the world] to be placed under the attribute of strict justice, but He realized that the world could not thus endure and therefore gave precedence to Divine mercy allaying it with Divine justice."
33. Cf. S. R. Hirsch, commentary on Genesis 2:4. It is interesting to note Hirsch's comment on "Eternal." He writes: "Our sages already tell us to take it [*Havayah*] as the management of God exercised in love, as God being the God of love for humanity. This already shows us how far off the idea 'Eternal' from the real meaning, and how this conception, which this name is usually taken to imply, is not in the least adequate, and certainly does not express anything like the whole meaning."

nized by them by My attribute of faithfulness, by reason of which My name is called *Havayah*." The Patriarchs knew the name *Havayah*, but they were not destined to witness Divine faithfulness, i.e., the fulfillment of the Divine promise that the nation of Israel would descend from them. It is interesting to note that according to the Talmud a Divine promise is never rescinded, even in situations when man fails to fulfill the conditions under which that promise had been made.[34] Divine faithfulness also manifests itself in rewarding the righteous measure for measure for their fulfillment of the commandments. As we have already noted, the realization of this promise may take place in this world or may not take place until the hereafter.[35]

There is still another notion implied in the name *Havayah* that is worthy of mention. As a manifestation of the name *Havayah* that represents Divine concern and compassion, man has been granted the gift of self-renewal. When he returns to the Lord in sincere repentance for his sins, he is forgiven. His former behavior is wiped away, and for all intents and purposes he is reborn. He starts his life anew with a clean slate. This manifestation of Divine compassion is called *teshuvah* (literally "Return"). We shall have more to say on this topic in our chapter on providence.[36] Interestingly, the miracle of self-renewal has been granted to nations as well. Israel is the classic example. Having lost all hope in being redeemed from Egyptian slavery, the Israelites were in the depths of despair. They cried out to the Lord, and He heard their lament. In Exodus 2:24 we read: "God heard their moaning, and God remembered His covenant with Abraham, and Isaac and Jacob. God looked upon the Israelites, and God took notice of them." Then, in Exodus 6:1, Moses was informed: "Now you shall see what I will do to Pharaoh . . ." The time for redemption had arrived. Not only would the Israelites be redeemed; they would experience self-renewal for they would be given a new existence as a kingdom of priests and a holy nation.[37]

---

34. Cf. *Berakhot* 17a; also M. Maimonides, *Mishneh Torah: Foundations of the Torah* 10:4, and the gloss of *Lehem Mishneh* ad loc.
35. Cf. M. Maimonides, op. cit., Laws of Repentence 8:1.
36. Chapter VI.
37. Cf. D. Z. Hoffmann, commentary to Leviticus 1:1, pp. 74–75.

The Significance of the Names of God

The late Rabbi Dr. Eliezer Berkovits, one of the most profound contemporary Jewish thinkers, understands the names *E-lohim* and *Havayah* quite differently, and it behooves us at least to mention his approach. Berkovits suggests that the name *E-lohim* signifies Divine immanence in contradistinction from *Havayah*, which signifies transcendence. Focusing on the text in Deuteronomy 4:35, which reads: "You have been shown to know that the Lord alone is God; there is none beside Him," he explains that the text means to teach us that *Havayah*, the transcendent Supreme Being of the universe, is none other than *E-lohim*, the God whom we recognize as immanent in the world and who is intimately concerned with man.[38]

Adney

Adney is a substitute expression for the sacred Divine name composed of the letters *aleph, daled, nun, yud*. The name derives from the word *adon* meaning "master" or "lord." An interesting statement is found in the Talmud concerning this name: "From the day that the Holy One blessed be He created the world there was no man that called the Holy One blessed be He *Adon* until Abraham came and called Him *Adon*."[39] Abraham regarded himself as a "tool" in the service of the Supreme Being. It was no more than fitting that he refer to Him as *Adon*.[40] There is an important lesson to be learned in this name. The world belongs to *Adney*; He is its Master. As such He has the right to give parts of the land permanently or temporarily to whomever He chooses. The Torah

---

38. E. Berkovits, *Man and God* (Detroit: Wayne State University Press, 1969), pp. 22–30.

39. *Berakhot* 7b. Notwithstanding this statement, Judah Halevi, op. cit., Part IV, pp. 176–177, writes: "The first man would not have known Him if He had not addressed, rewarded and punished him, and had not created Eve from one of his ribs. This gave him the conviction that He was the Creator of the world whom he designated by words and attributes and styled 'Lord' . . . Cain and Abel were made acquainted with the nature of His Being by the communication of their father as well as by prophetic intuition. Then Noah, Abraham, Isaac and Jacob, Moses and the prophets called Him intuitively 'Lord.'"

40. Cf. S. R. Hirsch, commentary on Genesis 15:2.

reveals that God promised the land of Canaan to Abraham. However, the promise was not realized until centuries later when the Jewish people took possession of the land. Thus is the claim the Jewish nation has to the land of Israel substantiated. In the words of R. Yitzhak: "He created it and gave it to whom He pleased."[41]

At such times as *Adney* occurs in the Torah juxtaposed to the name *Havayah*, the latter is vocalized and pronounced *E-lohim* (i.e., *segol, holom, hirik*). According to those who contend that the name *E-lohim* signifies the attribute of strict justice and *Havayah* signifies the attribute mercy or compassion, the implied meaning of this juxtaposition would be "the God who tempers justice with mercy in His judgment of mankind."[42] Others contend that the juxtaposition is meant to enlighten man as to God's ways in the world: though God's acts appear to the human mind to be rather harsh at times, in reality they are manifestations of His great love and mercy.[43] The fact that these two Divine names appear together in the Abraham narrative has special significance. It was the omnipotent Creator and Master of the universe (*Adney Havayah*) who blessed Abraham in his old age with a son, a truly supernatural act. By doing so He manifested His providential hand and His unbounded love for His trusted servant Abraham.[44]

Ehyeh

In Exodus 3:13–14 we read:

> Moses said to God, "When I come to the Israelites and say to them, 'The God of your fathers has sent me to you,' and they ask me, 'What is His name?' what shall I say to them?" And God said to Moses, "*Ehyeh Asher Ehyeh*." He continued, "Thus shall you say to the Israelites, '*Ehyeh* sent me to you.'"

---

41. Quoted by Rashi on Genesis 1:1.
42. Rashi, commentary on Deuteronomy 3:24.
43. Cf. S. R. Hirsch, op. cit.
44. Cf. *Maharsha* on *Berakhot* 7a.

What is the meaning and significance of Moses' question? Maimonides points out that until the time of Moses there had not risen a prophet who spoke in the name of God claiming to have been assigned a mission. God communicated with Adam, Noah, and the Patriarchs only on matters that concerned them personally or their family.[45] Moses was the first prophet who was instructed by God to bring a message to the people of Israel. It is no wonder that he was very much concerned that the people believe him. The masses were ignorant, and they might have insisted that he prove the existence of God before they would be willing to accept the fact that God had communicated with him and had sent them a message.[46] What was God's reply? *Ehyeh Asher Ehyeh!* I am the Being, whose existence is absolute and eternal, says God. Maimonides explains: "The proof which he was to give consisted in demonstrating that there is a Being of absolute existence, that has never been and never will be without existence."[47]

Let us develop the significance of the name *Ehyeh* a bit more fully. The late Rabbi Dr. J. B. Soloveitchik writes: "God, in answer to Moses' inquiry gave His name as Ehyeh Asher Ehyehm—I what I am. God is free from the contradiction between potentiality and actuality, ideal and reality. He is pure actuality, existence par excellence."[48] There is no "becoming" in God. What He once *was,* He *is* and always *will be.* The Talmud posits that the words *Ehyeh Asher Ehyeh* also imply Divine providence. God tells Moses to inform the Israelites that He will always be with them. He is with them in Egypt, in servitude to the Pharaoh, and He will demonstrate this by redeeming them, and He will be with them in their servitude to other kings in the future.[49] Quite in line with

---

45. Cf. M. Maimonides, *Guide of the Perplexed,* op. cit., p. 238.

46. Ibid., p. 239. Cf. M. Nahmanides, commentary on Exodus 3:13, who disagrees with Maimonides and offers a different approach to the meaning of the name *Ehyeh.*

47. Ibid. This is in line with proposition twenty of the twenty-six propositions Maimonides offers to prove the existence of God found in his introduction to Part II of this work. It reads: "A thing which has in itself the necessity of existence cannot have for its existence any cause whatsover."

48. J. B. Soloveitchik, "Confrontation," *Tradition,* vol. 6, no. 2, p. 10.

49. Cf. *Berakhot* 9b.

this thinking is the explanation given by J. Halevi. He writes: "I am that I am, the existing one, existing for you whenever you seek Me. Let them look for no stronger proof than My Presence among them and name Me accordingly."[50]

There is another point that must be made here. In Psalms 48:11 we read: "The praise of You, God, like Your name, reaches to the end of the Earth; Your right hand is filled with beneficence." Unlike the term "man," that can be qualified—namely, a "good man," a "wise man," a "strong man"—the name *Ehyeh* is all-inclusive; it embraces all possible qualities and perfections.[51]

Sha-dai

The name *Sha-dai* is rendered "Almighty" in most English translations. It first appears in Genesis 17:1 where we read: "When Abram was ninety-nine years old, the Lord appeared to Abram and said to him, 'I am God Almighty. Walk in My ways and be blameless.'" Maimonides understands the name *Sha-dai* to be an appellation that derives from the word *dai* ("enough"). As such it would mean "The One, who is sufficient," which, among other things, implies that He does not require the existence of those things that He has created.[52]

The Midrash interprets the name *Sha-dai* somewhat differently. "I am He who called to My world 'sufficient!' says the Midrash. Had I not called 'sufficient' to Heaven and Earth, they would be continuously evolving."[53] Accordingly, the name *Sha-dai* designates God as He who created, sustains, and *limits* the development of the universe. Indeed, it is He who set the nature or pattern of all things in Heaven and on Earth,

---

50. J. Halevi, op. cit., p. 178.
51. Cf. M. Malbim, commentary on Exodus 3:13.
52. M. Maimonides, op. cit., p. 240. The derivation of this name is subject to differing interpretations. Ibn Ezra in his commentary on Genesis 17:1 explains that the name derives from the term *shoded* and means "victor and prevailer over the host of Heaven. Cf. M. Nahmanides, ad loc. who agrees with this interpretation.
53. Genesis Rabbah 46. Cf. *Hagigah* 12a.

and who ordained that they would not develop beyond the limited potential that He had set for them.[54] Understandably, as the omnipotent Creator of the universe, God has the ability to contravene the laws of nature if He so chooses. This is likewise implied in the name *Sha-dai*.[55] When God chooses to contravene the laws of nature, how frequently He makes that choice and under what conditions, are matters to which man is not privy.

Lastly, there are those who opine that the name *Sha-dai* derives from *shadayim* ("breasts"). Notwithstanding His great power, He is a merciful God. In Job 37:23 we read: "The Almighty—we cannot attain Him; He is great in power and justice and abundant in righteousness; He does not torment." He is perfect and forgiving.[56] God is depicted as the One who nourishes the world like a mother who nurses her child. He supplies the world not only with food but also with all the needs of its inhabitants, and He sustains them throughout their lives.[57] It is interesting to note that the name *Sha-dai* was known to the Patriarchs, for in Exodus 6:3 we read: "I appeared to Abraham, Isaac, and Jacob as God Almighty but I did not make Myself known to them by My name the Lord."

Kadosh

The word *kadosh* is usually rendered "holy," yet a more precise rendering would be "separate." An offering that one dedicates to the Temple in Jerusalem is separated from the rest of one's possessions, and at that moment it becomes prohibited for any other purpose unless it is redeemed. In Leviticus 19:1–2 we read: "The Lord spoke to Moses

---

54. Cf. S. R. Hirsch, op. cit., Genesis 17:1. Note that he disagrees with the opinion that the name *Sha-dai* derives from the word *shoded*.

55. Cf. D. Kimhi, commentary on Genesis 17:1.

56. Rabbenu B'haye, commentary on the Torah (Jerusalem: Mossad Harav Kook, 1973), Deuteronomy 32:4.

57. Cf. J. Z. Mecklenburg, *Ha-Ketav V'HaKabbalah* (New York: Ohm, 1946), Exodus 6:3.

saying: Speak to the whole community of Israel and say to them: You shall be holy for I, the Lord your God am holy." What is meant here is that the Jewish people were to be a nation whose statutes, ethical, and moral laws made them unique, i.e., separate from the rest of humanity.[58]

The term *Kadosh* as one of the Divine names is rendered "The Holy One." It appears many times in the Bible, particularly in the book of Isaiah.[59] Perhaps the most well-known verse in Isaiah is 6:3, which reads: "And one [angel] would call to the other: Holy, holy, holy the Lord of Hosts, His Presence fills the Earth," for it has been incorporated into our prayer service.[60] Note the words of J. Halevi: "Holy, holy, holy, which meant that God is too high, too exalted . . . and too pure for any impurity of the people in whose midst His light dwells to touch Him."[61] Let us go one step more. "Holy is, further, a description of the spiritual which never assumes a corporeal form, and which nothing concrete can possibly resemble."[62] Accordingly, the term implies Divine uniqueness, that God is separate in terms of His essence from all existing things. Halevi states further: "Holy expresses the notion that He is high above any attribute of created beings, although many of these are applied to Him metaphorically."[63] Divine uniqueness manifests itself in three realms: the highest Heaven, the realm of the planets and stars, and the Earth.[64] S. R. Hirsch adds: "His nature and His purpose are constant and unchanging."[65]

---

58. Cf. Rashi, commentary on Leviticus 19:2.

59. It is already found in Isaiah 1:4, which reads: "Ah sinful nation! people laden with iniquity! brood of evil doers! Depraved children! They have forsaken the Lord, spurned the Holy One of Israel [Kadosh Yisrael]."

60. It should be noted that Deuteronomy 6:4, "Hear O Israel the Lord our God, the Lord is One," perhaps the most well-known verse in the Bible, established the same point, i.e., God is unique!

61. J. Halevi, op. cit., Part IV, no. 3, p. 179.

62. Ibid.

63. Ibid.

64. D. Kimhi, commentary on Isaiah 6:3.

65. S. R. Hirsch, The Hirsch Siddur (New York: Feldheim Publishers, 1972), p. 203.

The Significance of the Names of God

Tsur

The Hebrew word *tsur* literally means "rock." It represents both strength and firmness. Note the words of Homer, "A small rock holds back a great wave."[66] A strong person is often referred to as a "rock." It is strength and steadfastness that is implied in the Divine appellation *Tsur*. In Deuteronomy 32:4 we read: "The Rock! His deeds are perfect." What is the implication of these words? Rashi explains: "Although He is strong, yet when He brings punishment upon those who transgress His will, He does not bring it in a flood of anger but rather in deliberate judgment, because His work is perfect.[67] With regard to Divine strength, our sages commented that just as rock is the foundation of the Earth, God is the foundation of the world.[68] Just as a structure cannot stand unless it has a strong foundation so it is with the Earth. Without the support of the Supreme Being, the Earth, indeed the universe, could not survive.

There is another approach to the meaning and significance of the Divine name *Tsur*, for the word also means "to shape" or "to form." On the verse, "There is no Holy One like the Lord, truly there is none beside You; there is no rock [*tsur*] like our God,"[69] our sages remarked, "There is no 'former' [*tsayar*] like our God."[70] In this sense, we refer to God in the *Amidah* as "He who forms our lives" (*Tsur hayenu*).[71] S. R. Hirsch understands the name to designate Divine omnipotence. He writes: "Applied to God, *tsur* is the allegorical for the unchangeable and the absolute power of overcoming everything. He is the absolute origin of all existence. What He has decided to exist finds in Him its eternal hold and support, and every form that He intends it to take becomes realized with absolute certainty."[72]

---

66. Homer, *The Odyssey*, Book I, line 296.
67. Rashi, commentary on Deuteronomy 32:4.
68. Rabbenu B'haye, commentary on Deuteronomy 32:4.
69. I Samuel 2:2.
70. *Berakhot* 10a.
71. Cf. J. Z. Mecklenburg, *HaKetav V'HaKabbalah*, op. cit., Deuteronomy 32:4.
72. S. R. Hirsch, commentary on Deuteronomy 32:4. See also J. Z. Mecklenburg, op. cit., who suggests this interpretation among several others.

The last two names we will discuss here are *Av* ("Father") and *Melekh* ("King"). They play a vital role in our understanding of Divine rule in the universe, and each suggests a different approach to the way we must relate to God both in deed and in worship.

Av

In Isaiah 63:16 we read: "Surely You are our Father . . . You O Lord are our Father; from of old, Your name is our Redeemer," and in Isaiah 64:7 we read: "But now. O Lord, You are our Father; we are the clay and You are the potter, we are all the work of Your hands." In Malakhi 1:6 God Himself asks, "A son should honor his father, and a slave his master. Now if I am a father, where is the honor due to Me? And if I am a master, where is the reverence due to Me?"

What is the significance of designating God as the Father of humanity? The question can be answered with a single word—compassion. If there is a common theme to all the petitions in the Jewish liturgy it is the quest for Divine compassion, and there is no greater degree of compassion than that which a parent feels for his or her child. As such Psalms 103:13 is very much on target: "As a father has compassion for his children so the Lord has compassion for those who fear Him." Is it then not interesting to find in *Shaharit* ("Morning Service") the words: "O our Father, merciful Father, ever compassionate, have mercy upon us."[73] In a single verse that speaks of God as "Father" there are three references to Divine compassion.

But there is more for us to consider in this Divine appellation. A father teaches his child to be ethical and moral because he knows that this will make him a better human being. An ethical and moral person will bring honor to himself and will engender peace and harmony among men. God, the Father of humanity, has revealed the Torah, which is the standard of ethics and morality, to the nation of Israel. He has charged them with the mission to set the example for the nations of the world. If they heed this example and live by Divine law, peace and

---

73. The verse is found in the *Ahavah Rabbah* prayer of *Shaharit*.

harmony will prevail in the world. The symbolism can be taken still further. Just as a father's punishment of his child may at times seem a bit harsh, so too might Divine punishment seem harsh to the recipient, even cruel. But just as we know that a father's discipline will benefit the child in the long run, so too will God's discipline of mankind benefit all those who are its recipients. Lastly, just as a father who loves his child will ultimately forgive his wrongdoing, so it is with God. He loves all of mankind whom He regards as his children, and He will ultimately forgive their wrongdoing.

Melekh

We refer to God as our King. In Isaiah 33:22 we read: "For the Lord shall be our Ruler, the Lord shall be our Prince, the Lord shall be our King: He shall deliver us." In Psalms 47:7 we read: "Sing O sing to God; sing O sing to our King; for God is King over all the Earth; sing a hymn." In point of fact, at times we refer to God as the King of Kings. A powerful king generates fear in the hearts of his subjects, and fear engenders submission to his rule. God, the omnipotent King of the universe, on the other hand, inspires reverence in the hearts of humanity, and reverence for God inspires submission to His law. Recognizing God as King of the universe has other ramifications. Note the following: God created everything in the universe; it belongs to Him exclusively. As such one might rightfully ask, "By what right do we partake of that which belongs to God?" Jewish law teaches that before we partake of the bounties of this world we must recite a blessing to God acknowledging that He is King and rightful owner of all. This earns us the right to partake of His bounties.[74]

In Deuteronomy 6:5 we read: "You must love the Lord your God with all your heart and with all your soul and with all your might." Eight verses later (6:13) we find, "Revere only the Lord your God and worship

---

74. Cf. *Berakhot* 35a: "It is forbidden for a man to enjoy anything of this world without a benediction, and if anyone enjoys anything of this world without a benediction, he commits sacrilege."

Him alone, and swear only by His name." Would it be presumptuous to say that these two verses are sequentially addressed to the two names *Av* and *Melekh*? Acceptance of God as the Father of mankind inspires love within our hearts; accepting Him as King inspires reverence. Now some suggest that reverence is subsumed under love, for to love someone is also to revere him, for one doesn't want to displease him. Be that as it may, love is certainly not subsumed under reverence. There are many reasons for reverence; love is not necessarily among them.[75]

It is interesting to note that there are times when the names *Av* and *Melekh* are juxtaposed. On Fast Days and during the High Holiday period from Rosh Hashanah through Yom Kippur, it is customary to recite a series of petitions after the Amidah. They begin with the words "Our Father our King" *(Avinu Malkenu)*. We also find this juxtaposition in the *tahanun* prayer recited in the weekday *Shaharit* service on Mondays and Thursdays. In the weekday Amidah we also find: "Cause us to return O our Father to our Torah; draw us near O our King to Your service," and again: "Forgive us O our Father for we have sinned, pardon us O our King for we have transgressed." What is the reason for the parallelism?

Perhaps the answer is as follows: To proclaim God as the transcendent King of the universe is the epitome of adoration and praise, and Divine transcendence is a major principle in Jewish thinking. But it is somewhat disheartening to be reminded of this aspect of Divinity when petitioning the Almighty for forgiveness. At such times one would like to focus on Divine immanence, that is, His nearness and accessibility to man. Perhaps this is the rationale for parallelism in the *Amidah* as well as the juxtaposition of the names *Av* and *Melekh (Avenu Malkenu)* in our prayers when we approach God for forgiveness. It establishes the principle that while it is true that God is transcendent, in a sense very distant from us, He is also immanent; near to us and willing to hear our prayers when we call out to Him sincerely like children to their father.

A fitting conclusion to our discussion of these two names is a prayer from the *Mussaf* of Rosh Hashanah:

---

75. Cf. Rabbenu B'haye, op. cit., Deuteronomy 6:13. 20

The Significance of the Names of God

This day the world was called into being; this day all the creatures of the universe stand in judgment before You, as children or as servants. If as children, have pity upon us as a father pities his children; and if as servants, we call upon You to be gracious upon us and merciful in judgment of us, O revered and holy God.

In the chapters that follow, we shall peruse the Torah and some of the other books of the Bible. We will focus on the Divine names in the context and order in which they appear in the text, and we shall delineate the significance of these names. We shall discover that they are appellatives, that they were placed in the text systematically and reflect the message of the verse or verses in which they appear. In point of fact, at times they clarify or give us new insight into the meaning of these verses. Our findings will add one more link to the chain of unimpeachable proofs for the single authorship of the Torah.

2

THE THIRTEEN DIVINE ATTRIBUTES

Man must be mindful of his behavior at all times for how he acts defines not only his own nature but also the nature of humanity itself. Moreover, man's behavior reflects on God for man was created in God's image. Considering the potential consequences, what should be man's guide to proper behavior? In Deuteronomy 13:5 we read: "Follow none but the Lord your God, and revere none but Him; observe His commandments alone, and heed only His orders; worship none but Him and hold fast to Him" In *Sotah* 14a, we find the following explanation:

> What does the text "Follow none but the Lord your God" mean? Is it possible for a human being to follow the Divine Presence; for has it not been said, "For the Lord your God is a devouring fire?" But [the meaning is] to walk after the attributes of the Holy One blessed be He. As He clothes the naked . . . so should you clothe the naked. The Holy One blessed be He visited the sick . . . so should you visit the sick. The Holy One blessed be He comforts the mourners . . . so should you comfort the mourners.

Teach Me about God

The Divine attributes teach us how God acts on the world; they serve as a model for man. Having been created in God's image, man is charged to mimic his Creator in the way he treats his fellow man. To do as God does would be considered proper behavior. What else do we know about God?

Although the Divine essence is beyond human comprehension, in Deuteronomy 6:4 we read the definitive statement: "Hear O Israel; the Lord our God the Lord is One." These words affirm the principle of monotheism and put forth the notion that God is unique. The point is made in Isaiah 46:5 as well, where we read: "To whom can you compare Me or declare Me similar? To whom can you liken Me so that we seem comparable?" Maimonides explains: "God is One in every respect, containing no plurality or any element superadded to His essence; and that the many attributes of different signification applied in Scripture to God, originate in the multitude of His actions, not in a plurality existing in His essence."[1] Moreover, it must be understood that no potentiality can be attributed to God, for potentiality implies nonexistence. To attribute potentiality to God would imply that at some time God was not absolutely "Perfect," only potentially so. Such a posture would, of course, be untenable.[2]

ANTHROPOMORPHISM IN THE BIBLE

A firm tenet of Judaism is put forth in Deuteronomy 4:12–15. There it is stated: "The Lord spoke to you out of fire; you heard the sounds of words but perceived no shape—nothing but a voice . . . For your own

---

1. M. Maimonides, *Guide of the Perplexed*, trans. by M. Friedlander (New York: Hebrew Publishing Company), Part I, p. 185. Cf. Saadya Gaon, *The Book of Beliefs and Opinions* (New Haven: Yale University Press, 1948), p. 94; also Judah Halevi, *The Book of the Kuzari* (New York: Pardes, 1946), p. 74, who writes: "We take the term One . . . not to establish unity as we understand it. For we call a thing one, when the coherent parts are coherent and of the same materials, e.g., *one* bone *one* sinew . . . The Divine Essence is exempt from complexity and divisibility and *one* only stands to exclude plurality."
2. M. Maimonides, op. cit., p. 199.

sake, therefore, you must be careful . . . not to act wickedly and make for yourselves a sculptured image in any likeness whatever . . ." No physical form may be attributed to God. Given this prohibition, it becomes incumbent upon us to offer a rationale for the many anthropomorphic terms that are found in the Bible.

Terms such as the head of God, the eye, ear, mouth, lips, face, hand, heart, and foot of God are found throughout the Bible. Does this imply that the Bible postulates that God has a physical form? Absolutely not! The Bible means to convey a notion about God in language that would stimulate the imagination through the use of terms and expressions that would be most meaningful to the reader. A case in point is Isaiah 59:17, which speaks of God as follows: "He donned victory like a coat of mail, with a helmet of triumph on His head." Clearly, what the prophet wished to convey here is *not* that God dons a coat or that He wears a helmet, but rather an image of nobility, distinction, and elevation that these words engender. To cite another example, Deuteronomy 11:12 reads: "It is a land which the Lord your God looks after, on which the Lord your God always keeps His eye, from year's beginning to year's end." The term "eye" is clearly figurative; it is not meant to imply that God has eyes nor that he perceives things visually. What the text means to convey is Divine concern for the land. Lastly, Numbers 6:25 reads: "The Lord make his face shine upon you and be gracious to you." The term "face" in this context is meant to convey favor or good will such as in Proverbs 16:15, which reads: "In the light of the king's face is life." The principle that has been put forth here applies to all anthropomorphic expressions in the Bible.[3]

COMMON MISCONCEPTIONS

Let us take the matter of anthropomorphism a bit further. Just as the parts of the human body ascribed to God in the Bible are meant to be taken figuratively, so, too, are all functions connected with these parts

---

3. Saadya Gaon, op. cit., pp. 116–118.

such as the expression "He heard our voice" in Deuteronomy 26:7 and "His heart was saddened" in Genesis 6:6. When the Bible tells us that a particular action that God has commanded is lovable or hateful to Him, it means that the action is designated by God as lovable or hateful since He has made the love or hate of that action obligatory upon us. It should likewise be understood that whenever the Bible informs us that God is pleased with a particular action it means that happiness or reward has been decreed for some of God's creatures, which is characterized as Divine pleasure. This principle also applies to God being depicted as angry when He punishes man.[4]

With regard to such emotions as desire and fear, Saadya Gaon states: "They can be possessed only by beings that desire and fear. It is out of the question, however, that the Creator of all things should entertain a desire for ought that He has created or be in fear of it."[5] It is important to recognize, says Saadya Gaon, that when the Torah employs the expressions "God made" and "God rested," in the Creation narrative, they are meant to be taken figuratively. God brought things into existence. Having done so, He ceased from that activity.[6] To contend that God expended energy or exerted Himself physically in order to create the universe or that at a given time He rested from such exertion would be sacrilege and contrary to our understanding of the nature of God.

Another common misconception is that God dwells in Heaven, says Saadya Gaon. How would such a notion jibe with I Kings 8:27, which reads: "Even the Heavens to their uttermost regions cannot contain you." Here again the Bible meant to indicate God's greatness and His elevation, says Saadya Gaon.[7] Lastly, the Bible consistently asserts that God spoke to the prophet. What is meant here is not that God has a voice and speaks but rather that He created speech, which He conveyed to the hearing of the prophets.[8]

---

4. Ibid., p. 122–123.
5. Ibid., p. 123.
6. Ibid., p. 128.
7. Ibid., p. 124.
8. Ibid., p. 128.

The Thirteen Divine Attributes

In Exodus 33:18 we read that Moses implored the Lord with the words: "O let me behold Your Presence." The Lord answered "You cannot see My face for man cannot see Me and live" (Exodus 33:20). Indeed, the request to know God's essence was even beyond the intellectual and spiritual potential of Moses, the chief of all prophets. Parenthetically, one must not misconstrue the Lord's response. It is not an admonition. It does not indicate that Divine punishment will be exacted upon one who perceives God's essence. It simply avers that God's essence is incomprehensible to mortal man.

Invoking the adage of the sages, "The Torah speaks in the language of men,"[9] Maimonides explains that the object of passages in the Bible that speak of Divine attributes is to designate God as the Perfect Being. They are not meant to imply that He possesses these attributes, "which are only perfections in relation to created living beings."[10] Moreover, the fact that the attributes express different kinds of behavior does not imply differences of any kind in God.[11] The truth of the matter is that the definition and classification of the Divine attributes exists only in the thoughts of men.[12] In the words of Maimonides:

> Whenever any one of His actions is perceived by us, we ascribe to God that emotion which is the source of the act when performed by ourselves and call Him by an epithet which is formed by the verb expressing that action. We see how well He provides for the life of the embryo of living beings; how He endows with certain faculties both the embryo itself and those who have to rear it after its birth, in order that it may be protected from death and destruction . . . Similar acts when performed by us are due to a certain emotion and tenderness called mercy. God is, therefore, said to be merciful.[13]

Great care must be taken in the way we conceptualize the ways of God. To contend that He is at times motivated to act out of a feeling of

---

9. *Berakhot* 31b.
10. M. Maimonides, op. cit., p. 187.
11. Ibid.
12. Ibid., p. 191.
13. Ibid., pp. 194–195.

mercy would be untenable, says Maimonides, for it would imply a change in God. "The same is the case with all Divine acts," says Maimonides, "though resembling those acts which emanate from our passions and psychical dispositions, they are not due to anything superadded to His essence."[14]

The late Rabbi Dr. Eliezer Berkovits makes an interesting observation on the significance, indeed, the importance of anthropomorphic references. Creation is a bond between God and the world, says Berkovits; it is the ultimate proof that He is a caring God for to be involved is to care. Note the following:

> God's involvement in the world is the cause of all anthropomorphism. The God who cares loves; because He cares, He punishes and forgives too. All this is no less understandable than that He should create...Since God's involvement in the destinies of man is the precondition of religion, "anthropomorphism" is, indeed inseparable from religion. That God does care is not merely an allegory but a statement of fact, which one makes on the actual experience of the encounter.[15]

Accordingly, it is not that man attributes human characteristics to God but rather that "in his experience [i.e., the encounter between man and God] Divine intentions and actions whose likeness he also finds among men were revealed to him," says Berkovits. Lastly, "Anthropomorphism is the making of God in man's image; it is certainly to be rejected as vile idolatry. But the discovery of the likeness of the 'relational' attributes among men is the reflection of the truth that man is formed in the image of God."[16]

It is to be understood, of course, that the Divine acts in the world that

---

14. Ibid., p. 196. Comp. J. Halevi, op. cit., p. 73 who writes: "They attribute to Him mercy and compassion, although this is in our conception, surely nothing but a weakness of the soul and a quick movement of nature. This cannot be applied to God, who is a just Judge, ordaining the poverty of one individual and the wealth of another. His nature remains quite unaffected by it."

15. E. Berkovits, *God, Man and History* (New York: Jonathan David, 1959), p. 63.

16. Ibid., pp.63–64.

are for man's benefit are innumerable. However, only those that God deemed necessary for man to assimilate into his personality and for which he was charged in Deuteronomy 28:9, "And you shall walk in His ways," were revealed to him. Let us now proceed to the Divine attributes.

THE DIVINE ATTRIBUTES

After the revelation of the Ten Commandments to the entire nation of Israel, Moses remained on Mount Sinai for forty days and forty nights where he received the remaining commandments and their details. Awaiting his return to the camp, the people became impatient. They gathered against Aaron and insisted that he make them a god to lead them, for they did not know what had happened to Moses. Pressed by the people, Aaron had no alternative; he complied with their request. He threw their gold and silver into the fire and a golden calf was formed. The people brought offerings; they ate and drank and made merry before it. When Moses descended the mountain and witnessed what God had informed him was happening in the camp, he became enraged. He hurled the tablets of the law that he had received to the ground and shattered them at the foot of the mountain. Punishment was clearly in order.

Moses burned the golden calf, and he had the perpetrators of this abominable act executed. Some 3,000 of the people fell that day. Moses then ascended the mountain once more to win forgiveness from God for the horrendous sin that the people had committed. God informed him that from that day forward the people would no longer be led by God directly; an angel would lead them instead. Moses was dismayed. He petitioned God to rescind the harsh edict, and he prevailed. Encouraged by his accomplishment, Moses made two other requests. The first is found in Exodus 33:13 where we read: "Now, if I have truly gained Your favor let me know Your ways, that I may know You and continue in Your favor." It was in response to this request that God revealed the

"Thirteen Attributes."[17] They are found in Exodus 34:6–7 and read as follows:

> *Havayah, Havayah, E-l, Rahum, vehanun, erekh apayim, v'rav hesed, ve'emet, notser hesed la'alafim, nosei avon, va'fesha, ve'hata'ah, ve'nakei, lo yinakei, poked avon avot al banim, ve'al b'nei vanim, al sheleishim, ve'al ribeim.*

> The Lord! The Lord! A God compassionate and gracious, slow to anger, rich in steadfast kindness, extending kindness to the thousandth generation, forgiving iniquity, transgression, and sin; yet He does not remit all punishment, remembering the sins of the parents for children and children's children for the third and the fourth generation.[18]

The sages differ as to what precisely constitutes the thirteen attributes. The commonly accepted enumeration is as follows:

> 1. Lord 2. Lord 3. God 4. Compassionate 5. Gracious 6. Slow to anger 7. Rich in kindness 8. Rich in truth 9. Extending kindness to the thousandth generation 10. Forgiving iniquity 11. Forgiving transgression 12. Forgiving sin 13. Not remitting all punishment.[19]

Nahmanides postulates that the first three words here are proper nouns denoting God's essence and should not be counted among the attributes. Consequently he counts only ten Divine attributes in the biblical verse.[20] Others opine that the Divine attributes begin with the second reference to God as "Lord" *(Havayah)*. They count thirteen

---

17. Cf. Ibn Ezra, commentary on Exodus 34:6; also *Rosh Hashanah* 17b and Rashi ad loc.

18. This is the translation by S. R. Hirsch. Most English translations read: "visits the iniquity of the fathers upon children and children's children upon the third and fourth generation."

19. This is the enumeration according to *Rabbenu Tam*. Cf. *Rosh Hashanah* 17b in the *Tosafot* commentary s.v. *shalosh*. See also Ibn Ezra, commentary on Exodus 34:6.

20. Cf. M. Nahmanides, commentary on Exodus 34:6.

by dividing the ninth attribute into two attributes.[21] Still others retain the unity of the ninth attribute, but consider the words "remembering the sins of the parents for children and children's children for the third and the fourth generation" to be the thirteenth attribute.[22] Let us now focus on each of these Divine attributes and bring to light some of the comments of our sages.

1. *Havayah* 2. *Havayah*

We have already analyzed the meaning and significance of the name *Havayah* in the previous chapter. But what is the reason why the name appears here twice? Our sages explain the repetition as follows: "I am the Lord before man sins, and I am the Lord after a man sins and repents."[23] The name *Havayah* symbolizes compassion. The Lord's compassion is infinite, says the Talmud; it manifests itself upon man at all times. Just as the Lord is compassionate to man before he sins so is He compassionate to man after he sins. Now one might rightfully ask, "Why does man need Divine compassion before he sins?" Some suggest that it is to prevent him from committing a sin. Having been given freedom of will, the path of good and the path of evil are equally open to him. He needs God's help to keep him from acquiescing to the pressures of temptation.[24] Others contend that it indicates the Lord's limitless patience with man. He is compassionate to man despite the fact that He knows that man will eventually sin.[25] Even when man sins and he deserves to be despised by God, he is treated with compassion. Perhaps the greatest and most obvious manifestation of Divine compassion is the gift of *teshuvah* ("repentence"), for it teaches man that he will attain Divine forgiveness if he sincerely repents his sin.

---

21. Cf. Rabbenu Nissim on *Rosh Hashanah* 17b, s. v. *v'katav*, who designates the words "extending kindness to the thousandth generation" as two attributes.
22. M. Maimonides, *Responsa of Maimonides* (Levov, 1859), p. 19b.
23. *Rosh Hashanah* 17b.
24. *Daat Zekanim*, commentary to Exodus 34:6.
25. Cf. Rabbenu Asher glosses to *Rosh Hashanah* 17a. See also *Sifte Hahamim* to Rashi commentary on Exodus 34:6.

3. E-l

We have also discussed this name fully in the previous chapter. Let us only add here that although the name *E-l*, like the name *Havayah*, alludes to Divine compassion, according to some commentators,[26] it is compassion of a lesser degree than that which is alluded to in the name *Havayah*.[27]

4. Rahum

Rahum when applied to the Supreme Being denotes *hashgahah klalit* ("general providence"), i.e., Divine mercy that manifests itself in the maintenance and the preservation of *all* the species in nature. As the psalmist said: "The Lord is good to all, and His mercy is upon all His works."[28] In a very real sense, the Lord's mercy for His creations is very much like a mother's mercy for her child. It is unqualified and unlimited. In this light we can well understand why the words *rahum* ("merciful"), *rahamim* ("mercy"), and *rehem* ("womb") all derive from the same root, and why some opine that this attribute refers specifically to the mercy shown by God to the fetus in the womb.[29] Additionally, our sages explained that this attribute has specific application to the sinner. When he calls upon God in sincere repentance, God eases his punishment.[30]

5. Hanun

According to some, Divine graciousness applies exclusively to man for this attribute implies *hashgahah pratit* ("personal providence"), and

---

26. Cf. Rashi, commentary on Exodus 34:6.
27. Cf. *Sifte Hahamim* ad loc.
28. Cf. Rabbenu B'haye, commentary on Exodus 34:6.
29. Cf. I. Abravanel, commentary on Exodus 34:6, p. 339.
30. Cf. O. Seforno, commentary on Exodus 34:6.

man is the sole recipient of this Divine gift.[31] Others opine that while it is the suffering of the oppressed that activates Divine compassion, it is man's grace, namely, his belovedness to God for no other reason than the fact that he is "man," that activates Divine graciousness.[32] Let us note that when Moses entreated the Lord to gain entrance into the Promised Land, he referred to his prayer with the term *va-et'hanan*.[33] Rashi explains the term as a request for an "unearned gift." The word *va-et'hanan* has the same root as *Hanun*.[34] Others add that Divine graciousness refers specifically to the insight and knowledge with which man has been endowed by his Creator. This is man's unearned gift.[35]

6. *Erekh Apayim*

God is long-suffering to the righteous as well as the wicked. This means that the habitual sinner is given the same opportunity to repent as the first-time sinner.[36] God waits for the sense of morality that He has implanted within man to motivate him to repent. For every human being, even the habitual sinner, has been endowed by the Creator with a sense of morality. At times, God punishes the sinner in small doses perchance it might bring him to repent.[37] It should be understood, however, that if the sinner does not repent, he will surely be punished.

Some opine that God delays the reward earned by the righteous, that their merit is not requited until the World to Come. This position is stated in the Talmud, "There is no reward [for following the precepts] in this world."[38] Others opine that Divine patience with the sinner applies only to the child. They contend that the fact that the child is not considered liable for punishment until he reaches maturity, i.e., the age

---

31. Ibid.
32. Cf. M. Malbim, commentary on Exodus 34:6.
33. Deuteronomy 3:23.
34. Cf. Rashi, commentary on Deuteronomy 3:23.
35. Cf. I Abravanel, op. cit.
36. Cf. *Eruvin* 22a.
37. Cf. Isaac Arama, *Akedat Yitzhak* (Jerusalem, 1969), Exodus Gate 54, p. 191.
38. *Kiddushin* 39b.

of 13 in a terrestrial court and 20 in a Heavenly court, is a manifestation of the Divine patience.

6. Rav Hesed

God is exceedingly kind in His treatment of man. In His judgment of those whose good and bad deeds are equally balanced, He leans toward kindness rather than strict justice.[39] Moreover, God grants the righteous a special measure of kindness over and above that which they have earned for their righteousness. According to S. R. Hirsch, this special measure of kindness manifests itself in "giving to each one his own particular kind of satisfaction and happiness."[40]

7. Rav Emet

In His reward to man for his righteousness, God is truthful, namely, He rewards appropriately. But unlike man, whose love at times blinds him to the truth and is overly zealous in his rewards, God is exceedingly truthful. He tempers kindness with truth. One might say that He is mindful of the adage "Too much of a good thing can be harmful." Again, in the words of S. R. Hirsch, God "knows how to mix the most abundant granting of wishes with as much denial as will prevent the receiver of the desired blessing from his apparent good fortune having a deteriorating effect."[41]

8. Extending kindness to the thousandth generation

As we have already pointed out, there are times, for reasons beyond our understanding, that God withholds reward to the righteous during their

---

39. Cf. Rashi and *Sifte Hahamim* on Exodus 34:6; also *Akedat Yitzhak* ad loc.
40. S. R. Hirsch, commentary on Exodus 34:6.
41. Ibid.

lifetime. With others, He simply does not compensate them fully for their righteousness. Nevertheless, the merit of such individuals does not go unrequited. Quite the contrary, God retains, as it were, the memory of a person's righteousness and bestows reward to his children, grandchildren, or great-grandchildren, at times waiting even to the thousandth generation.[42] It is important to recognize the great benefit that ensues to mankind as a result of this Divine attribute. The younger generation inherits not only the knowledge of the older generation but its reward as well, which gives them a head start, so to speak, on the road to happiness and spiritual fulfillment. In the words of S. R. Hirsch: "God exercises His greatest love in allowing a good man to become a source, a root and "bud" of salvation and happiness to his children and children's children down the ages."[43] In light of this attribute we often appeal to God in the name of *zekhut avot*, "the [unrequited] merit of our forefathers."

10–12. *Forgiving iniquity, transgression, and sin*

There are three types of sin mentioned here, all of which are forgiven by God if the sinner truly repents. There is a difference of opinion, however, with regard to the precise meaning of each of these terms. According to some, *iniquity* is a wrong committed out of lust; *transgression* is a wrong committed in rebellion against God; *sin* is a wrong committed inadvertently.[44] Others opine that *iniquity* is an intellectual wrongdoing, i.e., improper thoughts or heresy; *transgression* is rebellion against God; and *sin* is simply lust.[45] Be that as it may, the remarkable thing about Divine forgiveness of those who are truly penitent is that the iniquity, transgression, or sin will be "lifted out" of the laws of cause

---

42. Cf. I. Abravanel, op. cit., p. 340.
43. S. R. Hirsch, op. cit. 4:7.
44. Cf. I. Abravanel, op. cit., p. 341. It should be noted that according to the Talmud, iniquity is deliberate wrongful behavior; transgression is rebellious acts, and sin is inadvertent wrongful behavior (*Yoma* 36b).
45. Cf. M. Malbim, op. cit, 34:7.

and effect.[46] In the words of S. R. Hirsch: "The sin will actually become as if it had not been committed, and the natural effects of sin will not take place."[47]

13. *Not remitting all punishment*

God remits punishment but only to those whose repentance is motivated by sincere regret for having committed an impropriety rather than out of fear of punishment.[48] Needless to say, those who do not repent are not forgiven. Others contend that there are two situations that are addressed by this attribute, both of which are manifestations of Divine compassion.[49] Where one's merits are more numerous than his sins, not only will God forgive him, but He will also wipe his slate clean; no sin will appear on his record. For all intents and purposes, it will be as if he had never committed a sin. In a situation where one's sins are more numerous than his merits, in consequence of which he deserves to die, he will be punished. God will cause him some suffering and anguish, but He will not destroy him.[50]

13. *Remembering the iniquity of parents for children and children's children to the third and fourth generation.*

As we pointed out above, according to Maimonides this is the thirteenth Divine attribute. The most common translation is "visiting the iniquity of the fathers upon the children." This means that the children are punished for the sins of their fathers. While this seems rather harsh, it is important to point out that it refers only to the sin of idolatry, and it

---

46. Cf. S. R. Hirsch, op, cit. The Hebrew for "forgives" here is *nosey*, which also means "lifts."
47. Ibid.
48. *Yoma* 86a. See also O. Seforno, op. cit.
49. Cf. I. Abravanel, op. cit.
50. Ibid.

applies only where the children have themselves committed this sin.[51] According to the translation that we have chosen,[52] the meaning here is quite different. God remembers the sins of the parents when He judges the children. He treats the children with forbearance for he recognizes that their idolatrous behavior is due to the bad influence of their parents. He waits until the fifth generation. By that time, that influence should have dissipated. If the children of that generation are still idolatrous, they are judged to be guilty and are punished.[53]

This concludes our discussion on the Thirteen Divine Attributes. In the next few chapters, we shall see how the names of God that appear in the Torah text reflect these Divine attributes and how this relates to the early history of the Jewish people.

---

51. Cf. *Berakhot* 7a.
52. This is the translation of S. R. Hirsch and is the implied translation in the commentary of O. Seforno.
53. Cf. S. R. Hirsch, op. cit.

3

THE GOD OF
ADAM AND NOAH

In the first chapter of the Creation narrative, the Divine appellative *E-lohim* is used exclusively. As we have already indicated, this name represents God the Creator. The story of Creation teaches man that the Supreme Being created the world and all its components. He created the law of nature that governs the world as well. It is not until Genesis 2:4 that we read: "Such is the story of Heaven and Earth as they were created, when the *Lord* God made Earth and Heaven." With the exception of the serpent that speaks of the Supreme Being simply as *E-lohim*, whenever the name *E-lohim* appears in chapters 2 and 3, *Havayah* precedes it. Let us attempt to understand the significance of this juxtaposition.

With the creation of man, the operation of the world changed. No longer would the law of nature alone effect the world. Providence entered the scene, and to the present, it figures significantly in the day-to-day implementation of the Divine plan. What this means is that man's attitude and his behavior are taken into careful consideration in the determination of the destiny of the world. Let us explain. As we have already indicated,[1] the name *Havayah* represents the Divine attribute of compassion. The fact that this name appears more frequently in the Torah than any other Divine name teaches us an important lesson. Contrary to Deism, which purports that God created the world and subsequently withdrew from it, no longer concerned with its destiny, Judaism purports that God is immanent in the world. He is very much concerned with the world, and Divine compassion is an ongoing manifestation of that concern.[2] The introduction of man in chapter 2 is marked by the introduction of the Divine name *Havayah* because from that point on the Torah focuses on man, his trials and his tribulations, his rewards and his punishments as they relate to his responsibility to his Creator.

THE CREATION OF MAN

The creation of man is already noted in chapter 1. Yet, in Genesis 2:7 we read: "The Lord God formed man from the dust of the Earth, and He blew into his nostrils the breath of life; and man became a living being." Is man created in chapter 1 or in chapter 2? Our sages were well aware of this difficulty, and they taught the following. The style of the biblical narrative is to proceed from the general to the particular. In chapter 1 we are told very briefly that man was created. The details of his creation and the creation of the woman as well as their initial encounter with temptation are all given in chapter 2. Although it appears to us that there are two different accounts of man's creation, in actuality the second account elaborates on the first.[3]

In chapter 2 we are told that man was created out of the dust of the Earth, and God subsequently endowed him with the breath of life. This indicates that man is a composite of the material and the spiritual, the Earthly and the Heavenly. The former is indicated by the appearance of the name *E-lohim*, the latter by the name *Havayah*. The association of

---

1. Cf. chapter 1 in this volume.
2. Cf. M. Malbim, commentary on Genesis 2:4, and S. R. Hirsch ad loc.
3. Cf. Rashi, commentary on Genesis 2:8.

The God of Adam and Noah

these names with the creation of man also teach us that if man is worthy, he will be judged with compassion; if not, strict justice alone will decide his fate.

In Genesis 2:16 we read: "And the Lord God commanded the man saying, 'Of every tree of the garden you are free to eat.'" There is much more to this verse than meets the eye. According to our sages, this single verse alludes to the seven Noahide commandments.[4] The appearance of the name *Havayah* here designates the special measure of Divine compassion that manifests itself in the relationship between man and his Creator. It is Divine compassion that inspired the revelation of the seven Noahide commandments, the observance of which would enable man to attain moral perfection and spiritual happiness. The close relationship between man and God precludes blasphemy, one of the Noahide commandments. The name *E-lohim* that appears here represents God as the Lawgiver, not only the ethical and moral law but the law of nature as well. Indeed, it is the latter that predetermines the behavior of all of God's creations with the exception of man. Man has the freedom of choice; he must choose to obey God. Deification of any other being is forbidden.[5]

In chapter 2 we are given the details of when and how the woman was created, and our sages made some important comments with regard to this event. The text in Genesis 2:22 reads: "And the Lord God fashioned into a woman the rib that He had taken from man, and He brought her to the man." Since the identical Divine names appear here as when the man was created, we must assume, said the sages, that just as the man is a composite of the physical and the spiritual, so, too, is the woman. Moreover, the sages commented: "'And the Lord God fashioned . . . the rib,' which teaches us that the Holy One blessed be He, endowed the woman with more understanding than the man."[6]

---

4. *Sanhedrin* 56a. The seven Noahide commandments are: to set up courts of law; and prohibition of blasphemy, idolatry, murder, illicit sexual relations, theft, and eating a limb from a living animal.

5. Cf. S. R. Hirsch, commentary on Genesis 2:16.

6. The Hebrew here, *va-yiven* ("built"), is analogous to the term *binah* ("understanding").

IN THE GARDEN OF EDEN

Adam and Eve, the first pair, were put into the Garden of Eden and charged not to eat from the tree of knowledge. The Bible tells us that presently, the serpent appeared, and he tempted Eve to eat from the tree. Now what do we know of this serpent? In Genesis 3:1 we read: "Now the serpent was the shrewdest of all the wild beasts that the Lord God had made. He said to the woman: 'Did God really say: You shall not eat of any tree of the garden?'" The serpent refers to the Supreme Being as *E-lohim*. This was the only name familiar to him. We have already indicated that the name *Havayah* is known only to man. When Eve speaks to the serpent about God she also refers to Him as *E-lohim*.[7] In point of fact, the discussion between them concerned the law, and as such the name *E-lohim* was certainly appropriate.

The serpent was successful and Eve gave in to temptation. She disobeyed God's command, and she ate from the fruit of the tree of knowledge. Of course, disobedience leads to punishment. Suddenly Adam and Eve experienced the presence of the Divine. In Genesis 3:8 we read: "They heard the sound of the Lord God moving about in the garden at the breezy time of day; and the man and his wife hid from the Lord God." The juxtaposed Divine names *Havayah E-lohim* are in order even when man is merely experiencing the presence of the Supreme Being. All the more so, when there is communication between the two.

In Genesis 3:9 we read: "The Lord God called out to the man and said to him, 'Where are you?'" These words, which are familiar to most of us, are pregnant with meaning. They have been interpreted in many different ways. We shall simply relate them to the Divine names that appear in the text. You have been created dust from the Earth, says God (*E-lohim*), but I have also endowed you with a soul, the breath of life, says the Lord (*Havayah*). You have been created in *My* image and in *My*

---

7. Genesis 3:2–3: "And the woman said to the serpent, 'We may eat of the fruit of the other trees of the garden. It is only about fruit of the tree in the middle of the garden that God [*E-lohim*] said: You shall not eat of it or touch it lest you die.'"

likeness.[8] What have you done to yourself by allowing desire to subdue your intellect? In a sense, one can say that these Divine components of the human personality call out to him whenever he sins, and they charge him to give an accounting of his behavior.

Let us attempt to resolve a contradiction. In Genesis 3:14 we read: "And the Lord God said to the serpent, 'Because you did this, banned shall you be from all cattle and all wild beasts . . . I will put enmity between you and the woman, and between your offspring and hers; they shall strike at your head and you shall strike at their heel.'" Have we not said that the name *Havayah* is reserved for man? Should the text not have read, "And God said to the serpent"? Perhaps the answer lies in the significance of the message rather than to whom it is addressed. It is not Divine communication with the serpent that the Torah wishes to emphasize here but rather the lesson that these words hold for man. Was not the Torah revealed to man exclusively? Given that this reasoning is correct, let us look to the lesson. S. R. Hirsch puts it very succinctly:

> From the point of view of the educational care for mankind, the strong antipathy implanted in man towards snakes may be meant to bring home to his mind that it was "animal wisdom" that led him astray . . . and at the same time, by concrete example, to keep the fact constantly before his eyes that there must be a different criterion for good and evil than the dictates of blind instinctive inclinations.[9]

There is another way we might resolve this difficulty. According to Isaac Abravanel,[10] the story of the Garden of Eden is an allegory. There never was an actual conversation between Eve and the serpent. Eve saw the serpent eating the fruit of the forbidden tree, and no harm came to him. She interpreted this as his way of telling her that if she were to

---

8. Cf. Genesis 1:26, 27.
9. S. R. Hirsch, commentary on Genesis 3:14–15.
10. Cf. I. Abravanel, commentary on Genesis 3:1; see also M. Maimonides, *Guide of the Perplexed*, op. cit., Part II, chap. xxx.

eat from the tree no harm would come to her either. Moreover the Supreme Being did not speak to the serpent; He simply designated the punishment.[11] The Torah, speaking in the language of man, wove the event into an allegory. Since the narrative was directed to mankind as a lesson in ethics, the name *Havayah E-lohim* is certainly in place.[12]

THE FIRST FAMILY

The natural birth of the first human being was surely a memorable event, and the Torah records this event in the words of Eve. In Genesis 4:1 we read: "Now the man knew his wife Eve, and she conceived and bore Cain saying, 'I have gained a male child with the help of the Lord.' She then bore his brother Abel." It is most noteworthy that Eve, the mother of mankind, invoked *Havayah* in naming her first child. Her words are not merely an expression of thanksgiving. Had that been the case, *E-lohim*, the name that focuses on the Divine creative powers, would certainly have been more appropriate. Eve recognized the miracle of birth as a manifestation of compassion of the greatest magnitude, perhaps the most significant Divine attribute represented by the name *Havayah*, and she invokes that name as she experiences the great joy of motherhood. As we have already noted, it is not merely coincidental that *rehem*, the Hebrew term for "womb," is the root of the word *rahamim*, which means "compassion."

We must also note the following. In the creation narrative, the Supreme Being is referred to as *E-lohim*, the creator of all that exists in the natural world, the Supreme Being who rules with strict justice. With the creation of man came the need for tempering justice with compassion, so the name *Havayah* was introduced and juxtaposed to *E-lohim*. With the formation of the first family and the introduction of the name *Havayah* as a separate Divine name, the Torah indicated that from this

---

11. Ibid.
12. The story of man in the Garden of Eden has been interpreted as a lesson in ethics by virtually all the biblical commentators. In addition to Maimonides and Abravanel mentioned in note 99, the reader is referred to the Hirsch commentary on Genesis chapter 3.

point in time and for the duration of all time to come, Divine compassion would prevail in the world.[13]

The Torah tells us that Cain entered into an argument with his brother Abel and killed him. In Genesis 4:25 we read: "Adam knew his wife again, and she bore a son and named him Seth, meaning, 'God has provided me with another offspring in place of Abel,' for Cain had killed him." The change in the Divine name here is significant. When Cain was born, Eve considered it a miraculous event, certainly a manifestation of Divine providence, and she invoked the name *Havayah*. When Seth was born, she had already come to the realization that birth is a manifestation of natural law; hence the name *E-lohim* was invoked. Moreover, Abel did not deserve to die. Cain had murdered him in a fit of anger. Eve considered the replacement of Abel with Seth a manifestation of Divine justice, the attribute represented by the name *E-lohim*.

IN THE TIME OF ENOSH

In the time of Enosh, a transformation occurred. In Genesis 4:26 we read: "And to Seth, in turn, a son was born, and he named him Enosh. It was then that men began to invoke the Lord by name." The term *huhal* is translated here as "began," the most literal rendering of the word.[14] Some differ with this translation and render the term "profane." For it was in the generation of Enosh that people began to profane the name of *Havayah*; it was the onset of idolatry.[15] Others contend that the masses felt themselves too lowly to offer prayers to the Lord. Instead, they offered their prayers to the Heavenly bodies: the sun, the moon, and the stars, which they felt would act as intermediaries. Calling upon *Havayah* Himself in time of need was considered an impropriety.[16] Be that as it may, the literal rendering of the term should also be considered. With the descendants of Cain and Seth, the name and the

---

13. Cf. M. Malbim, commentary on Genesis 4:1.
14. The term can also mean "profaned" or "desecrated."
15. Rashi, commentary on Genesis 4:26 and others.
16. Cf. J. Z. Mecklenburg, commentary on Genesis 4:26.

belief in *Havayah* as the One who guides human history and to whom all must submit had been completely forgotten. The time had come to regenerate these beliefs in the minds of the masses, to make reference to *Havayah* an integral part of their lives. Indeed, "it was then that men began to invoke the Lord by name."[17]

ENOKH AND NOAH

What now follows is for the most part a genealogical table with but two brief departures. The table is introduced in Genesis 5:1 with the words: "This is the record of Adam's line. When God created man, He made him in the likeness of God," and a fitting introduction it is. For it is through the process of procreation, a natural law with which man was endowed by *E-lohim*, the Creator of nature, that the families of the Earth emerged.

The first departure from genealogy concerns Enokh. In Genesis 5:21–24 we read: "When Enokh had lived sixty-five years, he begat Methuselah. After the birth of Methuselah, Enokh walked with God and he begat sons and daughters. All the days of Enokh came to 365 years. Enokh walked with God; then he was no more, for God took him." Since Enokh is singled out from among the descendants of Seth, he is clearly a person of note. The fact that the name *E-lohim* is mentioned twice in his regard hints to the following. Enokh came to the understanding that there exits a Supreme Being who created Heaven and Earth, by studying the nature of the Heavenly bodies, specifically the sun. This is alluded to in the Torah by the fact that he lived 365 years, the precise number of days that it takes the Earth to revolve around the sun.[18] The unique way in which the Torah records Enokh's death teaches us that he died before his time. Until he reached the age of 365, Enokh walked with both God and man. He worshipped his Creator, but he also engaged in normal behavior, namely, he fulfilled the

---

17. Cf. S. R. Hirsch, commentary on Genesis 4:26.
18. Cf. I. Abravanel, commentary on Genesis 5:23.

mitzvah of procreation. From that point on, however, he concerned himself exclusively with matters Divine. Finally, he left the world and his soul returned to its source "for God took him."[19]

The second departure from genealogy is with regard to Noah. In Genesis 5:28 we read: "When Lemech had lived 182 years, he begot a son. And he named him Noah, saying, 'This one will provide us relief from our work and from the toil of our hands, out of the very soil which the Lord placed under a curse." What is the significance here of the name "Lord"? Should the name not have been "God," the name that symbolizes creative activity? Perhaps the answer is as follows: *E-lohim* created the Earth and endowed it with natural properties. By nature, the Earth would have consistently yielded to man if he worked it properly. But man sinned, and the Supreme Being chose to punish him by placing the soil under a curse. He superimposed His will over nature so that it would not always yield to the labor of man's hands. The Divine name that represents an act that is contrary to nature is *Havayah*.

MAN'S WITHDRAWAL FROM GOD

Man began to multiply upon the Earth. In the beginning there were two separate families: the descendants of Cain and the descendants of Seth. At least to some extent, the Sethites served God. As such they were designated in the Torah as the "Sons of the Godly Race" (*B'ne E-lohim*). The Cainites, on the other hand, were not at all interested in God; they served only themselves; they were designated in the Torah as the "Sons of Men" (*B'ne Adam*).[20] So long as the two strains lived and developed separately from one another there was hope that the Sethites might prevail over the Cainites and put mankind back on track. But in Genesis 6:1–2 we read: "When men began to multiply on the face of the Earth and daughters were born to them, the sons of the godly race saw how

---

19. Ibid.; see also M. Malbim, commentary on Genesis 5:22–24.
20. Cf. S. R. Hirsch, commentary on Genesis 6:1.

beautiful the daughters of men were, and they took as wives any they liked."[21] When the two groups began to intermarry, all hope for the restoration of propriety to that generation was lost.

The result of all this is that in Genesis 6: 5–8 we read:

> The Lord saw how great was man's wickedness on Earth, and how every plan devised by his mind was nothing but evil all the time. And the Lord regretted that He had made man on Earth, and His heart was saddened. The Lord said, "I will blot out from the Earth the men whom I created . . . for I regret that I made them." But Noah found favor with the Lord.

In order to understand properly the expressions "The Lord saw," "The Lord regretted," and "His heart was saddened," we must again invoke a principle commonly referred to by our sages in their comments on biblical passages. The principle is: "The Torah speaks in the language of men."[22] In our context this principle teaches us that it was *as if* the Supreme Being experienced the movement of man toward self-centeredness, and this depressed Him. Were we to take these expressions literally, they would imply a change of heart, a condition that would certainly be contrary to our understanding of the Supreme Being.

Let us also note that it is *Havayah* that is spoken of here, not *E-lohim*. The families of man were about to be swept away by a flood that would encompass the world. They had been given 120 years to repent of their ways, but it was to no avail.[23] Divine justice demanded that they should be destroyed, and one would have expected the name *E-lohim* to appear here. This may be so, but we have already pointed out that with the creation of man, Divine compassion came into the world to temper strict justice. This is what is implied in the choice of the name *Havayah* here. It is *Havayah*, the compassionate Creator of man who saw man's wickedness, who regretted that He had created man, and who was

---

21. The translation of this verse is based on the S. R. Hirsch translation of the Bible.
22. Cf. M. Nahmanides, commentary on Genesis 6:1 and Ibn Ezra, commentary on Genesis 6:6.
23. Cf. Rashi, commentary on Genesis 6:3.

saddened in His heart that He had to destroy man, His most cherished creation. Noah was the exception. Noah found favor with *Havayah*. Of all the people who existed in that generation, he alone was worthy of being saved. As a manifestation of Divine compassion, *Havayah* saved Noah's entire family as well.

WALKING WITH GOD

With regard to Noah's righteousness, the Torah makes an interesting statement. In Genesis 6:9 we read: "This is the line of Noah. Noah was a righteous man; he was blameless in his age; Noah walked with God. Noah had three sons: Shem, Ham, and Japheth." What is the meaning of the expression "walked with God"? How does one walk with the Supreme Being of the universe? If we look back at Genesis 5:22 we see that Enokh also walked with God. Would it be presumptuous to contend that what was true of Enokh, namely, that he came to the understanding that there exists a Creator in the universe by observing the Heavenly bodies and the miracles of nature, was true of Noah as well?[24] In point of fact, a similar statement is made about Abraham, and our sages made the same comment about him.[25]

Let us go one step further in our comparison of Noah to Enokh. We must take notice of the fact that with Enokh we are first told that he had sons and daughters, and subsequently that he walked with God. With Noah, on the other hand, the fact that he had three sons is mentioned after we are told that he walked with God. Is this mere coincidence? Perhaps the Torah is telling us that unlike Enokh Noah did not give up living a normal life in order to walk with God. He walked with God, but he also engaged in the mitzvah of procreation.

---

24. Cf. I Abravanel, commentary on Genesis 5:23.
25. Ibid. Cf. Genesis 17:1, "When Abraham was ninety nine years old, the Lord appeared to Abraham and said to him, 'I am God Almighty. Walk in My ways and be blameless.'"

THE DESTRUCTIVE FLOOD

The corruption of society justified the cataclysmic event that was to take place, and in Genesis 6:12 we read: "When God saw how corrupt the Earth was, for all flesh had corrupted its ways on Earth, God said to Noah, 'I have decided to put an end to all flesh, for the Earth is filled with lawlessness because of them: I am about to destroy them with the Earth.'" Whenever the Divine name appears in connection with the flood it is *E-lohim*, for the flood was a manifestation of strict Divine justice, punishment inflicted upon an immoral society. In point of fact, even when the Torah records that Noah complied with all that he was charged to do in order to save him from the flood, the text reads: "Noah did so, just as God commanded him, so he did." It is not until the rains were about to begin and Noah had to enter the ark that a change occurred. Thus in Genesis 7:1 we read: "Then the *Lord* said to Noah, 'Go into the ark, you and all your household, for you alone have I found righteous before Me in this generation." What is the reason for this change? Saving Noah and his family was a manifestation of Divine compassion; it called for the name *Havayah*.[26]

Noah had been instructed by *E-lohim* to bring one pair of every animal with him into the ark. Then we read that *Havayah* instructed him to bring seven pairs of every clean animal into the ark. Why the discrepancy? Unlike the other animals that were saved in order to repopulate the Earth after the flood [which would call for the name *E-lohim*], the clean animals were saved for Noah's personal use. Clearly a manifestation of the providential hand of the Lord, they would serve as thanksgiving offerings.[27] For this reason, when the Torah records Noah's compliance with all that he was charged, the text in Genesis 7:5 reads: "And Noah did just as the Lord had commanded him."

Noah entered the ark with his family, and he took with him seven pairs of the clean animals. The other animals seem to have entered the ark of their own accord for in Genesis 7:15–16 we read: "They came to Noah into the ark, two each of all flesh in which there was breath of life.

---

26. Cf. M. Nahmanides, Genesis 7:1.
27. Rashi, commentary on Genesis 7:2.

The God of Adam and Noah

Thus they that entered comprised male and female of all flesh as God had commanded him. And the Lord shut him in." How interesting! Two different Divine names appear here. It was *E-lohim*, the Judge who rules the world in strict justice, who charged Noah to take with him a male and a female of every animal, but it was *Havayah*, the compassionate providential Supreme Being, who "shut him in" and thus saved him from drowning in the flood. Both names appear here in a single verse.

The rains fell upon the Earth for forty days and forty nights. In Genesis 8:1 we are told: "When the waters had swelled on the Earth for 150 days, "God remembered Noah and all the beasts and all the cattle that were with him in the ark, and God cause a wind to blow across the Earth and the waters subsided." Surely one would have expected the name Havayah to appear in this verse to indicate that it was Divine compassion that saved Noah.[28] Perhaps the rationale lies in the fact that with Noah's exit from the ark the world had a new beginning. Indeed, it was as if *E-lohim* had created the world anew.[29] What lends credence to this approach is the fact, in Genesis 8:15–16, when Noah is instructed to emerge from the ark, the text reads: "God spoke to Noah saying: 'Come out of the ark together with your wife, your sons and your sons' wives." It was *E-lohim,* the Creator, who addressed Noah. The final confirmation of this approach comes in Genesis 9:1, which reads: "God blessed Noah and his sons, and said to them 'Be fertile and increase and fill the Earth." These are the same words that were spoken to Adam in Genesis 1:28. Lastly, the Torah testifies that Noah was a righteous man; he deserved to be saved. It was not a manifestation of compassion; it was justice par excellence.

Be that as it may, Noah's offerings of thanksgiving were addressed to Divine compassion, and in Genesis 8:20 we read: "Then Noah built an altar to the Lord and, taking of every clean animal and of every clean bird, he offered burnt offerings on the altar." How does the Supreme Being react to this gesture? In Genesis 8:21 we read: "The Lord smelled

---

28. Cf. Rashi, commentary on Genesis 8:1, for an interesting approach to this problem.
29. Cf. M. Meiri, *Torah Me'irah* (London: Shapiro Vallentine & Co., 1958), Genesis 8:1.

the pleasing odor, and the Lord said to Himself: 'Never again will I doom the world because of man, since the divisings of man's mind are evil from his youth; nor will I ever again destroy every living being, as I have done.'" The response to Noah's gesture was a positive one. The context of this verse makes it quite clear. The choice of the name *Havayah* reinforces this contention. Indeed, the acceptance of Noah's offering was a manifestation of Divine compassion. There would never again be a flood upon the Earth that would destroy all living creatures. So spoke the Supreme Being of the universe. Indeed, in Genesis 9:12–15 we find the following declaration from *E-lohim* to mankind:

> This is the sign of the covenant that I set between Me and you . . . I have set My bow in the clouds, and it shall serve as a sign of the covenant between Me and the Earth. When I bring clouds over the Earth, and the bow appears in the clouds, I will remember My covenant between Me and you . . . so that the waters shall never again become a flood to destroy all flesh.

It was in His capacity as Creator of the world that *E-lohim* promised never again to inflict a flood upon the world to destroy it.

THE TOWER OF BABEL

There is a noteworthy incident recorded in the Torah, a brief story that bears analysis. In Genesis 11:1–8 we read:

> All the Earth had the same language and the same words. And as men migrated from the east, they came upon a valley in the land of Shinar and settled there. They said to one another, "Come let us make bricks and burn them hard." Bricks served them as stone and bitumen served them as mortar. And they said: "Come let us build us a city and a tower with its top in the sky, to make a name for ourselves; else we shall be scattered all over the world." The Lord came down to look at the city and tower which man had built, and the Lord said, "If as one people with one language for all, this is how they have begun to act, then nothing that they may propose to

do will be out of their reach. Let Me then go down and confound their speech there . . ." Thus the Lord scattered them from over the face of the whole Earth; and they stopped building the city.

What was the sin of the tower builders and what is the significance of the Divine name that appears in this context?

The story takes place in the days of Peleg, who was born 101 years after the flood.[30] Noah and his family were still alive. Until that time, the world consisted of simple people who were concerned mainly with their survival and the survival of their families.[31] The people were united in their thinking and in their ways.[32] Then a change took place. The younger generation was not happy with the status quo, and they decided to leave the community and try to make it on their own. They traveled eastward. In truth, they distanced themselves not only from their birthplace but from their Creator as well.[33] "Let us make for ourselves a tower that will reach the Heavens," they said, "and we will ascend to the Heavens and make war with Him who dwells therein."[34]

The Torah then tells us that *Havayah* came down to look at the city and the tower. Rashi comments: "He really did not need to do this, but the Torah intends to teach the judges that they should not proclaim a defendant guilty before they have seen the case and thoroughly understand the matter in question." What does Rashi mean here, and on what basis did he make this comment? Perhaps Rashi's comment is based on the fact that the Divine name that appears here is *Havayah*, indicative of Divine compassion. Just as compassion motivated the Lord to "go down," so to speak, and to examine the situation firsthand, to see if the tower builders were really guilty before He punished them, so

---

30. Genesis 10:25 reads: "Two sons were born to Eber: the name of the first was Peleg, for in his days the Earth was divided; and the name of his brother was Joktan."
31. Cf. M. Malbim, commentary on Genesis 11:1.
32. Ibid.
33. The Midrash in Bereshit Rabbah 38:7 comments that the people traveled away from the "originator of the world," a play on the word *kedem* which can imply either "east" or "first."
34. Cf. Bereshit Rabbah 37:6; also Rabbenu B'haye and Rashi in their commentaries on Genesis 11:4.

should compassion motivate every judge to investigate his cases meticulously, perhaps even personally, before rendering his decision.

The Lord confounded the language of the tower builders so that they could no longer communicate with one another, and they were forced to abandon the project. The Torah tells us that the people were scattered over the face of the whole Earth. Would this be the end of society? Would this be the final proof of the failure of the human experiment? It seems not. There was one man who together with his wife set out to change the world, to bring mankind back to its Creator once again. It was Abraham and his wife was Sarah.

4

THE GOD OF THE PATRIARCHS

NOAH AND ABRAHAM

In Exodus 6:3 we read: "I appeared to Abraham, Isaac, and Jacob as God Almighty, but I did not make Myself known to them by My name Lord." We have already explained that the names *E-l Shad-dai* (God Almighty) symbolize the Divine attributes of omnipotence or power, loving-kindness, and self-sufficiency that create, sustain, and set limits to the development of the universe. We have also noted that, according to Rashi, the name *Havayah* symbolizes the attribute of faithfulness.[1] God promised Abraham that he would inherit the land of Canaan, and that this land would belong to the Jewish people as a permanent inheritance. This is clearly established in Genesis 17:8 where we read: "I give the land you sojourn in to you and your offspring to come, all the land of Canaan, as an everlasting possession. I will be their God."

---

1. Cf. Rashi on Exodus 6:3.

Abraham had no doubts about God's faithfulness, to be sure; nor did Isaac and Jacob. But they were not privileged to see the fulfillment of the Divine promise in their lifetime. As such they could not bear witness to Divine faithfulness on a national level.[2]

What do the Bible and the biblical commentaries tell us about Abraham's perception of God? How did God interact with him? It is our contention that this can be discovered from the Divine names that appear in the text, those that he addressed and those that were addressed to him. So let us proceed to trace the interaction of God and Abraham from these texts.

After the flood that devastated the world, Noah became the physical progenitor of mankind. Ten generations later, Abraham became its spiritual father. Some have attempted to contrast Noah with Abraham. In Genesis 6:9 we read: "This is the line of Noah.—Noah was a righteous man; he was perfect in his generation; Noah walked with God." Rashi makes the following comment:

> Some of our Rabbis explain it to his credit: he was righteous even in his generation; it follows that had he lived in a generation of righteous people, he would have been even more righteous. Others, however, explain it to his discredit; in comparison with his own generation he was considered righteous, but had he lived in the generation of Abraham, he would have been accounted as of no importance.[3]

How did Abraham come to understand God? The Midrash points out that Terah, Abraham's father, did not tell him about God, nor did he

---

2. Others resolve the problem presented here by the biblical text differently. I. Abravanel in his commentary on the text explains that although God did appear to the patriarchs as *Havayah*, they did not recognize Him as such. They did not perceive God "face to face" as Moses had perceived Him. I. Karo in his *Toldot Yizhak* (Jerusalem: Vardi, 1940), p. 70 contends that the patriarchs believed that God created the universe, but it was never demonstrated to them. Moses and the Israelites had it demonstrated to them through the miracle of the rod that turned into a serpent. This supernatural act could only have been performed by the Creator. (See the text of the commentary proper for a fuller explanation.)

3. Rashi on Genesis 6:9.

have a teacher to enlighten him on these matters.[4] Though Noah and his son Shem were still alive in Abraham's day, they lived too far away from Abraham for there to be any interaction between them.[5] At first, the Midrash tells us, Abraham was no different in his worship than the rest of the people of his generation.[6] Indeed, his father manufactured idols. But as Abraham matured he began to realize that the thinking of the people of his time about God and the idolatrous worship in which they engaged was false.[7] After much contemplation he concluded that there is only One Just God in the universe. Maimonides explains:

> After he [Abraham] was weaned, while still an infant, his mind began to reflect "How is it possible that this celestial sphere should continuously be guiding the world and have no one to guide it . . ." He had no teacher, no one to instruct him in anything. His father and mother and the entire population worshiped idols, and he worshiped with them. But his mind was busily working and reflecting till he attained the way of truth . . . and knew that there is One God . . . that He created everything, and that among all that exists, there is no god beside Him . . . Abraham was forty years old when he recognized his Creator.[8]

Abraham and his wife Sarah became the teachers of ethical monotheism to the masses, and they succeeded in influencing many people to accept the notion that there is One Just God in the universe. This is confirmed in Genesis 12:5 where we read: "And Abram took his wife Sarai[9] and his brother's son Lot, and all the wealth that they had amassed, and the persons that they had acquired in Haran; and they set out for the land of Canaan." On the words "the souls that they had acquired in Haran," Rashi comments: "The souls which he had brought

---

4. *Bereshit Rabbah* 61.
5. Cf. Ibid., 48.
6. Cf. Ibid., 29 and 46.
7. Cf. Maimonides, *Mishneh Torah: Laws of Idolatry* 1:3.
8. Ibid.
9. Sarai was her given name. See Genesis 17: 5,15. When God changed Abram's name to Abraham, Sarai's name was changed to Sarah.

under the sheltering wings of the *Shekhinah* [Divine Presence]. Abraham converted the men and Sarah converted the women."

TRAVELS AND TRAVAILS

In Genesis 12:1 we find the first encounter between God and Abraham. "The Lord said to Abram,[10] 'Go forth from your native land and from your father's house to the land that I will show you.'" Intrinsically, revelation is an act of Divine concern for man. The message, which in the initial period of Abraham's prophecy came to him in a dream, is a manifestation of Divine compassion. As such the name *Havayah* is most fitting. Moreover, we must recognize that travel was a dangerous undertaking in Abraham's day. Long-distance travel to an unknown destination would have been particularly threatening and stressful. The name *Havayah* would be reassuring to him. What is implied in the text here is that Abraham was not merely to leave his birthplace and his parents' home physically; he was to abandon their idolatrous influence as well.[11] The Lord assuaged Abraham's fears by assuring him that the journey would be for his benefit and for his good.[12] His name would become great, and he would be a blessing to all the families of the Earth.[13]

When Abraham arrived in Canaan, he passed through the land as far as the site of Shekhem. Once more *Havayah* appeared to him and informed him that this is the land that would be inherited by his children.[14] Our sages tell us that this time *Havayah* appeared to Abraham in a vision, which is a higher form of revelation than a dream.[15] This teaches us, say the sages, that an encounter with the Divine that takes place in the land of Israel is of a higher form than that which takes place outside the land. Additionally, the text states that

---

10. At this point in the Torah narrative Abraham was still called Abram.
11. Cf. M. Malbim, commentary on Genesis 12:1.
12. Rashi, commentary on Genesis 12:1.
13. Genesis 12:2,3.
14. Genesis 12:7.
15. Ibid., in the commentary of Nahmanides.

Abraham built an altar to "the Lord who had appeared to him," which teaches us that each of the patriarchs perceived God according to his level of understanding at a given time.[16]

Moving on to the hill country east of Bethel, Abraham pitched his tent and once more built an altar to the Lord. Here the Torah tells us that he "invoked the Lord by name."[17] Interestingly, it was not the name *E-lohim* but *Havayah* that he invoked. The reason for this is that an offering must be brought to the Supreme Being alone. The name *E-lohim* at times refers to angels or to judges; the name *Havayah* refers to the Supreme Being exclusively. It is thus quite evident that the meanings and usage of these names of the Supreme Being were clear to him.

There was a famine in the land of Canaan, and Abraham and Sarah were forced to go down to Egypt and sojourn there. Sarah was a beautiful woman. Fearing that the Egyptians might kill him in order to take Sarah for themselves, Abraham instructed her to say that she was his sister. When the Egyptians saw how beautiful she was they brought her before Pharaoh, and she was taken into his palace, a move that Abraham had not anticipated. In Genesis 12:17 we read: "But the Lord afflicted Pharaoh and his household with mighty plagues on account of Sarai, the wife of Abram." Pharaoh summoned Abraham and confronted him: "What is this you have done to me? Why did you not tell me that she was your wife?"[18] What is the significance of the name *Havayah* that appears in the text above? Pharaoh was being punished. Wouldn't the name *E-lohim* have been more appropriate? Ordinarily, yes, but since this was clearly indicative of Divine intervention in the historical process on behalf of Abraham and Sarah, a clear manifestation of Divine compassion or providence, the name *Havayah* was more appropriate.

Abraham left Egypt together with his wife Sarah and his nephew Lot. They traveled up into the Negev as far as Bethel, to the place where his tent had been formerly, to the site of the altar that he had built there at

---

16. Cf. M. Meiri, *Torah Me'irah* (London: Shapiro, Vallentine & Co., 1960), on Genesis 12:7.
17. Genesis 12:9.
18. Genesis 12:18.

first. Once again Abraham invoked *Havayah* by name. This time it was in thanksgiving for having returned him unharmed to the land that had been promised to him and his children as an inheritance.[19] Considering what Abraham had endured in Egypt, it was truly indicative of Divine compassion. Abraham and Lot had amassed large flocks and herds and tents, and there was quarreling between the shepherds of Lot and those of Abraham over the grazing land. Most unfortunate for Lot, the disagreement became so pronounced that the two men were forced to separate. Abraham was greatly saddened by this turn of events. He felt very lonely for Lot was his only family, and this made him feel regret for what he allowed to happen. After all, Lot may very well have been destined to be his inheritor. So the Lord appeared to him saying, "Raise your eyes and look out from where you are . . . for I give all the land that you see to you and your offspring forever." This encounter was a clear manifestation of Divine compassion, as if to reassure him that he need not be concerned with Lot for his own children would be his heirs.[20] As such the name *Havayah* was most appropriate.

Abraham moved his tent and came to dwell in the terebinths of Mamre, which were in Hebron. Once again, he built an altar to the *Havayah*. This time it was to thank Him for the promise that he would be the father of a great nation and inherit the land of Canaan.[21]

VICTORIOUS IN BATTLE

Lot settled in the cities of the Plain, pitching his tents near Sodom, notwithstanding the fact that the inhabitants of Sodom were wicked sinners against the Lord. A battle broke out in the vicinity: four kings made war against five. The invaders took the wealth of Sodom and Lot was taken captive. When the news was brought to Abraham, he gathered a small force of 318 men and went out in pursuit of the invaders. Victorious in battle, Abraham brought back his nephew Lot

---

19. Cf. Ibn Ezra, commentary on Genesis 13:4.
20. Cf. Don Isaac Abravanel, commentary ad loc.
21. Cf. Ibid., Genesis 13:18.

and his possessions, the women, and the rest of the people. The King of Sodom implored Abraham to allow the Sodomites to return to their homes. "Give me the persons, and take the possessions for yourself," he said. Abraham replied: "I swear to the Lord Most High, Creator of Heaven and Earth, that I will not take as much as a thread or a sandal strap, or anything that is yours, lest you say, 'It is I who made Abraham rich.'" This is the first time Abraham refers to the Supreme Being by the name "Lord Most High" (*Havayah E-l Elyon*), and it is important that we understand the significance of this reference. I raise my hand to *Havayah E-l Elyon*, to sanctify His name and to declare that He alone is the Creator of Heaven and Earth, says Abraham. I testify that the idols of the nations are worthless, and that their idolatrous practices are for naught. Only the Lord Most High shelters and protects all those who trust in Him as a manifestation of compassion and providence of the highest order.[22]

After his miraculous victory over the five kings, Abraham became apprehensive about the future. Perhaps this victory was his reward, the Lord's compensation to him for all the good that he had accomplished in his life.[23] To put his anxiety to rest, the Lord appeared to him and in Genesis 15:1 we read: "After these things, the word of the Lord came to Abram in a vision saying, 'Fear not Abram, I am a shield to you; your reward shall be very great.'" You will not be punished on account of all the people you have killed in battle, said the Lord, moreover, your reward will be exceedingly great.[24] Quite in keeping with the name *Havayah*, this promise was truly a manifestation of Divine compassion in Abraham's behalf.

THE GREAT REWARD

Abraham responded somewhat skeptically to the Lord's reassuring words, and in Genesis 15:2 we read: "But Abram said, 'O Lord God,

---

22. Cf. M. Malbim, commentary on Genesis 14:22.
23. Cf. Rashi, commentary on Genesis 15:1.
24. Ibid.

what can You give me seeing that I continue childless, and the one in charge of my household is Dammesek Eliezer.'" This is the first time the two names *Adney* and *Havayah* are juxtaposed in the Torah, and we must probe the sources for a logical explanation. Our sages point out that Abraham was the first person to refer to God as *Adney*,[25] and as we have already indicated, the name depicts God as the Master of the world and designates all of humanity as His servants. Abraham was the first person to understand that man's role in life is to serve God freely, without demanding or even expecting a reward. But since God had promised him that his reward would be great, Abraham focused on the only reward that would be meaningful to him—a son who would walk in his ways. At the same time, he felt unworthy of a miracle. For only through Divine intervention in the law of nature would it have been possible for a man of his age to have a son. It is for this reason that Abraham made his request known to God indirectly with the words, "what can you give me seeing that I go childless."[26] With this in mind, let us return to the juxtaposition of the names *Adney Havayah*. Abraham turned to God as *Adney*, Creator and Master of the universe, the omnipotent One within whose power it is to act either in consonance with the law of nature or contrary to it. But he also appeals to Him as *Havayah*, the compassionate One. (Is it not interesting that when these two names are juxtaposed, the name *Havayah* is vocalized and read like *E-lohim*?) To grant an old man's request for a son could only be accomplished by the omnipotent God. It would have to be a supernatural act, and one of Divine compassion in Abraham's behalf.

The response to Abraham's request came swiftly and directly. In Genesis 15:4 we read: "The word of the Lord came to him in reply, 'That one shall not be your heir; none but your very own issue shall be your heir.'" This was not the first time that the Lord promised Abraham that he would have a son to inherit him. Yes, he and Sarah were old, and the promise had not yet been fulfilled, but Abraham did not lose faith in the quality of Divine compassion. He knew that someday the promise

---

25. Cf. *Berakhot* 7a.
26. Cf. D. Z. Hoffmann, *Torah Commentary* (B'nei B'rak, Israel: Nezach, 1971), Genesis 15:2.

would be fulfilled. Indeed, unshakable faith was one of Abraham's most outstanding qualities. This is confirmed in Genesis 15:6 where we read: "And because he put his trust in the Lord, He [the Lord] reckoned it to his merit."

THE PROMISE OF NATIONHOOD

The fact that he would have a son to inherit him was only the first part of a threefold promise the Lord had made to Abraham. He was to be the father of a great nation[27] who would inherit the land of Canaan. Concerning the latter we read: "Then He said to him, 'I am the Lord who brought you out of Ur of the Chaldeans to give you this land as a possession." My concern for your welfare and the welfare of society at large prompted Me to exercise My compassion and bring you out of Ur of the Chaldeans, says the Lord. It also prompted Me to give you and your children the land of Canaan as a permanent inheritance.

God allayed Abraham's fears; He made a treaty with him. A treaty differs from a promise in that the former is unconditional. Worthy or unworthy, the children of Israel would inherit the land.[28] Alas, Abraham would not live to see it. For it would be several generations before the treaty would be fulfilled. In Genesis 15:13, 15–16 we read:

> And He said to Abram, "Know well that your offspring shall be strangers in a land not theirs, and they shall be enslaved and oppressed four hundred years . . . As for you, you shall go to your fathers in peace; you shall be buried in a ripe old age. And they shall return here in the fourth generation, for the iniquity of the Amorites will not be fulfilled until then."

On first reading, Abraham's response to the words of *Havayah* is enigmatic. In Genesis 15:8 we read: "And he said, 'O Lord God how shall I know that I am to possess it?'" What is the meaning of this question? Did Abraham need proof? Did he need reassurance from the

---

27. Genesis 15:5.
28. Ibid.

Lord that He would fulfill His promise? This is not the Abraham we know from his previous encounters with the Lord. Here again, we must focus on the names by which Abraham addressed the Supreme Being. "You are, indeed, the Creator [*E-lohim*] and Master of the universe, said Abraham. As such there is nothing that is beyond Your ability. Your compassion [*Havayah*] like Your essence is eternal. While I do not question Your ability and Your intent to fulfill the promise that my children will inherit the land of Canaan, I am apprehensive about the future. Perhaps when the time comes my children will have sinned rendering them unworthy of Your benevolence."[29]

SARAH'S PLAN

Despite the repeated Divine promises that Abraham would have a son, none was born to him, and Sarah became distressed. What distressed her even more than her inability to bear Abraham a son was the fact that the Divine promise was not being fulfilled. Convinced that it was her fault, she approached Abraham with a plan. In Genesis 16:2 we read: "And Sarai[30] said to Abram, 'See the Lord has kept me from bearing. Consort with my maid; perhaps I shall be built up through her.'" What is the meaning of Sarah's words? Sarah trusted Hagar who had been a devoted servant. After all, Hagar was the daughter of Pharaoh, a woman of noble stock. The Supreme Being, the Lord of compassion who promised you a son, said Sarah, has kept me from bearing that son. A son born to my trusted handmaid Hagar would grow up in my house. I would be able to raise him in the Abrahamite tradition. Who knows, perhaps this gesture would find favor in God's eyes, and in His boundless compassion He would subsequently grant me a son in reward for my selflessness.

Abraham complied with Sarah's wishes. Much to Sarah's dismay, however, things did not work out as she had anticipated. When Hagar became pregnant her attitude toward Sarah changed. She felt that she

---

29. Cf. Nahmanides, commentary on Genesis 15:8.
30. At this point in the Torah narrative Sarah was still called Sarai.

should be the mistress of the house, not the handmaid. Even Abraham felt that Hagar could no longer be considered a mere handmaid.[31] Sarah was distraught. In Genesis 16:5 we read: "And Sarai said to Abram, 'The wrong done me is your fault! I myself gave my maid into your bosom; now that she sees that she is pregnant, I am lowered in her esteem. Let the Lord decide between you and me.'" Sarah was unsure whom to blame for the friction that now existed between herself and Hagar. She was perplexed, and Abraham could not resolve her dilemma. So she called upon *Havayah* who perceives the past, present, and future simultaneously, who judges mankind with compassion and understanding, to settle the matter and advise them how to proceed.

Abraham told Sarah to handle Hagar as she saw fit, and the Torah tells us that Sarah treated Hagar harshly, causing her to flee into the wilderness. There an angel confronted her. How interesting that in the brief conversation between Hagar and the angel, recorded in the Torah in five verses, the phrase "angel of the Lord" appears four times. Some opine that a series of four or five different angels appeared to Hagar, each with its own message.[32] Depending on its purpose, an angel takes on different forms.[33] In any case, it should be understood that the word of the angel here is the word of *Havayah*.

The angel delivers the word of the Lord. Hagar must return to the home of Abraham and submit to the will of Sarah her mistress. She was Sarah's handmaid; to serve her was a matter of propriety. The text in Genesis 16:9 reads: "Go back to your mistress and submit to her harsh treatment." Hagar refused. Then came a second revelation indicating that the Lord would multiply Hagar's descendants if she returned to the house of Abraham. The text in Genesis 16:10 reads: "I will greatly increase your offspring, and they shall be too many to count." Again Hagar refused. Finally, the angel revealed that if she returned, Sarah

---

31. Cf. M. Alshikh, commentary on Genesis 16:5.
32. Cf. *Bereshit Rabbah* 45. This is in accordance with the opinion that an angel has only a single message to deliver; it then dissipates.
33. For a discussion on the meaning and significance of angels, the reader is referred to M. Maimonides, *Guide of the Perplexed*, trans. by M. Friedlander (New York: Hebrew Publishing Company), Part II, chaps. 6 and 7.

would no longer torture her.³⁴ The text in Genesis 16:11 reads, "For the Lord has paid heed to your suffering." Now Hagar acquiesced, and she returned to the home of Abraham and Sarah. Each of these promises reveals God as the merciful *Havayah* who is concerned with the welfare of His children. This is further confirmed by the text in Genesis 16:13, which reads, "And she called the Lord who spoke to her, 'You are a God of seeing,' for she said, 'have I not gone on seeing after He saw me!'" The text here is somewhat obscure, but the commentaries enlighten us.

You are the God (*"E-l"*) who has seen my affliction, said Hagar, for your providential hand is always upon me.³⁵ Hagar did not refer to the Supreme Being who spoke to her as *Havayah* but rather as *E-l*. The reason is obvious: the name *Havayah* is used exclusively by Israel. It would seem that in a certain sense, the name *E-l* also represents the Divine attribute of compassion. The key is in the words of Hagar. In astonishment, Hagar exclaimed, "Have I not gone on seeing after He saw me!" She had been accustomed to seeing angels in Abraham's house; she had not expected to see one in the wilderness. It was her understanding that the Supreme Being appeared only to the worthy ones like Abraham, for He is concerned with their welfare. She now knew that the He is compassionately concerned with the welfare of all his children.³⁶

THE COVENANT OF CIRCUMCISION

Abraham was 86 years old when Hagar gave birth to a son. Abraham named his son Ishmael. In Genesis 17:1 the Torah records: "When Abram was 99 years old, the Lord appeared to Abram and said to him, 'I am God Almighty. Walk in My Presence and be perfect.'" This is the first instance in the Torah where the names God Almighty (*E-l Sha-dai*) are juxtaposed. Although we have mentioned these names before we

---

34. Cf. S. R. Hirsch, commentary on Genesis 16:11,12, who opines that the promise was that her son "would become the freest man in the world."
35. Cf. Ibn Ezra and Seforno commentaries on Genesis 16:13.
36. Cf. *Bereshit Rabbah* 45 and Rashi commentary on Genesis 16:13.

must probe the meaning and significance of their appearance together in this context.

Havayah appeared to Abraham and affirmed the promise that he would be the father of a multitude of nations, and that he would inherit the land of Canaan as an everlasting possession. Even though both you and Sarah are along in years, said the Supreme Being of the universe, I am *E-l Sha-dai*. Nature is in My hand; there is nothing beyond My power. I know that your deepest desire is to have a son to inherit you, and, as a manifestation of My loving-kindness, I am ready to fulfill the promises I made to you in this regard. But first, you must perform an act that demands great courage. "Walk in My Presence and be perfect," said *Havayah*. I know that what I ask of you is dangerous, but it will make you perfect.[37] Conform to what I ask of you, and I will protect you from harm. Kindness and protection from harm were the two aspects of Divinity that are implied in the names *E-l Sha-dai*. With these reassuring words, God introduced Abraham to the mitzvah of circumcision (*Berit Milah*).

A covenant was made between God and Abraham. In Genesis 17:4–5, 7–11 we read:

> As for Me, this is My covenant with you: You shall be the father of a multitude of nations. And you shall no longer be called Abram, but your name shall be Abraham, for I make you the father of a multitude of nations . . . I will maintain My covenant between Me and you and your offspring to come, as an everlasting covenant throughout the ages to be a God to you and to your offspring to come . . . God further said to Abraham, "As for you, you shall keep My covenant, you and your offspring to come throughout the ages . . . every male among you shall be circumcised. You shall circumcise the flesh of your foreskin, and that shall be the sign of the covenant between Me and you."

This is the first time that the Torah states that God revealed Himself to Abraham as *E-lohim*, and it is most fitting. As we have already

---

37. Cf. *Nedarim* 32a.

mentioned, the name *E-lohim* represents the Supreme Being as the Creator of Heaven and Earth and the law of nature that governs all that exists on the Earth. It appears here to emphasize the importance of the mitzvah of circumcision, and to remind us of the statement in the Talmud: "Great is circumcision, since but for it Heaven and Earth would not endure."[38] For by performing the act of circumcision Abraham became a partner with God in Creation, in a sense, in setting the foundation of the world.[39] For action speaks louder than words. As noble as one's thoughts might be, when such thoughts are translated into action their nobility increases many times over. It is one thing to have faith and trust in the Supreme Being; it is quite another to demonstrate such faith by putting one's life on the line. Even more! *E-lohim* creates man, and man recreates himself. Through the act of circumcision, man becomes a Jew. The mission of the Jewish people as a nation is to teach humanity how to live a dignified life. As such he becomes a partner with the Supreme Being in Creation.

The mitzvah of circumcision marked Abraham's entry into the covenantal community. To symbolize the fact that he had now become the father of a multitude of nations,[40] Abraham is given a new name. As a partner with *E-lohim* in Creation, the letter *he*, one of the letters in God's name, is added to Abram's name. He is now "Abraham." Sarah's name is also changed. And in Genesis 17:15 we read: "And God said to Abraham, 'As for your wife Sarai, you shall not call her Sarai, but her

---

38. Ibid.
39. Cf. *Bereshit Rabbah* 14.
40. The notion that Abraham and Sarah were equal in status is already hinted to in the biblical text and picked up by Rashi. On the words in Genesis 12:5, "and the souls that they had made in Haran," Rashi comments: "Abraham converted the men and Sarah converted the women." The point is made here by the fact that the same letter *he* is added to her name and for the same reason. As we read in Genesis 17:15, "I will bless her so that she will give rise to nations." Later, when Sarah advises Abraham to send Hagar and Ishmael away, Abraham is perturbed. He turns to God (*E-lohim*) for a just resolution to the problem, and God tells him, "whatever Sarah tells you do as she says." Rashi makes an even stronger point and comments, "Abraham was inferior to Sarah in prophetic ability." Sarah was, indeed, a woman of considerable importance in her own right. Cf. M. Meiri, *Torah Meira* op. cit., Genesis 17:15, note 12.

name shall be Sarah. I will bless her; indeed, I will give you a son by her. I will bless her so that she will give rise to nations; rulers of peoples shall issue from her.'" True to form the letter *he* is added to her name as well.[41]

Abraham is overwhelmed by the promise that Sarah will have a child. In utter humility, he turns to God with a strange request. In Genesis 17:18 we read: "And Abraham said to God, 'O that Ishmael might live by Your favor.'" Sensitive to Abraham's words, Rashi explains: "Would that Ishmael would live. I [Abraham] am unworthy to receive such a reward." It is our contention that the Divine attribute of strict justice represented by the name *E-lohim* is the key to understanding Rashi's comment here. You (God) have promised me a child through Sarah, says Abraham. For a man of my age, this can only be accomplished through a miracle. You have indicated that in my case a miracle would be a manifestation of strict justice, implying that I have earned the right to such a miracle. In my estimation, however, I am unworthy. Strict justice would preclude a miracle being performed in my behalf. Considering this, I would be satisfied with Ishmael as my inheritor. Responding to Abraham's humble request, God promised Abraham that He would provide for Ishmael. As for his inheritor, Isaac, the son born to him through Sarah, would be his inheritor. All of this having been said, in Genesis 17:22 we read: "And when He was done speaking with him, God went up from Abraham." On that very day, Abraham took to fulfilling God's command; he circumcised himself and Ishmael as well as all the males of his household.

THE THREE VISITORS

Only three days later, Abraham was sitting outside his tent in the heat of the day, when *Havayah* appeared to him. What prompted this visit? Perhaps it was in consideration of the name *Havayah* that the Midrash

---

41. Ibid.

comments: "It was the third day after his circumcision, and the Holy One blessed be He came and inquired as to his well-being."[42] This was, indeed, a manifestation of Divine compassion. Subsequently, Abraham looked up and saw three men approaching. Unaware of the fact that they were angels in disguise, he ran to greet them. He invited them into his tent, and he provided for them. One of the men told him that at this time in the following year Sarah would have a son. Sarah, who had overheard this prediction, laughed in astonishment, and the Lord reacted to her gesture with displeasure. In Genesis 18:13 we read: "Then the Lord said to Abraham, 'Why did Sarah laugh saying, "Shall I in truth bear a child, old as I am?" Is anything too wondrous for the Lord?'" It is most likely that this remark was made by the Lord Himself rather than the angel, although there are differences of opinion on this matter.[43] Be that as it may, the name *Havayah* is apropos since the promise here as it was previously is clearly a manifestation of Divine compassion.

THE DESTRUCTION OF SODOM AND GOMORRAH

The angels took leave of Abraham, on their mission to destroy the wicked cities of Sodom and Gomorrah, and we are told that *Havayah* appeared to Abraham to inform him that the cities were about to be destroyed. In Genesis 18:20 we read: "Then the Lord said, 'The outrage of Sodom and Gomorrah is so great, and their sin so grave! I will go down to see whether they have acted altogether according to the outcry that has come to Me; if not, I will know.'" We must bear in mind that *Havayah* had promised Abraham that he would be a great and populous nation and that all the nations of the Earth would bless themselves by him. Surely Abraham would be concerned with their welfare. But should it not have been *E-lohim*, the God of strict justice, who appeared

---

42. *Tanhuma Vayeira* 1.
43. Cf. *Bava Metsiah* 77a and Nahmanides, commentary to Genesis 18:10. Others opine that it was the angel who spoke to Abraham. Cf. *Bereshit Rabbah* 48 and the commentaries of Ibn Ezra, Kimhi, Rashbam, and Rabbenu B'haye on Genesis 18:13.

to Abraham with this bad news? Why does the name *Havayah* appear in the biblical text?

Some opine that the destruction of Sodom and Gomorrah was a manifestation of Divine compassion, not for the people of these wicked cities, of course, but for the rest of mankind. Much as a gangrenous limb must be amputated in order to save a person's life, the cities of Sodom and Gomorrah needed to be destroyed and their inhabitants killed in order to prevent them from spreading their evil ways to the rest of mankind.[44]

Perhaps there is an additional rationale for the name *Havayah* that appears here. Informing Abraham that Sodom and Gomorrah were to be destroyed would motivate him to show concern for their welfare. He would plead with *Havayah* in their behalf, and this would be to his credit. In the end, of course, the cities would be destroyed, but Abraham would have earned Divine favor for his noble gesture. Seen from this perspective, the revelation that Sodom and Gomorrah were to be destroyed was clearly an act of Divine compassion in behalf of Abraham. Perhaps this is what the name *Havayah* means to convey to the reader. It is noteworthy that in a dialogue that consists of a mere seventeen verses (Genesis 18:17–33), the name *Havayah* appears seven times. Would this not confirm our contention?

It is also interesting to note that when Abraham speaks to the Supreme Being in this dialogue,[45] he refers to Him as *Adney*. We have already explained that this name, which derives from *Adon* (master), symbolizes Divine mastery over the universe and as such the attribute of strict, uncompromising justice. Knowing that the decree to destroy these cities with all their inhabitants could only have been issued forth as a matter of strict justice, Abraham addresses the Supreme Being by that name.[46]

Abraham is not successful in his plea. Divine compassion does not prevail in this matter. The wicked cities of Sodom and Gomorrah are to be destroyed. How subtly this is conveyed in the biblical text. In Genesis

---

44. Cf. M. Meiri, op. cit., Genesis 18:20 note 11.
45. Genesis 18: 26, 30–32.
46. Cf. Rabbenu B'Haye, commentary to Genesis 18:27.

18:33 and 19:1 we read: "When the Lord had finished speaking to Abraham, He departed; and Abraham returned to his place. The two angels arrived in Sodom in the evening, as Lot was sitting in the gate of Sodom." *Havayah* departed, and the two angels whose mission it was to destroy the wicked cities arrived in Sodom. Divine compassion withdrew from the scene, leaving the attribute of strict judgment to prevail against Sodom.[47]

The angels bade Lot and his family to escape, and in Genesis 19:13 we read: "For we are about to destroy this place; because the outcry against them before the Lord has become so great that the Lord has sent us to destroy it." Upon hearing the news, Lot lingered somewhat. It was not so easy for him to abandon his home and the members of his family who had refused to go with him. The angels grasped him by the hand and took him, his wife, and his two daughters out of the city. It was a Divine gesture of compassion as the biblical text in Genesis 19:16 comments, "in the Lord's mercy on him." But it was not compassion alone that was operating for Lot; it was just as much the merit of Abraham.[48] In Genesis 19:29 we read: "Thus it was that, when God destroyed the cities of the Plain and annihilated the cities where Lot dwelt, God was mindful of Abraham and removed Lot from the midst of the upheaval." The Divine name here is *E-lohim* to teach us that Abraham truly deserved to have his nephew Lot and family saved. It was a manifestation of Divine justice in Abraham's behalf coupled with Divine compassion for Lot. Much to Abraham's dismay, the wickedness of the people of these two cities was so great that even Divine mercy could not save them.[49]

---

47. Ibid., Genesis 18:33.
48. Cf. M. Malbim, commentary to Genesis 19:29.
49. Cf. B'er Mayim Hayyim (New York: 1953), on Genesis 19:13. A noteworthy comment is made by Samson Raphael Hirsch, who writes: "It is significant that in this whole story God is called by the name *Havayah*—God in His care for the future of mankind—as the One Who is bringing destruction to Sodom. To such a depth of depravity, complete annihilation itself is an act of merciful love" (Genesis 19:13). Note Genesis 19:24: "The Lord [*Havayah*] rained upon Sodom and Gommorah sulfurous fire from the Lord [*Havayah*] out of Heaven."

The God of the Patriarchs

THE INCIDENT WITH AVIMELEKH

In his journey to the South, Abraham stopped in a place called Gerar. Here again Sarah was instructed by Abraham to tell anyone who inquired about her status that she was his sister, and here again the King took her. This time it was Avimelekh of Gerar. God appeared to Avimelekh in a dream and warned him not to violate Sarah, that he would die unless he returned her to Abraham unharmed. In Genesis 20:7 we read: "But you must restore the man's wife—since he is a prophet, he will intercede for you—to save your life." Avimelekh complied, and in Genesis 20:17–18 we read: "Abraham then prayed to God, and God healed Avimelekh, his wife and his slave girls, so that they bore children; for the Lord had closed fast every womb of the household of Avimelekh because of Sarah the wife of Abraham."

It is important to note that both names, *E-lohim* and *Havayah*, appear here. Abraham prays to *E-lohim* in behalf of Avimelekh, for it was not mercy that he sought but justice. Avimelekh did not know that Sarah was Abraham's wife, and when *E-lohim* threatened his life he claimed innocence. In point of fact, *E-lohim* recognized his innocence and in Genesis 20:6 we read: "And God said to him in the dream, 'I know that you did this with a blameless heart, and so I kept you from sinning against Me.'" Avimelekh heeded the word of *E-lohim*, and he returned Sarah to Abraham. He sent them away with gifts. It was, therefore, *E-lohim*, the attribute of strict justice, that was invoked by Abraham and was responsible for the healing of Avimelekh.[50] It was *Havayah* who acted with compassion in behalf of both Avimelekh and Sarah and closed fast every womb of the household of Avimelekh. This was to save him from committing a sin inadvertently, but it was also to save Sarah from being violated against her will.

---

50. Cf. D. Z. Hoffmann, op. cit., Genesis 21:1.

THE BIRTH OF ISAAC

In Genesis 21:1 we read: "The Lord took note of Sarah as He had promised, and the Lord did for Sarah as He had spoken." It was the concern of *Havayah* for the personal happiness of Abraham and Sarah and His desire to fulfill His plan for the formation of the nation of Israel that motivated Him to superimpose His will over the law of nature. Granting Sarah a child was a clear manifestation of Divine providence acting in compassion.[51] As promised, a son was born to Abraham and Sarah, and Abraham named him Isaac. In Genesis 21:4 we read: "And when his son Isaac was eight days old, Abraham circumcised him, as God had commanded him." The last phrase seems redundant here. Are we not aware of the fact that it was *E-lohim* who had commanded Abraham to perform circumcision? The point is that notwithstanding the potential threat to life that is involved in this act, Abraham circumcised his son Isaac, the long-awaited child of his old age, because *E-lohim* the Creator and Supreme Authority over all had commanded him to do so. *E-lohim* would surely protect Abraham from danger.[52]

What was Sarah's reaction to the birth of Isaac? In Genesis 21:6–7 we read: "Sarah said, 'God has brought me laughter; everyone who hears will laugh with me.' And she added, 'Who would have said to Abraham that Sarah would suckle children! Yes, I have borne a son in his old age.'" The key to understanding Sarah's reaction here is her reference to the name *E-lohim*. But there is a difference of opinion among the sages as to the meaning and significance of laughter here. Some opine that the laughter to which Sarah referred was that which results from happiness. All who hear of this miracle performed for me by *E-lohim* the Creator of nature who supersedes nature when He desires to do so will laugh with me in joy, says Sarah.[53] Others opine that Sarah openly expressed her guilt. She had laughed in disbelief when the angel told Abraham that at this time in the following year she would have a son. It

---

51. Cf. S. R. Hirsch, commentary to Genesis 21:1.
52. Cf. I. Abravanel, commentary to Genesis 21:1.
53. Cf. commentaries of D. Kimhi, and Samuel ben Meir (Rashbam) ad loc.

was a sinful reaction, and now she was being subjected to strict judgment by *E-lohim*. She felt that when this child is born, the world would laugh *at* her, not *with* her. *E-lohim* had made a mockery of her.[54]

THE EXPULSION OF HAGAR AND ISHMAEL

Isaac grew up and was weaned, and Abraham made a great feast on that day. The Torah tells us that Ishmael mocked Isaac. Sarah noticed what had transpired, and she knew then that Ishmael would be a bad influence on Isaac. Recognizing that the association of the two boys would imperil Isaac's future as the second patriarch of the Jewish people, she told Abraham to send Hagar and Ishmael away immediately. The matter distressed Abraham for he was concerned for their welfare. Should he heed Sarah's words? The answer came in Genesis 21:12 where we read: "But God said to Abraham, 'Do not be distressed over the boy or your slave; whatever Sarah tells you, do as she says, for it is through Isaac that offspring shall be continued for you.'" The matter must be handled according to strict justice, says *E-lohim*. Do not get emotionally involved. Sarah has spoken objectively, and I agree with her judgment. Do as she says, for Isaac shall be your spiritual inheritor, not Ishmael.

Abraham heeded the words of Sarah as *E-lohim* had instructed him to do. He took some bread and a skin of water and gave them to Hagar and sent her and Ishmael away. They wandered about in the wilderness of Beer-sheba, and when the water from the skin was gone Hagar became distraught. She left the child under one of the bushes and sat down at a distance and wept. In Genesis 21: 17–20 we read the following:

> God heard the cry of the boy, and an angel of God called to Hagar from Heaven and said to her, "What troubles you, Hagar? Fear not. For God has heeded the cry of the boy where he is. Come, lift up the boy and hold him by the hand, for I will make a great nation of him." Then God opened her eyes and she saw a well of water. She

---

54. Cf. I. Arama, *Akedat Yitzhak*, vol. 1 (Jerusalem: 1961), p. 147.

went and filled the skin with water, and let the boy drink. God was with the boy, and he grew up; he dwelt in the wilderness and became a bowman.

Two things about this brief incident are puzzling: What is the meaning of the words "where he is," and why does the name *E-lohim* appear here no less than five times? There is reason to believe that these matters are interrelated. Let us begin our query with a statement in the Talmud: "Man is judged only according to his actions up to the time of judgment, as it says, 'God has heeded the cry of the boy where he is.'" Rashi in his commentary on the text writes: "Because the ministering angels accused him [Ishmael] saying, 'Master of the Universe, for him whose descendants will at one time kill Your children with thirst will You provide a well?' He asked them, 'What is he now, righteous or wicked?' They replied to Him, 'Righteous.' He said to them, 'According to his present deeds will I judge him.'"

The prophet Isaiah wrote, "For My thoughts are not your thoughts, neither are your ways My ways, says the Lord." Every decision man makes is colored by his emotions and his prejudices. Only the Supreme Being is totally objective in His judgment. He provided for Ishmael because at that point in time Ishmael did not deserve to die or even to be punished. As such helping Hagar and Ishmael was not a manifestation of Divine compassion but strict Divine justice, thus the name *E-lohim*. It seems that even the angels found this difficult to fathom.

A TREATY SIGNED

The people around him recognized Abraham as a man of prominence. Avimelekh, the king of Gerar, was impressed with Abraham's greatness in the eyes of the leaders of the surrounding nations for they had attended the great feast when Isaac was weaned. What must have impressed him even more was the fact that his wife and his slave girls were cured through Abraham's prayers.[55] It was a case of mixed

---

55. Cf. M. Meiri, op. cit., Genesis 21:22 note 11.

emotions for at the same time; Avimelekh feared Abraham's power. He came to Abraham with a suggestion. In Genesis 21:22–23 we read:

> At that time Avimelekh and Phikhol, chief of his troops, said to Abraham, "God is with you in everything that you do. Therefore swear to me here by God that you will not deal falsely with me or with my offspring nor with my kith and kin, but will deal with me and with the land in which you have sojourned, as loyally as I have dealt with you."

Swear to me in the name of *E-lohim,* who (justly) enriched you and made you a prominent personality in the land and who gave you the ability to cure the sick, said Avimelekh [56] Swear to me that we will be friends and that our children and grandchildren will live in peace with each other. Abraham agreed, and the pact was made.

THE SACRIFICE OF ISAAC

Quite some time later,[57] Abraham and Isaac, his son, two men of inscrutable faith, faced the most difficult decision of their lives. In Genesis 22:1–2 we read: "Some time afterward, God put Abraham to the test. He said to him, 'Abraham,' and he answered, 'Here I am.' And He said, 'Take your son, your favored one, Isaac, whom you love, and go to the land of Moriah, and offer him there as a burnt offering on one of the heights which I will point out to you.'" Let us try to imagine what went through Abraham's mind when he received this charge. All of his life he had preached ethical monotheism, that there is only One Supreme Being in the universe, and He is just in all His ways. He detests the practice of human sacrifice. To Him, human sacrifice is a grievous sin. This same Supreme Being now demands that Abraham bring his beloved son Isaac as a burnt offering. How can this be? There is a second inconsistency. Abraham had been promised that Isaac would

---

56. Ibid., Genesis 21:23 note 7 in the name of A. Saba, Tsror Hamor (Warsaw: 1979).
57. Our sages tell us that by this time Isaac was already 37 years old.

be his heir.[58] How can this promise be fulfilled if Isaac is brought as a burnt offering? To heed the Divine command would be both immoral and illogical. On the other hand, to disobey the Divine command would be contrary to everything in which Abraham believed. This was Abraham's dilemma! Let us keep in mind that the matter could not be left for further consideration. A decision had to be made immediately. How does Abraham react?

In Genesis 22:3–4 we read: "So early the next morning, Abraham saddled his ass and took with him two of his servants and his son Isaac. He split the wood for the offering, and he set out for the place of which God had told him." Interestingly, there is no indication in the text whatsoever that would suggest that he in any way questioned the veracity of the command or its logic. Neither did he plead for compassion. Eager to fulfill the Divine command, Abraham arose early in the morning, and without hesitation he set out on the journey. There is no way of knowing for sure what moved Abraham to act, but we will offer some food for thought.

Let us first note that it is *E-lohim* who puts Abraham to the test and it is *E-lohim* to whom Abraham answers. It is our contention that the key to the resolution of Abraham's dilemma lies in the meaning and the significance of the name *E-lohim*. As noble and as sophisticated as the human mind may be, in the final analysis, man must recognize that revelation takes precedence over reason! Due to man's limited knowledge and understanding, the commands of the Supreme Being may, at times, appear illogical, even immoral. But the ultimate judgment of whether an act is moral or immoral, whether it is logical or illogical, is not man's prerogative. That decision is in the hands of *E-lohim*, the Supreme Judge of the universe whom all human beings must acknowledge and obey without question.

Now this position presents some difficulty. Perhaps the greatest gift with which the Creator has endowed the human being is the ability to reason. With this gift man has been able to discover many of the secrets of nature. With his intelligence, he has created technology in all fields

---

58. Cf. Genesis 21: 12.

of endeavor, virtually performing miracles. Considering this, how can he simply suspend that which reason dictates in favor of that which is revealed to him in an encounter with the Divine? The answer is really quite obvious. Man must accept the fact that as noble and as sophisticated as his intellect may be; it is not without limitation. In the final analysis, he must recognize that revelation must supersede reason, for Divine knowledge supersedes human knowledge. Should revelation contradict reason, the former must take precedence.

Together with Isaac and his servants, Abraham proceeded on his journey. On the third day, he saw in the distance the place of which he had been told. From that point on, he continued with Isaac alone. In Genesis 22:9 we read: "They arrived at the place of which God had told him. Abraham built an altar there; he laid out the wood; he bound his son Isaac; he laid him on the altar, on top of the wood. And Abraham picked up the knife to slay his son." According to the biblical account, Abraham was not hesitant: he did not pause or reflect, but proceeded methodically to do what he had been told. As he was about to slaughter his son Isaac, an angel appeared on the scene. In Genesis 22:11 we read: "Then an angel of the Lord called to him from Heaven: 'Abraham! Abraham!' And he answered, 'Here I am.' And he said, 'Do not raise you hand against the boy, or do anything to him. For now I know that you fear God, since you have not withheld your son, your favored one, from Me.'"

What do the Divine names tell us here? For all intents and purposes, they tell us the whole story. *Havayah* is merciful. He never meant for Abraham to sacrifice his son Isaac for He does not demand human sacrifice. But in light of the fact that Abraham was commanded by *E-lohim* to bring his son Isaac as an offering, he could not take this for granted. He had to demonstrate by his actions that revelation takes precedence over reason, no matter what the consequences might be, and so he did. The biblical text tells us that this was a test. It was a means through which Abraham would actualize his faith potential. Of course, there was no way that Abraham could have known this. By his decision to fulfill the Divine charge, Abraham demonstrated his supreme faith ("for now I know that you fear God"), and for this, the last of a series of ten such tests, he earned great reward.[59] Finally, in Genesis 22:14 we read: "And Abraham named the site 'the Lord sees,' which today is expressed by 'on the mount the Lord will see.'" To commemorate the fact that the true nature of Divinity was revealed to him at this place, Abraham named it accordingly. *Havayah*, the compassionate Supreme Being of the universe, sees all and reacts accordingly. He recognizes the value, indeed the sacredness of human life, and as such will never demand human sacrifice. He tempers His judgment with mercy, and treats man in accordance with his merit. *Havayah will see*! This is His nature for all time to come.

PROVIDING A WIFE FOR ISAAC

Sarah died in Hebron, and Abraham mourned for her and bewailed her. He buried her in the cave of Machpelah that he had purchased from Ephron the Hittite. In Genesis 24:1 we read: "Abraham was now old, advanced in years, and the Lord had blessed Abraham in all things." Whether the phrase "in all things" is to be taken to mean material wealth or is an allusion to his son Isaac, as the sages point out,[60] the blessing was surely a manifestation of Divine compassion—thus the name *Havayah*. The time had now come for Abraham to concern himself with his descendants, i.e., the future of the nation of Israel. This meant finding a suitable wife for Isaac. He was sure that the compassionate *Havayah* who had provided him with all that he had materially and spiritually would also guide him in finding the right woman for Isaac.[61] How tactfully Abraham conveyed these thoughts to his trusted servant Eliezer. In Genesis 24:3 we read: "And I will make you swear by the Lord, the God of Heaven and the God of the Earth, that you will not take a wife for my son from the daughters of the Canaanites among whom I dwell." The dominion of *Havayah* is not limited to Heaven. His providential hand reaches out to the Earth to guide man and to treat

---

59. Cf. Genesis 22:15–18.
60. Cf. Rashi on Genesis 24:1.
61. Cf. D. Hoffmann, op. cit., Genesis 24:1.

him with compassion. He will guide you to the right woman, says Abraham.

Where would the right woman for Isaac be found? Surely she would not be found among the immoral idolaters of Canaan. Abraham would send Eliezer to Haran, the home of his nephew Betuel in Ur of the Chaldeans. There he would find the right woman for Isaac. If she agreed, he would bring her back to Canaan to become Isaac's wife. What if he finds the right woman, but she refuses to go to Canaan, asks Eliezer; should he bring Isaac to Haran? By no means, says Abraham. He was confident that *Havayah* who had guided him in his life almost from the beginning would guide Eliezer to the right woman. Thus in Genesis 24:7 we read: "The Lord the God of Heaven, who took me from my father's house and from the land of my birth, who promised me under oath saying, 'I will give this land to your offspring'—He will send His angel before you, and you will get a wife for my son Isaac from there.'"

THE ENCOUNTER WITH REBECCA

Eliezer set out on his journey. Had it been left entirely in his hands to choose the right woman for Isaac, it would have been an impossible task. Every parent with marriageable daughters would have welcomed him with open arms and would have offered him all sorts of gifts to win his favor.[62] How could he be sure that he would make the right choice? In the evening he approached the city. It was that time of the day when the women come out to draw water from the well. The camels that were with him needed drink, so Eliezer had them kneel down by the well. He offered a prayer to *Havayah* to guide him and provide a sign for him to know when he had met the right woman. The woman, who would offer to draw water not only for him but for his camels as well, let her be the one whom *Havayah* had chosen for Isaac, pleaded Eliezer. He had barely finished his prayer when he noticed that Rebecca, the daughter of Betuel, had approached the well. She offered to draw water for both

---

62. Cf. S. R. Hirsch, op. cit., Genesis 24:27.

him and his camels, and did so. Eliezer must have been astonished because we read in Genesis 24:21, "The man meanwhile stood gazing at her in silence, to learn whether the Lord had made his errand successful or not."

Rebecca identified herself, and in Genesis 24:26–27 we read: "The man bowed low in homage to the Lord and said, 'Blessed be the Lord the God of my master Abraham, who has not withheld His steadfast kindness from my master. For I am on the road on which the Lord has guided me—to the house of my master's kinsmen.'" Eliezer uses the name *Havayah* twice in this brief statement to express his thanksgiving and to acknowledge that it was the Supreme Being who had been introduced to him by Abraham, who answered his prayers, and who guided him to Abraham's family.

Recognizing Rebecca as the potential wife for Isaac, Eliezer gave her rings and bracelets and she escorted him home to meet her family. Seeing Rebecca and Eliezer approaching, Laban, her brother, could not help but notice her bedecked with jewelry. Hoping that there would be more where this came from, Laban ran out to greet the stranger. In Genesis 24:31 we read his rather surprising expression: "Come in O blessed of the Lord." According to our sages, what Laban alluded to was the material wealth with which Eliezer had come.[63] What is surprising is his use of the name *Havayah*. The simplest explanation is that Abraham's family already knew the name and its significance.[64] Rebecca's family welcomed Eliezer. His camels were provided for, and he was made comfortable. He was given food, but he refused to eat until he revealed the purpose of his journey. The family listened intently as he related his story.

In the Torah Eliezer's story consists of fifteen verses (Genesis 24: 34–48) in which the name *Havayah* appears six times. It is evident from the context that Eliezer was a true believer in the teachings of his master, and that he had adopted these teachings into his own life style, for he attributed the success of Abraham in life as well as his own success

---

63. Ibid. 24:31.
64. D. Hoffmann, op. cit., Genesis 24:31.

in finding Rebecca entirely to the providential hand of *Havayah*. Moreover, he attempted to convince Rebecca's family of the truth of his convictions. Perhaps he was somewhat successful in this regard for in Genesis 24:50–51 we read: "Then Laban and Betual answered, 'The matter stems from the Lord; we cannot speak to you bad or good. Here is Rebecca before you; take her and go, and let her be a wife to your master's son, as the Lord has spoken.'"

Be that as it may, it seems that Laban had second thoughts about sending Rebecca—perhaps he felt that he had responded too quickly to Eliezer's request—so he resorted to some delay tactics. In Genesis 24:55 we read: "But her brother and her mother said, 'Let the maiden remain with us some ten days; then you may go.'" Eliezer would not agree, and in Genesis 24:56 we read: "He said to them, 'Do not delay me, now that the Lord has made my errand successful.'" It was the bidding of *Havayah* that he return with the potential wife for Isaac as soon as possible, said Eliezer. How would this dilemma be resolved? It was decided to ask Rebecca what her preference would be. When she agreed to go with Eliezer, the family acquiesced, and they sent her off with their blessing. Isaac was favorably impressed when he saw Rebecca. He took her as his wife and was comforted through her over the loss of his mother Sarah.

The Torah tells us that at the age of 140, Abraham took another wife. Her name was Keturah. According to the Midrash, Keturah was none other than Hagar.[65] Perhaps Abraham felt that with Isaac married he could now remarry Hagar, who was a pious woman in her own right. Abraham lived for thirty-five more years and had many children through whom the Divine promise that he would be the father of many nations was fulfilled. He died at the age of 175.[66]

---

65. *Bereshit Rabbah* 61:5 in the name of R. Judah. Cf. Ibn Ezra and D. Hoffmann who posit that it had to be someone else.

66. D. Hoffmann, op. cit., Genesis 24:16 makes an interesting point. Abraham was 140 years old when he married Hagar. He had thirty-five more years to live, a fifth of his life. This would be equivalent to a fifty-six-year-old man today. Such a person would still be quite virile, certainly capable of having more children.

REBECCA'S DILEMMA

Isaac was forty years old when he married Rebecca. For twenty years Isaac tried to have a child, but Rebecca failed to conceive. He knew that the promise made to Abraham "It is through Isaac that offspring shall be continued for you,"[67] would eventually be fulfilled, but perhaps it was to be fulfilled through someone other than Rebecca. Isaac did not want this to happen so he appealed to Divine compassion. In Genesis 25:21 we read: "Isaac pleaded with the Lord on behalf of his wife, because she was barren; and the Lord responded to his plea, and his wife Rebecca conceived." Isaac appealed to *Havayah* for compassion, and He answered him. All did not go smoothly, however. In Genesis 25:22 we read:

> But the children struggled in her womb, and she said, "If so, why do I exist?" She went to inquire of the Lord and the Lord answered her, "Two nations are in your womb, two people apart while still in your body; one people shall be mightier than the other, and the older shall serve the younger."

There are differences of opinion among the sages as to precisely what was happening in Rebecca's womb. Whatever it was that worried her, she needed compassion, so she went to inquire of *Havayah*. What do we know of Rebecca, and what was her query?

Whether Rebecca was three years old when she became Isaac's wife as some opine[68] or she had already reached the age of fourteen as others insist,[69] when she conceived she was a mature woman. It is only logical to assume that through the years Isaac had introduced her to the principles of ethical monotheism that he had learned from his father Abraham. When she felt abnormal movement within her womb, she feared that she might lose the child.[70] This distressed her greatly, and she decided to seek advice. The Torah records that she "went to inquire

---

67. Genesis 21:12. Cf. S. R. Hirsch commentary ad loc.
68. Cf. Rashi on Genesis 25:20.
69. Cf. *Daat Zekanim* commentary ad loc.
70. Cf. H. Ben Atar, *Or HaHayyim* on Genesis 25:21.

of the Lord." What does this mean? Precisely where did she go? Second, why doesn't the text read "to inquire *from* the Lord"?

Rebecca was perplexed. She went to Shem, the son of Noah, in the hope of resolving her dilemma. Her purpose was to inquire of the *nature* of the Divine. Would the compassionate *Havayah* have allowed her to conceive and subsequently lose the child through a miscarriage? Had she sinned, and would she need atonement? *Havayah* put her concerns to rest. Whether the prediction that she would have twin boys, each of whom would have his own agenda, was revealed to Shem who subsequently told it to Rebecca,[71] or it was revealed directly to Rebecca,[72] is irrelevant. The dilemma was resolved, and Rebecca was at peace with herself.

ISAAC'S DESTINY

Rebecca bore Esau and Jacob. In Genesis 25:27 we read: "When the boys grew up, Esau became a skillful hunter, a man of the outdoors; but Jacob was a mild man, who stayed in camp." There was a famine in the land and Isaac went to Avimelekh king of Gerar. He had in mind to travel to Egypt as his father had done, but this was not to be. In Genesis 26:2-4 we read:

> The Lord had appeared to him and said, "Do not go down to Egypt; stay in the land, which I point out to you. Reside in this land, and I will be with you and bless you; I will give all these lands to you and to your offspring . . . I will make your descendants as numerous as the stars of Heaven, and give to your descendants all these lands, so that all the nations of the Earth shall bless themselves by your offspring . . ."

Isaac was commanded by *Havayah* not to leave Canaan. A holy man, Isaac was destined to live his entire life on holy land, the land promised to him and his descendants. Indeed, the providential hand of *Havayah*

---

71. Cf. Rashi and Rashbam, commentaries on Genesis 25:23.
72. Cf. D. Hoffmann, op. cit., Genesis 25:23.

would provide for him and his family for all their days. In compliance with the Divine command, Isaac lived in Gerar, where he prospered greatly, acquiring flocks and herds and a large household. He reopened the wells that his father Abraham had dug, which the Philistines had sealed after Abraham's death. There was friction between the herdsmen of Isaac and those of Gerar, each claiming that the water was theirs. Finally, Isaac opened a well concerning which there was no strife. He named it *Rehovot*, saying, "Now at last the Lord has granted us ample space to increase in the land."[73] It was an acknowledgment of Divine compassion, an attestation to the fact that *Havayah* had fulfilled His promises to him.

Isaac traveled to Beer-sheba, the place where his father Abraham had built an altar to *Havayah*. In Genesis 26:24 we read: "That night the Lord appeared to him and said, 'I am the God of your father Abraham. Fear not, for I am with you, and I will bless you and increase your offspring for the sake of Abraham My servant.'" As an expression of thanksgiving, Isaac built an altar to *Havayah* who had shown him such compassion.

Avimelekh, king of Gerar recognized that Isaac, like his father before him, was successful in all his endeavors. He wanted to ensure the covenant he had made with Abraham by reestablishing it with Isaac. Accompanied by his councilor and the chief of his troops he came to Isaac with this goal in mind. In Genesis 26:28 we read:

> And they said, "We see now plainly that the Lord has been with you, and we thought: Let there be a sworn treaty between our two parties, between you and us. Let us make a pact with you that you will not do us harm, just as we have not molested you but have always dealt kindly with you and sent you away in peace. From now on be you blessed of the Lord!"

It is strange that Avimelekh would refer to the Supreme Being as *Havayah*. Perhaps it was his long association with Abraham that taught

---

73. See Genesis 26:22

The God of the Patriarchs

him the significance of the name. It may very well be that he and many Philistines with him converted and adopted the teachings of Abraham.[74] Be that as it may, Isaac agreed to the treaty and in Genesis 26:31 we read: "Early in the morning they exchanged oaths, Isaac then bade them farewell, and they departed from him in peace."

THE BLESSING

When Isaac grew old, he summoned his elder son Esau. He told Esau to prepare a fine meal and bring it to him. This mitzvah would set the scene for Esau, the potential head of the family, to be blessed by Isaac. Rebecca overheard the conversation between the two men. She knew that Isaac favored Esau over Jacob, but she also knew that Jacob was eminently more fit than Esau to inherit the spiritual leadership of the family. She felt that she had no choice but to formulate a plan of action to enable Jacob to receive what rightfully belonged to him. In Genesis 27:6 we read: "Rebecca said to her son Jacob, 'I overheard your father speaking to your brother Esau, saying, "Bring me some game and make me a tasty dish to eat that I may bless you, with the Lord's approval before I die." It is interesting to note that the biblical text does not tell us that Isaac used the words "with the Lord's approval" when he spoke to Esau, although he must surely have implied it.[75] Of course, it is also possible that Esau was not sensitive to this name or concerned with its implications.

Isaac's eyesight was failing. Rebecca was well aware of this so she prepared one of Isaac's favorite dishes, dressed Jacob up to appear like Esau, and covered his arms with animal skins so that they would appear hairy. She instructed Jacob to bring the meal to Isaac while his brother was still out hunting. With some reluctance, Jacob obeyed his mother and appeared before Isaac his father. Isaac was surprised to see who he thought was Esau return from the hunt so soon. "How did you succeed so quickly, my son?" he asked. "Because the Lord your God granted me

---

74. Cf. D. Hoffmann, op. cit., Genesis 26:28.
75. Cf. S. R. Hirsch, commentary on Genesis 27:7, and D. Hoffmann ad loc.

good fortune," Esau replied. Now one would have thought that *E-lohim*, the name that designates the Creator of nature, would be more fitting here. Yet if we scrutinize Jacob's words we see that this is not so. Ordinarily, it would have taken me much longer, said Jacob, but Havayah granted me good fortune, and the animal appeared before me seemingly out of nowhere. It was, indeed, the Lord's providential hand at work.[76] It was not at all like Esau to use such language, and this may very well be the reason why Isaac asked Jacob to come closer so that he could feel his hairy arms. Apparently convinced that it was Esau who stood before him, Isaac blessed him.

The opening lines of the blessing are relevant to our discussion. In Genesis 27:27–28 we read: "See the smell of my son is as the smell of the field that the Lord has blessed. May God give you of the dew of Heaven and the fat of the Earth, abundance of new grain and wine." Here again, one might have expected *E-lohim*, the name that designates the Creator of nature, to appear in the first verse, but this would be incorrect. S. R. Hirsch enlightens us. "We know already what predilection Isaac had for agriculture under God's blessing," says Hirsch; ". . . my son . . . exhales the fragrance, not of the wild, not of the forests, but of the cultivated fields that God has blessed; so may God then give thee all the blessings of productivity and abundance."[77] In verse 27, Isaac refers to the fields that man has cultivated, not the forests that grow wild. The success of these fields is in some measure due to man's efforts, to be sure; but it is the providential hand of the *Havayah* that blesses man's work and makes it successful. In verse 28, the name *E-lohim* is more appropriate. For as the head of the family, the firstborn son of Isaac deserved that blessing from *E-lohim* as a manifestation of Divine justice.[78]

---

76. Cf. M. Malbim, commentary on Genesis 27:20, and *Daat Zekanim* ad loc.
77. S. R. Hirsch, commentary on Genesis 27:27. It should be noted that the English translation quoted here does not differentiate among the various names of God. All the Divine names are translated as "God."
78. Cf. D. Hoffmann, op. cit., Genesis 27:28.

JACOB LEAVES HOME

When Esau returned from the fields and became aware of the fact that Jacob had received the blessing that was reserved for the firstborn, he was very distraught. Although Isaac blessed him as well, Esau was not appeased. On the contrary, he was angry with Jacob and threatened to kill him. Aware of Esau's plans, Rebecca instructed Jacob to escape to Haran, where her brother Laban lived, to stay there until it would be safe for him to return. She may have felt that Laban would protect Jacob from Esau.[79] Isaac agreed to her plan. In Genesis 28:2–3 we read:

> Up, go to Padan—Aram, to the house of Betuel, your mother's father, and take a wife there from among the daughters of Laban, your mother's brother. May God Almighty bless you, make you fertile and numerous, so that you become a community of peoples. May He grant you the blessing of Abraham, to you and your offspring; that you may possess the land where you are sojourning, which God gave to Abraham.

This is the second time the name *E-l Sha-dai* (God Almighty) is found in the Torah. It appears previously regarding the covenant of circumcision,[80] where we pointed out that it refers to the Divine attributes of omnipotence and self-sufficiency. Here it may also refer to God as He who nourishes the world. Jacob was instructed to leave Canaan and go to Haran. He went with nothing but the clothes on his back. In his prayer to the Supreme Being for protection, for he was about to be confronted by Esau, Jacob himself admitted: "with my staff alone I crossed this Jordan."[81] What would become of Jacob? How would he be able to survive, let alone marry and prosper? Isaac reassured him that the omnipotent self-sufficient *E-l Sha-dai* who is the provider of the world would provide for him as well. As S. R. Hirsch

---

79. Cf. H. Ben Atar, *Or HaHayyim*, Genesis 27:43.
80. Genesis 17:1.
81. Genesis 32:11.

explains, "You need take nothing with you but God, He will bless you."[82] This blessing that would provide a wife for Jacob and give him the means to support a family and to bring up children who would be the future nation of Israel would come from *E-lohim*. It would be a manifestation of strict Divine justice, for Jacob deserved the blessing.[83]

THE DREAM OF THE LADDER

Jacob left Beer-sheba and set out for Haran. It was a lengthy journey so he stopped at a place for the night. In Genesis 28:12–15 we read:

> He had a dream; a ladder was set on the ground and its top reached the sky, and the angels of God were going up and down on it. And the Lord was standing beside him and He said, "I am the Lord, the God of your father and the God of Isaac: the ground on which you are lying I will give to you and to your offspring. Your descendants shall be as the dust of the Earth; you shall spread out to the west and to the east to the north and to the south. All the families of the Earth shall bless themselves by you and your descendants. Remember, I am with you: I will protect you wherever you go and will bring you back to this land. I will not leave you until I have done what I have promised you."

We must try to understand the significance of the multiple Divine names that are found here. Reassurance from his father Isaac that all would go well with him must have been encouraging to Jacob; reassurance from the Supreme Being Himself must clearly have relieved any and all fears concerning the future. In His unbounded compassion, *Havayah* revealed to Jacob how He interacts with the world. Everything that transpires on the Earth is effected by means of the angels of *E-lohim*, the Creator. The angels traverse the Earth and report their findings to their Maker. He subsequently instructs them, for they are forbidden to do anything on their own. Then they return to

---

82. S. R. Hirsch, commentary on Genesis 28:3.
83. Cf. Ibid.

the Earth to do His bidding. This is all a manifestation of strict Divine justice, the law of nature. For the angels, in this context, are none other than the forces of nature created by *E-lohim*.[84] Angels, however, would not determine Jacob's destiny. By revealing Himself as the Lord God of Abraham and Isaac, the Supreme Being informs Jacob that he will not be under the rule of strict justice, the only rule that the angels are empowered to enforce. Jacob will be subject to the providential hand of *Havayah* that will protect him and provide for him always.[85] Although he had nothing with him but his staff, *Havayah* stood beside him.

Jacob awakened from sleep. In Genesis 28:16 we read: "Jacob awoke from his sleep and said, 'surely the Lord is present in this place, and I did not know it.'" Shaken, he said, "How awesome is this place! This is none other than the abode of God, and this is the gateway of Heaven." Again, we are confronted with both names of the Divine in a single context, and we must determine the significance of each in its place. The promise that all the nations of the world would be blessed with Jacob and that his destiny would be determined by the providential hand of the Divine rather than the angels clearly called for the name *Havayah*. But what was it that Jacob knew now that he had not known before? Perhaps it was the fact that Divine compassion does not only manifest itself in formal worship at an altar, but that one can perceive Divine compassion everywhere, as evidenced by the words "And the Lord was standing beside him." But he is reminded of something else as well, and this disturbs him.

The Midrash points out that the angels of *E-lohim* ascended to Heaven and there they saw the picture of Jacob engraved as Israel glorifying *E-lohim*. When they descended to the Earth, they saw him sleeping in the place that should have bestirred in him thoughts of his glorious mission and kept him awake. On that account his life was threatened. Immediately *Havayah* stood beside him to protect him.[86] The ladder that Jacob saw joined Heaven and Earth. The angels of

---

84. Cf. D. Hoffmann, op. cit., Genesis 28:12.
85. Cf. Nahmanides, commentary on Genesis ad loc.
86. Cf. *Bereshit Rabbah* 68:18 and *Hullin* 91b.

E-lohim note man's behavior on the Earth. They report his behavior to the Heavenly court, and man is judged by *E-lohim*, in strict justice. Considering that he was still far from having fulfilled his Divinely ordained destiny, Jacob must have feared that he would not fare well in such judgment.

Jacob marked the place with a stone pillar, and he named the site Bethel. In Genesis 28:20–22 we read that he made the following vow:

> If God remains with me, if He protects me on this journey that I am making, and gives me bread to eat and clothing to wear, and if I return safe to my father's house—the Lord shall be my God. And this stone which I have set up as a pillar, shall be God's abode; and of all that You give me, I will always set aside a tithe for You.

Still very much concerned with his ability to fulfill his destiny, Jacob made a vow. *Havayah* had promised to be with him, to protect him, to sustain him, and to return him to his home. As such it was a matter of true justice that he be protected. Perhaps this is why he refers to *E-lohim* here. The one thing that Jacob was not promised is that he would serve *Havayah* always. He was not given the reassurance that he would maintain his loyalty to *Havayah* for the rest of his life as his father and grandfather had done before him. Of course, this is the one thing that could not be promised to him. Allegiance to the Supreme Being is subject to man's free will. As our sages commented: "All is in the hands of Heaven with the exception of the fear of Heaven."[87] Given that I will maintain my allegiance to *Havayah*, says Jacob, this stone which I now set up as a memorial shall become a permanent place for Divine inspiration in recognition of the fact the *Havayah* is *E-lohim* (a God of justice).[88]

There is another meaning implied in the words "The Lord shall be my God." If (better, "when")[89] *Havayah* who had promised to be with me and protect me and sustain me through my journey fulfills that

---

87. *Berakhot* 33b.
88. Cf. M. Malbim, commentary on Genesis 28:22.
89. Cf. H. Ben Atar, *Or HaHayyim* 28:20.

promise, then He will be for me *E-lohim*, a God of justice. In the words of S. R. Hirsch: "The God who showers all His love on me shall be, to me, in my mind, a God who not only gives, but who demands, who wants to know that with all that He gives His will is furthered."[90] This calls for the name *E-lohim*.

RACHEL AND LEAH

Jacob arrived in Haran. Outside the city he met Rachel, Laban's daughter, with whom he was very favorably impressed. He identified himself as Rebecca's son, and Rachel ran to tell her father of the news. Laban invited Jacob to stay with the family, and he accepted the invitation. Laban had two daughters: Leah and Rachel. Jacob loved Rachel, and he agreed to work for Laban for seven years for the right to marry her. At the end of the seven years, Laban substituted Leah for Rachel, claiming that it was the custom in his land that the elder daughter marry before the younger. However, he would allow Jacob to marry Rachel as well if Jacob agreed to work for him for another seven years. Jacob agreed. He married Leah and Rachel, but it was clear that he favored Rachel over her sister Leah. In Genesis 29:31–35 we read:

> The Lord saw that Leah was unloved and he opened her womb; but Rachel was barren. Leah conceived and bore a son, and named him Reuben; for she declared, "It means: The Lord has seen my affliction; it also means: Now my husband will love me. She conceived again, and bore a son, and declared, "This is because the Lord heard that I was unloved and has given me this one also"; so she named him Simeon. Again she conceived and bore a son and declared, "This time my husband will become attached to me, for I have borne him three sons." Therefore, he was named Levi. She conceived again and bore a son, and declared, "This time I will praise the Lord." Therefore she named him Judah. Then she stopped bearing.

---

90. Cf. S. R. Hirsch, commentary on Genesis 28:21.

Havayah showed great compassion for Leah. It was His providential hand that opened her womb for she, too, was barren.[91] Leah knew this and reacted accordingly. With sons, she would not only be fulfilled as a mother, but as the matriarch of the nation of Israel as well. She felt that this would please Jacob greatly, and would bring him closer to her. All this is eminently clear from her references to *Havayah* in the naming of her children.

Needless to say, Rachel was not pleased with what was happening and in Genesis 30:1 we read: "When Rachel saw that she had borne Jacob no children, she became envious of her sister; and Rachel said to Jacob, 'Give me children or I shall die.' Jacob was incensed with Rachel and he scolded her saying: "Can I take the place of God who has denied you fruit of the womb?" Let us understand the significance of this brief but resolute conversation. Rachel was upset with Jacob because she thought that he didn't pray for her to have a child as his father Isaac had prayed on behalf of Rebecca. Her barrenness was intolerable. It was to emphasize the pain that she was suffering that Rachel confronted Jacob with the words, "Give me children or I shall die." From his use of the name *E-lohim*, it is clear that Jacob was telling Rachel one of two things. Either it was that *E-lohim* the Creator of the world who fixed the laws of nature had made her barren or it was that *E-lohim* who conducts the world according to strict justice had seen fit to deny her children as punishment for her sins. In either case there was nothing that he could do about it. Perhaps he was telling her both these things.

It would certainly seem that Rachel eventually gave up on having her own child. As Sarah before her had done with Hagar, she gave Bilhah, her handmaid, to Jacob as a wife. Rachel could raise the child of Bilhah as her own. When Bilhah subsequently had a son, Rachel named him. In Genesis 30:6 we read: "And Rachel said, 'God has vindicated me; indeed, He has heeded my plea and given me a son.' Therefore she named him Dan." Recalling the chiding words of Jacob, that she had been treated with strict justice, Rachel now felt that *E-lohim* had found some merit in her, the result of which He had given her a child through her handmaid Bilhah. When Bilhah had another son, Rachel once more

---

91. Cf. D. Hoffmann, op. cit., Genesis 29:31.

invoked the Divine name, and in Genesis 30:8 we read: "And Rachel said, 'Wrestlings of God have I wrestled with my sister; yes, and I have prevailed.' So she named him Naftali." Rachel referred to the rivalry between her and her sister to contribute to Jacob's family as "wrestlings of God."[92] Perhaps this is because she knew that their childbearing was for a noble purpose, namely, the formation of the nation of Israel. By giving her maidservant to Jacob for a wife she performed a deed no less noble than that of Sarah, and as such she had earned the right to bring up another child as a manifestation of strict Divine justice (*E-lohim*) rather than compassion.

Leah was not passive on this matter. Thinking, perhaps, that she had stopped giving birth, she gave Zilpah, her maidservant, to Jacob as a wife; and Zilpah had two sons, Gad and Asher. Then Leah herself had another son. In Genesis 30:17 we read: "And God heard Leah, and she conceived and bore him [Jacob] a fifth son. And Leah said, 'God has given me my reward for having given my maid to my husband. So she named him Issachar." Leah also felt that she had earned the right to bear Jacob another child for she, too, had given her maidservant to Jacob for a wife. It seems that her feelings were valid as well, for the Torah tells us that it was *E-lohim* rather than *Havayah* who heard Leah, a manifestation of strict justice.

Leah had still another son. In Genesis 30:20 we read: "Leah said, 'God has given me a choice gift; this time my husband will give me presents, for I have borne him six sons.'" At last Leah felt that by bearing Jacob six sons she had earned his love and devotion, and honor, which she *justly* deserved. Finally, Leah had a daughter whom she named Dinah.

In all this time, Rachel had no children, but she was not forsaken. In Genesis 30:22 we read: "Now God remembered Rachel; God heeded her and opened her womb. She conceived and bore a son and said, 'God has taken away my disgrace.' So she named him Joseph, which is to say, 'May the Lord add another son for me.'" What is the significance of the two Divine names addressed by Rachel here? Jacob and Rachel anticipated that Laban might try to substitute Leah for Rachel on their

---

92. Cf. D. Hoffmann, op. cit., Genesis 30:7; also S. R. Hirsch ad loc.

wedding night. To prevent this from happening, they agreed upon certain secret signs that would identify Rachel to him. That night, Rachel regretted the plan. Seeing that her fears had materialized, she felt that Leah would be terribly embarrassed if she were discovered. To avoid this, Rachel revealed the signs to Leah. Her act betrayed great compassion to be sure, and *E-lohim* rewarded her for it. It is our contention that the Torah is telling us that it was not Divine mercy but rather Divine justice that was responsible for Rachel having conceived. She justly deserved a child. Of course, her request for a second child would have to be an appeal to Divine compassion. By addressing her prayer to *Havayah* she made this clear.

THE AGREEMENT

By now Jacob was ready to return home to Canaan, but he would not go without asking permission from Laban. In Genesis 30:27–28, we read Laban's response: "But Laban said to him, 'If you will indulge me, I have learned by divination that the Lord has blessed me on your account.' And he continued, 'Name the wages due from me and I will pay you.'" Jacob confirmed the fact that *Havayah* had blessed Laban, enriching him through Jacob's merit. And in Genesis 30:29 he responded: "But he said, 'You well know how I served you and how your livestock has fared with me. For the little you had before I came has grown too much, since the Lord has blessed you wherever I turned. And now, when shall I make provision for my own household?'"

The two men came to an agreement. Jacob would take for himself every speckled and spotted animal, every dark-colored sheep, and every spotted and speckled goat. This would be his wages. Laban tried to outsmart him by removing all such animals from his flock that very same day, but as we shall see, *Havayah* intervened on Jacob's behalf. He enriched Jacob with large flocks, maidservants and menservants, camels and asses. In Genesis 31:3 we read: "Then the Lord said to Jacob, 'Return to the land of your fathers where you were born, and I will be with you.'" Knowing that Jacob would feel somewhat uneasy about returning to his father's house, having to face his brother Esau, he was reassured that the providential hand of *Havayah* would protect him.

THE CONSULTATION

Jacob was ready and able to abide by the charge that had been given to him by *Havayah*, but out of respect to his wives, he chose to consult with them on the matter. He spoke to them frankly and sincerely. He explained that Laban had tried to trick him regarding the spotted and speckled animals despite the agreement they had made, but it was to no avail. In Genesis 31:9 we read: "God has taken away your father's livestock and given it to me." How much more meaningful these words become when we consider the fact that the name *E-lohim* appears here. It was an act of strict Divine justice that Jacob was given Laban's livestock since according to their agreement it truly belonged to him.[93] This is further confirmed in Genesis 31:10–12 where Jacob recalls:

> Once, at the mating time of the flocks, I had a dream in which I saw that the he-goats in the flock, as they mated, were streaked, speckled, and mottled. And in the dream an angel of God said to me, "Jacob!" "Here," I answered. And he said, "Note well that all the he-goats in the flock which are mating are streaked, speckled, and mottled; for I have noted all that Laban has been doing to you."

Lastly, the angel told Jacob to leave Haran. It was time for him to fulfill his part of the vow that he had made at Bethel and dedicate a house to *Havayah*.[94]

Rachel and Leah agreed that their father had dealt dishonorably with Jacob. What's more, they felt that Laban had cheated them as well. Clearly, all the material wealth that *E-lohim* had given them was justifiably theirs. As we read in Genesis 31:14–15:

> Then Rachel and Leah answered him, saying, "Have we still a share in the inheritance of our father's house? Are we not reckoned by him as outsiders? For he sold us and then used up our purchase

---

93. Cf. S. R. Hirsch, commentary on Genesis 31:9.
94. Cf. Nahmanides, commentary on Genesis 31:13 and S. R. Hirsch ad loc.

price. Truly, all the wealth that God has taken away from our father belongs to us and to our children. Now then, do just as God has told you."

Satisfied with his wives' response, Jacob put his children and his wives on camels. He took all the wealth that he had amassed in Haran, and he set out for Canaan. Perhaps out of fear that Laban would try to stop him, Jacob did not inform Laban that he was leaving. In an attempt to wean her father from idolatry, Rachel stole his idols.[95] On the third day, Laban was told that Jacob had fled, so he took some of his kinsmen and pursued Jacob a distance of seven days. What would Laban say to Jacob when he met him? The night before, Laban had a dream.[96] In Genesis 31:24 we read: "But God appeared to Laban the Aramean in a dream by night and said to him, 'Beware of attempting anything with Jacob, good or bad.'" Clearly, this warning came from *E-lohim* who punishes the wicked and rewards the righteous. The warning was a manifestation of strict justice.

THE ENCOUNTER WITH JACOB

Laban met up with Jacob at Gilead. He told Jacob that God had appeared to him the night before and had warned him not to speak to Jacob, good or bad. Notwithstanding the warning, Laban took the opportunity to chastise Jacob for leaving without notice, and he accused Jacob of stealing his idols. Though these words angered Jacob, he allowed Laban to search for the idols among his belongings and the belongings of his wives. Laban found nothing. Incensed and deeply hurt, Jacob took the opportunity to vent his anger. He expressed his disappointment at the way he had been treated by Laban all these twenty years. After all, he had been a loyal and a diligent worker. He concluded with the words in Genesis 31:42: "Had not the God of my

---

95. Cf. Rashi, commentary on Genesis 31:19.
96. Cf. Ibn Ezra on Genesis 31:24.

father, the God of Abraham and the Fear of Isaac,[97] been with me, you would have sent me away empty-handed. But God took notice of my plight and the toil of my hands, and He gave judgment last night." The name *E-lohim* is mentioned here three times, clearly indicating that as far as Jacob was concerned all that he had taken with him, his wives and children and his flocks, were earned in honesty. God gave them to him as a manifestation of Divine justice. Laban responded audaciously: "The daughters are my daughters, the children are my children, and the flocks are my flocks; all that you see is mine."[98] Notwithstanding this, the two made a treaty that neither would ever do harm to the other, and they parted.

THE ENCOUNTER WITH ANGELS

In Genesis 32:2 we read: "Jacob went on his way and angels of God encountered him. When he saw them, Jacob said, 'This is God's camp.' So he named the place Mahanayim." The angels who had encountered Jacob were *Malakhe E-lohim* ("angels of God") who were sent to accompany him on his journey home. True, it was *Havayah* who had promised to protect him and to return him safely to Canaan as a manifestation of Divine compassion. But twenty years had passed since then. Jacob was returning to Canaan a righteous man despite his mistreatment by Laban. He was unimpressed and untainted by the idolatry he had seen in Laban's house. Tested in the crucible of evil and temptation, Jacob emerged refined and pure.[99] He did not have to depend on Divine compassion to bring him home safely. He had earned the right to be protected; it was a manifestation of Divine justice.

---

97. The words "the Fear of Isaac" mean "the God of Isaac." For an explanation of the significance of this phrase cf. Nahmanides on Genesis 31:42.
98. Genesis 31:43.
99. Cf. Rashi on Genesis 32:4. "Though I have sojourned with Laban, the wicked, I have observed the 613 Divine commandments, and I have learned nought of his evil ways."

THE ENCOUNTER WITH ESAU

Jacob sent messengers ahead to his brother Esau, who was in the land of Seir in the country of Edom. Esau was informed that Jacob had spent time with Laban, and he had acquired both animals and slaves. The message was delivered, and Esau set out with 400 men to meet Jacob. Frightened at the prospect of a confrontation, Jacob divided his people into two camps with the hope that if one camp was attacked and destroyed the other would escape. In Genesis 32:10 Jacob offered the following prayer:

> O God of my father Abraham and God of my father Isaac, O Lord, who said to me, "Return to your native land and I will deal beautifully with you!" I am unworthy of all the kindness that You have so steadfastly shown Your servant: with my staff alone did I cross this Jordan, and now I have become two camps. Deliver me, I pray, from the hand of my brother, from the hand of Esau; else, I fear, he may come and strike me down mothers and children alike . . .

Jacob referred to the "God of Abraham and Isaac." This is how *E-lohim* revealed Himself to Jacob outside of Haran.[100] But the appeal itself was to *Havayah* for it was Divine compassion that Jacob had sought.[101] There is another reason why Jacob referred to the "God of Abraham and Isaac." There is a fundamental difference between a Divine promise made to an individual on the merit of his forefathers

---

100. See Genesis 28:13.
101. In point of fact, Jacob appeals here to both attributes of the Divine. As Rashi points out: "Jacob said to the Holy One blessed be He, 'You made me two promises. One was when I left my father's house at Beer-sheba when you said to me (28:13), "I am the Lord, the God of Abraham your father and the God of Isaac," and on that occasion You promised me (verse 15) "I will protect you wherever you go." Then again in Laban's house You said to me, "Return to the land of your fathers where you were born and I will be with you." There You revealed Yourself to me by Your Proper Name alone . . . Relying on these two promises, I now come to You invoking You as "the God of Abraham and the God of Isaac" and also simply as "the Lord" under which names You made me these two promises respectively.'" Cf. also *Rashbam* ad loc.

and one made to him on his own merits. The former will not be broken even if the individual sins; that is not the case with the latter. In utter humility, Jacob felt that he was unworthy and could not depend upon Divine protection in his own merit.[102]

Jacob selected animals from his flock and set them up in droves. He put his servants in charge of the droves and had them walk ahead. He told them that when Esau confronted them, they should say that the animals were a gift from Jacob who is behind them. That night, Jacob took his family and his possessions across the ford of the Jabbok River. He remained alone on the other side. A man wrestled with him that night, and when the man saw that he could not prevail over him, he wrenched Jacob's hip at its socket. The dawn was coming and the man pleaded with Jacob to release him, but Jacob insisted that the man first bless him. He did. And in Genesis 32:29 we read: "He said, 'Your name shall no longer be Jacob, but Israel, for you have striven with beings Divine and human, and have prevailed.'"[103] Our sages point out that the man of whom the Torah speaks here was actually an angel.

The brothers finally met. They embraced each other, kissed, and wept. Jacob asked Esau to accept his gifts, but Esau refused saying that he had enough wealth of his own. Jacob insisted, and in Genesis 33:11 we read: "Accept, then, my blessing [offering] which has been brought to you, for God has favored me and I have plenty. And when he urged him, he accepted." Could it not be that Jacob was alluding to the blessing that he was given by his father Isaac that he was gladly relinquishing in atonement for what he had done?[104] At the same time, did he refer to his accumulated wealth as a gift from *E-lohim* who rules the world with strict justice, implying that what he had was the result of his own labor and as such it was justly deserved? Perhaps both of these are true.

---

102. Cf. M. Malbim, commentary on Genesis 32:10.

103. This was a prediction. Jacob's name was not changed to Israel; he was given an additional name. At Bethel, God gave him the name to indicate that had earned the right to be considered a prince and chief. See text and Rashi commentary on Genesis 35:10.

104. Cf. S. R. Hirsch, commentary on Genesis 33:11.

THE INCIDENT AT SHEKHEM

A brief dialogue ensued between the two brothers. Esau then continued on his way to Seir, and Jacob journeyed on and came to the city of Shekhem in Canaan. There he purchased a parcel of land from Hamor, the father of Shekhem. He set up an altar and called it *E-l E-lohe Yisrael* (God, the God of Israel). In doing so, Jacob acknowledged that it was the omnipotent hand of *E-lohim* that had protected him from the moment he left the home of his father until that day.[105]

Shekhem was not to be remembered as a pleasant experience in Jacob's life. The Torah records that Dinah, Jacob's daughter, went out to visit the daughters of the land. Shekhem, the son of Hamor, saw her and violated her. He was in love with her, and he wanted her for his wife so her told his father Hamor to make the necessary arrangements. When Jacob's sons heard that Shekhem had violated Dinah, they became distressed and very angry. They told Shekhem that only on the condition that he and all the other males in his community be circumcised would they permit such a marriage. For then, the two peoples would become one, and they could intermarry. Shekhem agreed. He spoke to his people and they agreed as well.

On the third day after their circumcision, when the people were still in pain, Simeon and Levi, two of Jacob's sons, came upon the city and slew all the males. They took Dinah and left. The other sons came and plundered the town taking everything that was of value (among which were idols of silver and gold)[106] because of the shame that Shekhem had brought upon their family. Jacob was distressed with what Simeon and Levi had done, and he conveyed his feelings to them. In Genesis 34:30 we read: "Jacob said to Simeon and Levi, 'You have brought trouble on me, making me odious among the inhabitants of the land . . . so that if they attack me, I and my house will be destroyed.'" Simeon and Levi responded, "Should our sister be treated like a whore?'"[107]

---

105. In this context, the name "Israel" refers not to the nation but to Jacob himself who had also been named Israel.
106. Cf. Rashi and Rabbenu B'haye on Genesis 35:2
107. Genesis 34:31.

THE RETURN TO BETH-EL

In Genesis 35:1 we read: "God said to Jacob, 'Go up promptly to Bethel and remain there; and build an altar there to the God [*E-l*] who appeared to you when you were fleeing from your brother Esau.'" The incident with Dinah and the unfortunate consequences that followed were clear indications that Jacob and his family did not belong there. He should have gone to Bethel first, to fulfill his vow, and subsequently to Hebron.[108] Perhaps it was to remind him of the yet-unfulfilled vow he made at Bethel that the Torah records that *E-lohim* appeared to him. For in Bethel he vowed, "If God remains with me." This may also be the reason for the appearance of the name *E-l* here, from which the name Bethel is taken.[109]

Jacob instructed his people to rid themselves of the strange gods that they had acquired, to purify themselves, and to change their garments. He buried the idols, and he set out for Bethel. Interestingly, in Genesis 35:5 the Torah records: "As they set out, a terror from God fell on the cities round about, so that they did not pursue the sons of Jacob." The fact that two men, Simeon and Levi, were able to vanquish all of Shekhem terrified the inhabitants of the neighboring cities, for they felt that this phenomenon had to be the workings of the omnipotent *E-lohim*.

Jacob arrived in Bethel, and in Genesis 35:7 we read: "There he built an altar and named the site *E-l*-Bethel for it was there that God had revealed Himself to him when he was fleeing from his brother." In Shekhem, Jacob named the altar that he had built *E-l E-lohe Yisrael* (the God of Israel) again indicating that the Supreme Being had appeared to him. Upon return to Bethel, he seemed to have gained a new insight, namely, that this place was special; it was predisposed to revelation. To indicate this he named *the place* rather than the altar.[110] Of course, he named the place in commemoration of the providential hand of the omnipotent *E-lohim* who had protected him from his brother Esau.

---

108. Cf. S. R. Hirsch, commentary on Genesis 35:1.
109. Cf. D. Hoffmann, op. cit., Genesis 35:1.
110. Cf. M. Malbim, commentary on Genesis 35:7.

FROM JACOB TO ISRAEL

God appeared to Jacob again, and He blessed him. In Genesis 35:10–12 we read:

> God said to him, "You whose name is Jacob, you shall be called Jacob no more, but Israel shall be your name." Thus He named him Israel. And God said to him, "I am God Almighty be fertile and increase; a nation, yea an assembly of nations, shall descend from you. Kings shall issue from your loins. The land that I gave to Abraham and Isaac I give to you; and to your offspring to come will I give the land." God parted from him at the spot where He had spoken to him.

The angel with whom Jacob strove had predicted that at Bethel *E-lohim* would appear to Jacob and change his name to Israel. "At that time," said the angel, "I will be there and testify that you merit that name in that you strove with and angel and a man and triumphed."[111] It is no more than fitting that *E-lohim*, the omnipotent Creator of the universe, give Jacob the name that designates him as the prince and chief among his people who strove with an angel and a man and triumphed. Indeed, it was *E-l Sha-dai* (God Almighty), the omnipotent all sufficient Supreme Being who nourishes the world through His providential hand, who informed Jacob (Israel) that nations will descend from him. He also promised him that he would inherit the land that had been promised to Abraham and Isaac. A sworn promise made by *E-lohim* to an individual can never be broken even if the individual sins and no longer merits reward.[112]

THE INCIDENT WITH JOSEPH

Together with his family, Jacob settled in Canaan, the land where his father had resided. We are told that of all his sons, Jacob loved Joseph

---

111. Cf. Rashi on Genesis 32:29.
112. Cf. Nahmanides, commentary on Genesis 35:12.

best. To show his affection, he made Joseph an ornamental tunic. This aroused the jealousy of the brothers, and they hated Joseph for it. The Torah tells us that Joseph had two dreams. He dreamed that he and his brothers were binding sheaves in the field. Suddenly, his sheaf stood erect and those of his brothers gathered around and bowed before it. He told the dream to his brothers and they hated him even more for now they thought that he planned to reign over them. In the second dream, the sun, the moon, and the stars bowed down to him. He told this dream to his brothers and his father as well. Upon hearing the dream, his father berated him. "Are we to come, I and your mother and your brothers, and bow low to you to the ground?" Jacob asked. Joseph's brothers became even angrier, but Jacob kept the matter in mind.

It happened that the brothers had gone to pasture their father's flock in Shekhem. Israel (Jacob) told Joseph to find them and return with news of how they were. The brothers saw him at a distance, and they conspired to kill him. They planned to throw him into a pit and report to their father that a wild beast had devoured him. Reuben knew that this would be an inexcusable evil act, and he tried to save Joseph. With the intention of eventually retrieving him and bringing him back to his father, Reuben told his brothers to throw him into the pit alive. The brothers agreed. When Joseph reached them, they stripped him of the ornamental tunic he was wearing, and they threw him into a pit. Later, some Midianite traders were passing by, and the brothers decided to sell Joseph to them. Eventually, Joseph ended up in Egypt where he was sold to Potiphar, the Pharaoh's chief steward. The brothers returned home. They showed their father the tunic, which they had dipped in the blood of a kid that they had slaughtered, and they told him that a wild beast had devoured Joseph. Jacob was devastated. He rent his clothes and mourned Joseph for many days.

JOSEPH IN EGYPT

In Genesis 39:2–5 we read:

> The Lord was with Joseph, and he was a successful man. He remained in the house of his Egyptian master; and when his master

> saw that the Lord was with him and that the Lord lent success to everything he undertook, he took a liking to Joseph. He made him his personal attendant and put him in charge of his household, placing in his hands all that he owned. And from the time that the Egyptian put him in charge . . . the Lord blessed his house for Joseph's sake, so that the blessing of the Lord was upon everything that he owned, in the house and outside.

The fact that the name *Havayah* appears five times in these four verses is a clear indication that everything that was happening to Joseph in Egypt until this point was a manifestation of Divine compassion. But we must see the broader picture in the series of events. It is quite clear that Joseph's destiny was being shaped by Divine providence step by step. Let us review the events that had transpired with Joseph.

The brothers heeded the words of Reuben, and instead of killing Joseph they threw him into a pit. Then they sold him to traders who resold him. Joseph ended up in Egypt, in the home of Potiphar, the steward of Pharaoh, who prospered because of him. All this was part of a Divine plan. In very general terms, this plan was revealed to Abraham. In Genesis 15:13–14 we read the following: "Know well that your offspring shall be strangers in a land not theirs, and they shall be enslaved and oppressed four hundred years; but I will pass judgment on the nation they shall serve, and in the end they shall go free with great wealth." In a sense, the destiny of the Jewish people began not with Jacob but with Joseph's settlement in Egypt.

Joseph did not fare well long in the home of Potiphar. Potiphar's wife tried to seduce him. When Joseph refused her advances she accused Joseph of toying with her. Potiphar was furious, and he had Joseph imprisoned. In Genesis 39:21–23 we read:

> The Lord was with Joseph; He extended kindness to him and disposed the chief jailer favorably toward him. The chief jailer put in Joseph's charge all the prisoners who were in that prison, and he was the one to carry out everything that was done there. The chief jailer did not supervise anything that was in Joseph's charge, because the Lord was with him, and whatever he did the Lord made successful.

Havayah was compassionate to Joseph. He did not relinquish His providential hand even when Joseph was in prison. What's more, He disposed the jailer favorably toward Joseph, in itself a sign of Divine compassion, for the jailers were always quite cruel.[113]

THE INTERPRETER OF DREAMS

During the period of his incarceration, the cupbearer and the chief baker of Pharaoh were imprisoned. They each had a dream, and Joseph offered to interpret them. He predicted that the cupbearer would be restored to his position and the baker would be executed. The dreams were fulfilled, but the cupbearer who was restored to his position did nothing for Joseph in return. He simply forgot him. Two years later, Pharaoh had two dreams. He asked his magicians and his wise men to interpret them, but they were unable to do so. Then the cupbearer remembered Joseph, and he told Pharaoh about him whereupon Pharaoh had Joseph removed from the prison and brought before him. He told Joseph that he had heard that he could interpret dreams, and Joseph responded: "Not I! God will see to Pharaoh's welfare."[114] Joseph listened intently as Pharaoh related both dreams, and in Genesis 41: 25, 32 we read: "And Joseph said to Pharaoh, 'Pharaoh's dreams are one and the same: God has told Pharaoh what He is about to do . . . As for Pharaoh having the same dream twice, it means that the matter has been determined by God and that God will soon carry it out.'"

The dreams were interpreted by Joseph to mean that Egypt would be faced with seven years of plenty followed by seven years of famine. At times, a severe decree that issues forth from God is conditional: if the people repent, the decree is withdrawn. In this case, the decree was irrevocable.[115] Perhaps this is the rationale for the name *E-lohim*, namely, that the seven years of famine was a matter of strict, irrevocable Divine judgment. Be that as it may, the die was cast, and Joseph told

---

113. Cf, M. Malbim, commentary on Genesis 39:21.
114. Genesis 41:16.
115. M Malbim, commentary on Genesis 41:32.

Pharaoh to appoint a man of wisdom and understanding and set him over the land of Egypt to supervise the storage of grain during the years of plenty. In Genesis 41: 38–40 we read:

> And Pharaoh said to his courtiers, "Could we find another like him, a man in whom is the spirit of God?" So Pharaoh said to Joseph, "Since God has made all this known to you, there is none so discerning and wise as you. You shall be in charge of my court, and by your command shall all my people be directed; only with respect to the throne shall I be superior to you."

Pharaoh appointed Joseph to the task. There cannot be anyone more suitable for the job than Joseph, said Pharaoh; for not only is he wise, he is Divinely inspired. How clearly the sequence of events that we have reviewed demonstrates that Divine providence was shaping the destiny of the nation of Israel. Indeed, it was *E-lohim* who would bring the final calamity upon Egypt in strict accordance with the attribute of justice.

The destiny of Israel continued to unfold. Joseph had two sons: Ephraim and Manasseh. In Genesis 41:51–52 we read: "Joseph named the first-born Manasseh, meaning, 'God has made me forget completely my hardship and my parental home.' And the second he named Ephraim, meaning, 'God has made me fertile in the land of my affliction.'" It seems rather strange that Joseph would be pleased to have forgotten his parental home. Perhaps what he is saying is that in giving him children, *E-lohim*, the Creator of the law of nature, had brought him great joy. For his children were a welcome distraction from the difficult work with which he had been involved in Egypt. The sheer joy he had experienced with his children had made him forget, if only temporarily, the pain he had suffered longing to return to his father's house.

FAMINE COMES UPON EGYPT

The seven years of plenty passed, and as Joseph had predicted, the seven years of famine came upon Egypt. Egypt was prepared for the famine, for Joseph had stored away a plentiful supply of grain. When

The God of the Patriarchs

Jacob heard that there was food in Egypt, he sent ten of his sons there to purchase grain. Benjamin remained at home. Of Rachel's two sons, Benjamin was the only one left, and his father feared that if he went to Egypt he might suffer disaster.

When the brothers came before Joseph, he recognized them but they did not recognize him. This was an opportunity for Joseph to test them to see whether their attitude had changed. Would the need for grain be a valid enough reason to deprive their father of Rachel's other son? Joseph accused them of being spies. When they told him that Benjamin, their youngest brother, had remained at home, Joseph insisted that they bring him to Egypt, but first he incarcerated them. After three days, he allowed them to return home to get Benjamin, but one of them would have to stay behind. Reuben scolded them for what they had done to Joseph, and insisted that the suffering that they now had to endure was punishment for that deed. Joseph kept Simeon to make sure that the brothers would return to Egypt.

The brothers returned to Canaan, and they told their father what had transpired in Egypt. Jacob at first refused to let Benjamin go, but when the food ran out, he had no choice. In Genesis 43:14 we read Jacob's words as they departed: "And may God Almighty dispose the man to compassion toward you that he may release to you your other brother, as well as Benjamin. As for me, if I am to be bereaved, I shall be bereaved." *Sha-dai*, namely, the "Being" who is sufficient in all things, whose providential hand nourishes the world with great compassion, may He dispose the man (Joseph) to compassion as well, so that he will send Simeon and Benjamin back to me, says Jacob.

Judah took responsibility for Benjamin, and the brothers returned to Egypt. Seeing Benjamin before him, Joseph was overcome with warm feelings toward him. He wanted to weep but could not do so in front of his brothers, for that might make them suspect what was happening. So he went into another room and wept. When he came out, he gave the order to serve a meal, and they all ate and drank together. But the matter did not end there. Joseph gave each of his brothers a bag of grain, and he instructed his steward to put a silver goblet in Benjamin's bag. In the morning, the brothers left for Canaan. Joseph instructed his steward to overtake them and accuse them of taking the silver goblet.

He did so, and they denied it saying, "Whichever of your servants it is found with shall die; the rest of us, moreover, shall be slaves to my lord."

REVEALED IDENTITY

The goblet turned up in Benjamin's bag, and the brothers were returned to Egypt. They pleaded guilty and vowed that they would be slaves to Joseph along with Benjamin. Joseph told them that Benjamin alone would be his slave, and upon hearing this they were panic-stricken. Judah pleaded with Joseph for mercy. He told him that Jacob would die if he were bereft of Benjamin. By now, Joseph was overcome with emotion. He had everyone in the room withdraw except the brothers, and he revealed his identity to them. "I am Joseph. Is my father still well?" he said. The brothers were speechless. Joseph told them not to be distressed, but more important, he explained that it was his destiny to be in Egypt. In Genesis 45:7, 8 we read: "God has sent me ahead of you to insure your survival on Earth, and to save your lives in an extraordinary deliverance. So now it was not you who sent me here, but God; and He has made me a father to Pharaoh, lord of all his household, and ruler over the whole land of Egypt."

Joseph informed his brothers that they should not be afraid. Although he may have harbored some ill feelings toward them when they threw him into the pit, he no longer felt that way. He was now privy to the greater picture, namely, that his exile to Egypt was not mere chance but part of a Divine plan. It was a manifestation of the intervention of *E-lohim*, the Supreme Judge of the universe, in the process of history. It was not the brothers who were responsible for his being brought to Egypt. They were merely the means through which the Divine plan was being implemented. Consequently, they should feel no guilt. In point of fact, said Joseph, it had gone well with him in Egypt. He had endeared himself to Pharaoh, his household, and all of Egypt.[116]

---

116. Cf. M. Malbim, commentary on Genesis 45:8; also *Or HaHayyim* ad loc.

THE EXILE BEGINS

Having made his peace with his brothers, Joseph was anxious to see his father. In Genesis 45:9 he instructed his brothers as follows: "Hurry back, then, to my father and say to him, 'God has made me lord over all Egypt; come down to me without delay." Should Joseph not have said, "Pharaoh has made me lord over all of Egypt"? Perhaps he wanted to convey to his father the reason why he could not return to Canaan to see him. It simply was not his destiny. The plan of *E-lohim*, the Supreme Judge of the universe, was for Joseph to remain in Egypt.

The brothers returned to Canaan with good news. They told their father that Joseph was alive and that he was ruler over the whole land of Egypt. At first, Jacob didn't believe them. So they told him more. When he saw the wagons of provisions, however, he was convinced, and in Genesis 45:28 we read: "Enough!" said Israel. "My son Joseph is still alive! I must go and see him before I die." Jacob began his journey to Egypt. When he came to Beer-sheba, he offered sacrifices to the God of his father Isaac. In Genesis 46:2–4 we read: "God called to Israel in a vision by night: 'Jacob! Jacob!' He answered, 'Here.' And He said, 'I am God [*E-l*], the God *of* your father. Fear not to go down to Egypt, for there I will make you a great nation. I Myself will go down with you to Egypt, and I Myself will also bring you back; and Joseph's hand shall close your eyes.'"

The Torah tells us that *E-lohim* revealed Himself to Israel. What is strange is that He called him "Jacob," the name he was given at birth. Had not *E-lohim* said to him, "You shall be called Jacob no more, but Israel shall be your name"?[117] If we consider the significance of the name "Israel," the fact that it was given to him because he had striven with beings Divine and human and had prevailed, we can understand why he was not called by that name in this instance. Jacob's journey to Egypt was the onset of the *galut*, the exile of the Jewish people to Egypt, which led to their enslavement. This depressing thought was not to be associated with the glorious name "Israel."[118] Be that as it may,

---

117. Genesis 35:10.
118. Cf. Nahmanides, commentary on Genesis 36:2.

says *E-lohim*, I am *E-l*, the omnipotent Supreme Being of the universe. I have the power to redeem you from bondage, and I will do so.

Jacob left Beer-sheba, and arrived in Egypt with his whole family, a legion of seventy souls. Joseph went out to greet them. When he reached his father he embraced him and wept. In Genesis 46:30 we read: "Then Israel said to Joseph, 'Now I can die, having seen for myself that you are still alive.'" Jacob settled in Goshen where he remained for the rest of his life. In Genesis 47:27 we read: "Thus Israel settled in the country of Egypt, in the region of Goshen; they acquired holdings in it, and increased greatly in numbers." Jacob lived there for seventeen years and died at the age of 147.

5

THE GOD OF MOSES

Time passed. Joseph, his brothers, and that entire generation died. The children of Israel (Jacob) were prolific; they multiplied and increased greatly. A new Pharaoh arose in Egypt who did not or would not recognize what Joseph had done for the country. He saw the growth of the Israelites (Hebrews) as a threat to his security, so he set taskmasters over them to oppress them with forced labor. Much to his dismay, the more they were oppressed the more they increased. To stem the tide, Pharaoh told the Israelite midwives to kill all the newborn males but to allow the females to live. To their credit, the midwives refused to follow Pharaoh's edict, and the Israelites continued to multiply greatly. Frustrated by his foiled plan, Pharaoh charged the entire Egyptian population to throw all newborn males into the Nile River while allowing the females to live.

THE BIRTH OF MOSES

Despite the cruel edicts, the Torah records that a man of the tribe of Levi married a Levite woman. She conceived and had a son whom she was able to hide for three months. Seeing that she could hide the boy no longer, she took a wicker basket and coated it with pitch. She then put the infant in it and set it on the Nile River. Miriam, the infant's sister, stood at a distance and kept a watchful eye on the basket. Before long Pharaoh's daughter who was bathing in the river saw the basket and she retrieved it. She knew that it must be an Israelite child. Miriam then asked her if she should call a Hebrew nurse to suckle the child, and Pharaoh's daughter answered, "Yes." Of course, Miriam brought the child's mother Yokheved, who nursed him and took him home. When he grew up, she brought him to Pharaoh's daughter, who adopted him as her own son and named him Moses (*Moshe*), which means "I drew him out of the water."

Some time later, Moses witnessed an Egyptian beating an Israelite slave. Enraged by what he saw, he struck the Egyptian down and hid him in the sand. The next day, Moses saw two Israelite men fighting. When he inquired of one of them why he was pummeling his friend he responded, "Who made you chief and ruler over us? Do you mean to kill me as you killed the Egyptian?" Frightened at the thought that what he had done had been discovered, Moses escaped to Midian. There he met Reuel, the priest of Midian, whose daughter Zipporah he eventually married. She bore him a son whom Moses named Gershom (meaning "a stranger there"), commemorating the fact that he was a stranger in a foreign land.

GOD REMEMBERS

Pharaoh died. The Israelites cried out to *E-lohim*, and in Exodus 2:24–25 we read: "God heard their moaning, and God remembered his covenant with Abraham and Isaac and Jacob. God looked upon the Israelites, and God took notice of them." The Divine plan for the children of Israel continued to unfold. In the above two verses, the name *E-lohim* appears four times. Why? It was judgment day for Egypt, and in punishment for their persecution and enslavement of the Israelites, *E-lohim* was about to initiate the first steps to redemption. *E-lohim* remembered His covenant with the Patriarchs in which He foretold that the Israelites would be enslaved, even persecuted. The redemption would, indeed, be a manifestation of strict justice. Through the centuries the Israelites had assimilated some of the practices of the Egyptians. Our sages tell us that the redemption took place somewhat before its time in order to prevent the Israelites from totally assimilating.[1]

THE MESSAGE OF THE BURNING BUSH

Moses was tending his flock in the wilderness. He came to Horeb, a place that was later to become known as the mountain of God. Suddenly, an angel of *Havayah* appeared to him in a blazing fire out of a bush. The bush was aflame but it was not being consumed. Moses went to see this strange phenomenon, and in Exodus 3:4–11 we read:

> When the Lord saw that he had turned aside to look, God called to him out of the bush: "Moses! Moses!" He answered, "Here I am." And He said, "Do not come closer. Remove your sandals from your feet, for the place on which you stand is holy ground. I am," He said, "the God of your father, the God of Abraham, the God of Isaac and the God of Jacob." And Moses hid his face for he was afraid to look at God. And the Lord continued, "I have marked well the plight of My people in Egypt and have heeded their outcry because of their taskmasters; yes, I am mindful of their sufferings. I have come down to rescue them from the Egyptians and to bring them out of that land to a good and spacious land, a land flowing with milk and honey . . . Come, therefore, I will send you to Pharaoh, and you shall free My people, the Israelites, from Egypt."

Both names of the Divine appear in this brief encounter, and we must seek out a rationale for this phenomenon. Moses' initial encounter with the Divine was through an angel of *Havayah*. Perhaps this is to indicate that prophecy, the encounter between God and man, is to be understood first and foremost as a manifestation of Divine compassion. The message that was conveyed in this encounter, however, was a

---

1. Cf. S. R. Hirsch, commentary on Exodus 2:24.

manifestation of strict justice for it was the fulfillment of the promise made to the patriarchs. Consequently, it came from *E-lohim* or, as some understand it, the angel of *E-lohim*.[2] Be that as it may, in terms of the Israelites, the redemption from bondage in Egypt was clearly a manifestation of Divine compassion, which explains why it is introduced in the biblical text with the name *Havayah*.

MOSES' DILEMMA

One of Moses' most outstanding qualities was his humility. Indeed, the Torah itself testifies to this in Numbers 12:3 where we read, "Now Moses was a humble man, more so than any other man on Earth." We are made aware of Moses' humility by his response at the burning bush, which was his initial encounter with *E-lohim*. In Exodus 3:11 we read, "But Moses said to God, 'Who am I that I should go to Pharaoh and free the Israelites from Egypt?'" He expressed his insufficiency on two counts: first, who is he, a mere shepherd, to appear before the powerful Pharaoh of Egypt, and second, even if he is deemed worthy enough to appear before the Pharaoh, he surely lacks the ability to convince him to free the Israelites from bondage.[3] *E-lohim* reassures Moses that he will have Divine assistance, and in Exodus 3:13–15 we read:

> Moses said to God, "When I come to the Israelites and say to them, 'The God of my fathers has sent me to you' and they ask me, 'What is His name?' what shall I say to them?" And God said to Moses, "*Ehyeh Asher Ehyeh*." He continued, "Thus shall you say to the Israelites, *Ehyeh* sent me to you." And God said further to Moses, "Thus shall you speak to the Israelites: The Lord the God of your fathers, the God of Abraham, the God of Isaac, and the God of Jacob, has sent me to you: This shall be My name forever, this My appellation for all eternity."

---

2. Cf. Ibn Ezra, commentary on Exodus 3:4.
3. Cf. Rashbam on Exodus 3:10.

The God of Moses

A NEW APPELLATION

We have already explained the meaning of the Divine name *Ehyeh*. We must understand its significance in the above context. Let us first clarify the meaning and implication of Moses' query. Nahmanides points out that for Moses to have requested the revelation of a Divine name that would make the people believe in him would make no sense. If the people already knew that name, the fact that Moses now repeated it to them would accomplish nothing. If, on the other hand, they did not know the name how would this prove that he spoke the truth? What proof would this be that they should now believe him?[4] What Moses wanted to know is by what Divine attribute he is being sent to the Israelites. Was it the attribute of omnipotence and self-sufficiency represented by the names *E-l Sha-dai* that were so well-known to the patriarchs? Perhaps it was the attribute of compassion represented by the name *Havayah*? The answer given to Moses was that it was the attribute of justice, within which is a measure of compassion.[5] This meant that the great miracles and wonders that would be performed for the Israelites through Divine compassion would be manifestations of strict justice against the Egyptians. This is the meaning of *Ehyeh Asher Ehyeh*; namely, "I will be in judgment that which I will be in compassion." This name is related to *Havayah*,[6] the name that we have consistently associated with the Divine attribute of compassion.[7]

There is another interpretation of the Divine name *Ehyeh Asher Ehyeh* that is noteworthy.[8] Moses had a double mission: he was to be the agent of the Divine in the redemption of the Israelites from bondage in Egypt, and he was to prepare the Israelite tribes to become the nation of Israel. This is implied in the closing words of Exodus 3:12, "And when you have freed the people from Egypt, you shall worship God at this mountain." It was with regard to his second mission that Moses asked, "What shall I say to them?" To this question the Supreme

---

4. Cf. Nahmanides, commentary on Exodus 3:13.
5. Ibid.
6. Ibid.
7. See my chapter on the names of God for other implications of the name *Ehyeh*.
8. Cf. S. R. Hirsch, commentary on Exodus 3:13.

Being responded, *"Ehyeh Asher Ehyeh."* Commenting on this Divine response, S. R. Hirsch writes: "If I [God] am to express an idea of Myself, which, if he comprehends it, and if he allows himself to be completely absorbed by it, will completely change a man, will raise him out of, and above all other creatures, and bring him into direct intimate relationship to Me, then I name Myself, I express Myself as: I shall be that which I Will be."[9]

The name designates the Supreme Being as totally free. He can be what He wishes to be in contradistinction from man whose ability and potential is limited. It implies that the future is completely in His hands and allows for continuous renewal in the world if such is His will. This designation is in total opposition to Deism, which tolerates the principle that God created the world but posits that once created the world is self-contained and operates strictly in accordance with the laws of nature. Moreover, the absolute freedom of the Supreme Being means that man, who is created in His image, is also free, albeit to a lesser degree. He is coworker with the Divine in building the future world. S. R. Hirsch adds: "The guarantee that this future will ultimately be absolutely achieved lies in the very fact that God, with the power of His absolute free and unbound will, created this world for this future, so that even the apparently most opposing conditions and events must be leading up to this one, great, sure goal."[10]

RESOLVING MOSES' INSECURITY

The Supreme Being instructed Moses to gather the elders of the people together and address them concerning their future. In Exodus 3:16–18 we read:

> The Lord the God of your fathers, the God of Abraham, Isaac, and Jacob has appeared to me and said, "I have surely taken note of you and of what is being done to you in Egypt, and I have declared: I

---

9. Ibid.
10. Ibid.

will take you out of the misery of Egypt to the land of the Canaanites . . . to a land flowing with milk and honey."

The appearance of the two names *Havayah* and *E-lohim* indicate that the redemption is to be a simultaneous manifestation of two Divine attributes—compassion and strict justice—compassion for the Israelites and strict justice for the Egyptians.[11] It also indicates that the Divine compassion that will bring about the redemption is likewise a manifestation of strict justice for it would be the fulfillment of the promise made to Abraham, Isaac, and Jacob.[12]

Moses was insecure in his mission, and in Exodus 4:1 we read: "But Moses spoke up and said, 'What if they do not believe and do not listen to me, but say: The Lord did not appear to you?'" Given that the elders and the people will listen to me and understand what I have to teach them about the nature of Divinity, says Moses, who is to say that they will believe that *Havayah* appeared to me? Given that they will believe that *Havayah* will redeem them from Egypt as a manifestation of His unbounded compassion, who is to say that they will believe that He has appointed me to be His agent? They may think that I am not a prophet at all, and that I have gained all this knowledge through personal study and investigation, says Moses.[13] *Havayah* recognized Moses' fears. Since the authenticity of a prophet was established in the minds of the people either through the actualization of a predicted event or the performance of miracles, God gave Moses the ability to perform three miracles that were contrary to the laws of nature.

The Midrash[14] points out that *Havayah* had spoken to Moses for six days to convince him to accept the mission to be the agent of redemption. On the seventh day we read in Exodus 4:10, "But Moses said to the Lord, 'Please O Master [*Adney*] I have never been a man of words, either in times past or now that You have spoken to Your servant; I am slow of speech and slow of tongue.'" It appears that Moses was still

---

11. Ibid.
12. Cf. M. Malbim, commentary on Exodus 3:17.
13. I. Abravanel, commentary on the Bible (Jerusalem: Sefarim B'nei Arbael, 1964), Exodus 4:1, p. 35.
14. Cf. *Vayikrah Rabbah* 11.

insecure about his ability to carry out his mission successfully. He sought the compassion of *Havayah* to relieve him of this responsibility. He offered the logical argument that one slow of speech and slow of tongue would make a poor impression on Pharaoh and thus dishonor the Divine name. Perhaps Moses focused on the name *Adney*, which like *Havayah* designates the Supreme Being as the omnipotent Master of the universe who may act contrary to nature if He so chooses, to indicate that He should have removed Moses' disability if He wanted him to accept this mission."

In Exodus 4:11 we read: "And the Lord said to him, 'Who gives man speech? Who makes him dumb or deaf, seeing or blind? Is it not I the Lord? Now go, and I will be with you as you speak and will tell you what to say.'" Moses addressed the Creator here in terms of His compassion, and the Creator responded to Moses in kind. You recognize that I may perform the supernatural, says *Havayah;* why did you not pray to Me asking that I remove your disability?[16] Since you did not ask that I heal you, says *Havayah,* I will not do so, but I will be with you so that you will be able to express correctly the words that I will put in your mouth.[17] In a sense, it was more fitting that Moses retain his disability when he appeared before Pharaoh. In the words of S. R. Hirsch, "Every word of this stuttering stammerer is itself a sign. If a man who ordinarily stammers speaks easily and flowingly in God's mission, every single word brings its own credentials with it."[18]

Still rather reluctant, Moses maintains his position. In Exodus 4:13 we read, "But he said, 'Please O Master, make someone else Your agent.'" True, You are *Adney* the omnipotent self-sufficient Master and nothing is beyond Your ability, says Moses, but would it still not be better if Your words were spoken by one who does not have a speech defect?[19] The Lord was *angry* with Moses for refusing to be the sole Divine agent to appear before Pharaoh. To placate Moses, He ap-

---

15. Cf. Nahmanides, commentary on Exodus 4:10.
16. Ibid.
17. Ibid.
18. S. R. Hirsch, commentary on Exodus 4:11. A more elaborate discussion on this point is found in the commentary of I. Abravanel, op. cit., Exodus 4:11, pp. 38–39.
19. Cf. M. Malbim, commentary on Exodus 4:13.

pointed Aaron, Moses' brother, to accompany him. But how would the word of *Havayah* be transmitted to Pharaoh? In Exodus 4:15–16 the Lord explains: "You shall speak to him and put the words in his mouth—I will be with you and with him as you speak, and tell both of you what to do—and he shall speak for you to the people. Thus he shall be your spokesman, and you shall be an oracle to him." The word of *Havayah* would be revealed to Moses who would tell it to Aaron. Aaron would in turn bring the message to the masses of Israel. Out of respect for royalty, however, Moses would himself speak the word of *Havayah* to Pharaoh.[20]

THE MESSAGE TO PHARAOH

Moses was told to perform the given signs before Pharaoh. *Havayah* would harden Pharaoh's heart, however, so that he would not release the Israelites. In Exodus 4:22–23 we read: "Then you shall say to Pharaoh, 'Thus says the Lord: Israel is My firstborn son. I have said to you, 'Let My son go, that he may worship Me,' yet you refuse to let him go. Hence I will slay your firstborn son.'" One would have expected the name *E-lohim* to appear here, for the slaying of the firstborn son of Pharaoh would surely be a manifestation of strict justice. Yet, there is something else to consider. Pharaoh had tortured the Israelites and had decreed that their newborn sons be thrown into the Nile River. These are sins between man and his fellow man. As such, punishment of Pharaoh would be a manifestation of Divine compassion for the Israelites, which calls for the name *Havayah*.[21] Here again, we see the dual aspect of the redemption: justice within the attribute of compas-

---

20. Cf. Nahmanides, commentary on Exodus 4:15. Although the original plan was for Moses himself to speak to Pharaoh, in the end that mission was given to Aaron as well for we read in Exodus 6:30–7:2 "Moses appealed to the Lord, saying, 'See, I am of impeded speech; how then should Pharaoh heed me!' The Lord replied to Moses, 'See, I make you an oracle to Pharaoh, and your brother Aaron shall be your spokesman. You shall repeat all that I command you, and your brother Aaron shall speak to Pharaoh, to let the Israelites depart from his land.'"

21. Cf. M. Malbim, commentary on Exodus 4:22.

sion.²² It is also important to note the expression "firstborn son." It is not one of exclusivity but of primacy in time only. The point is poignantly expressed by S. R. Hirsch: "When God speaks of Israel as 'My firstborn son' it expresses the idea that with Israel, the mother womb of humanity is opened, with Israel is commenced the list in which the names of all the nations should appear as 'My sons' . . . Israel is My first but not My only child [says the Lord]; it is only the first nation that I have won as Mine."²³

THE MEETING WITH AARON

Moses took his wife and children and went to Egypt. On the journey to Egypt, he met up with Aaron, his brother, and in Exodus 4:28 we read: "Moses told Aaron about all the things that the Lord had committed to him and all the signs about which He had instructed him." What is implied here in the name *Havayah*? Moses revealed the meaning and significance of the ineffable name of the Supreme Being to Aaron.²⁴ He enlightened Aaron as to the following: *Ehyeh Asher Ehyeh* alludes to the attribute of justice within compassion; the name *Ehyeh* is identical with the name *Havayah*; and the name *Adney* symbolizes the two names *Ehyeh* and *Havayah*, the *Alef* for *Ehyeh* and the last letter *yud* for *Havayah*. The two middle letters, *daled* and *nun*, make up the word *din* ("justice") and symbolize the Divine attribute of justice.²⁵

BEFORE THE PHARAOH

Moses and Aaron appeared before Pharaoh. In Exodus 5:1–2 we read:

> Afterward Moses and Aaron went and said to Pharaoh, "Thus says the Lord the God of Israel: Let My people go that they may

---

22. Cf. Nahmanides, commentary on Exodus 3:13.
23. S.R. Hirsch, commentary on Exodus 4:22.
24. Shir *HaShirim Rabbah* 4:12.
25. Cf. Rabbenu B'haye, commentary on Exodus 4:28.

celebrate a festival for Me in the wilderness." But Pharaoh said, "Who is the Lord that I should heed Him and let Israel go? I do not know the Lord, nor will I let Israel go."

Moses spoke in the name of *Havayah*, but since Pharaoh would not recognize that name, he had to identify Him as the God of Israel (*E-lohe Yisrael*).[26] The fact that Moses and Aaron spoke in the name of the God of Israel had little effect on Pharaoh. How powerful is this God? Surely He is not so strong that in fear of Him I will release the Israelites, said Pharaoh.[27]

Seeing that they could not prevail, Moses and Aaron tried another approach. In Exodus 5:3 we read, "They answered, 'The God of the Hebrews has manifested Himself to us. Let us go, we pray, a distance of three days into the wilderness to sacrifice to the Lord our God, lest He strike us with pestilence or sword.'" We are no different than You, said Moses. Just as you worship a deity, so do we. If we do not offer sacrifice to our Lord (*Havayah*), He will punish us with pestilence or sword and you will lose your slaves. It is for your benefit that you let us go into the wilderness for three days.[28]

Not only did Pharaoh refuse to heed Moses' request; he accused him of distracting the Israelites from their tasks. He charged the taskmasters and the foremen (who were Hebrews) to make the work more difficult by requiring the slaves to gather their own straw to make the bricks for the garrison cities of Pit'om and Raamses that they were building. This additional work was imposed upon the Israelites without reducing the quota of bricks they had to make in a given day. The foremen were quite agitated. When they left the presence of Pharaoh, they came to Moses and Aaron and said to them, "May the Lord look upon you and punish you for making us objectionable to Pharaoh and his courtiers—putting a sword in their hands to slay us."[29] We have no way of knowing whether the Lord has sent you or not, said the foremen. But He is *Havayah*, the

---

26. Cf. Ibn Ezra, commentary on Exodus 5:1.
27. Cf. H. Atar, *Or HaHayyim*, commentary on Exodus 5:2.
28. M. Malbim, commentary on Exodus 5:3. Cf. Also S. R. Hirsch ad loc.
29. Exodus 5:21.

Lord of the universe; He surely knows. Let Him judge you accordingly.[30]

Moses and Aaron were devastated, and they brought their feelings to the Lord. In Exodus 5:22–23 we read: "Then Moses returned to the Lord and said, 'O Master [*Adney*] why did You bring harm upon this people? Why did You select me? Ever since I came to Pharaoh to speak in Your name, it has gone worse with this people; yet You have not delivered Your people at all.'" In his dilemma, Moses turned to *Havayah*, the compassionate Supreme Being of the universe, in a plea for mercy, but when He mentioned the harm done to the Israelites, he could not refer to Him with the name that represents compassion. Perhaps this is why he referred to Him as *Adney*.[31] It is *Havayah* who answers Moses, however. In Exodus 6:1 we read: "Then the Lord said to Moses, 'You shall soon see what I will do to Pharaoh: he shall let them go because of a greater might; indeed, because of a greater might he shall drive them from his land.'" The name itself implies the answer. Divine compassion on behalf of the Israelites is about to enter the scene. Initially, it will manifest itself in terms of the plagues brought upon Egypt.

HAVAYAH AND PROVIDENCE

In Exodus 6:2–3 we read: "God spoke to Moses and said to him, 'I am the Lord, I appeared to Abraham, Isaac, and Jacob as God Almighty, but I did not make Myself known to them by My name Lord.'" We have already pointed out the difficulties in this verse, and we have discussed the approach of Rashi and others to resolve them.[32] But let us mention another approach to the problems.[33]

The words "I am the Lord" resolve Moses' dilemma concerning the treatment of the Israelites in Egypt. They explain the difference between what the patriarchs perceived about the methods and planning

---

30. M. Malbim, commentary on Exodus 5:20.
31. Nahmanides, commentary on Exodus 5:22.
32. See the beginning of "God of the Patriarchs."
33. Cf. S. R. Hirsch, commentary on Exodus 6:2.

of the Supreme Being and what Moses and the people were about to perceive. All the difficulties that the Israelites had encountered in Egypt, the degradation and the enslavement, were the results of power politics or that which occurs in the day-to-day process of world history. As yet, there had been no Divine intervention in this process. "I am *Havayah*," says the Lord. This is the name that represents, among other things, Divine providence. It indicates that the Supreme Being of the universe can and does intervene in the process of history when it is His will to do so. S. R. Hirsch writes: "With this moment a completely new world is to enter the realm of mankind, a world which is to be independent of all those conditions which hitherto had governed the events of world history."[34] All of this is part of a greater Divine plan that began in the time of Abraham. The patriarchs knew the name *Havayah*, in terms of many of its implications. It appeared frequently in the biblical texts that dealt with their lives. But they were unaware of God's method of intervention in the process of history that this name also represents.[35]

THE THREE STAGES OF REDEMPTION

Moses was to announce to the Israelites that they had entered a unique period in the history of the world. In Exodus 6:6–8 we read the following:

> Say, therefore, to the Israelite people: I am the Lord. I will free you from the burdens of the Egyptians and deliver you from their bondage. I will redeem you with an outstretched arm and through extraordinary chastisements. And I will take you to be My people, and I will be your God. And you shall know that I, the Lord am your God who freed you from the burdens of the Egyptians. I will bring you into the land which I swore to give to Abraham, Isaac, and Jacob, and I will give it to you for a possession, I the Lord.

---

34. Ibid.
35. Ibid.

Havayah would intervene in the historical process in behalf of the Israelites and bring about a multiplicity of supernatural events that had never been experienced by man heretofore. The Divine plan would manifest itself in three stages: redemption, revelation, and inheritance of the land of Canaan.[36]

The redemption would manifest itself in three steps: The first step would be initiated with the ten plagues. No sooner would the first plague come upon Egypt than the suffering of the Israelites would be eased. (They would no longer have to make their own bricks.) The release of the Israelites from enslavement would come after the tenth plague, the death of the firstborn. Then would come the drowning of the Egyptians at the Red Sea. This would be an act of retribution for the newborn male Israelites who had been thrown into the Nile River.[37] The second stage would be the revelation of the Torah at Sinai. With revelation, the Israelites would know that it was *Havayah* who redeemed them from Egypt with signs and wonders. In point of fact, the first of the Ten Commandments reads: "I the Lord am your God who took you out of the land of Egypt, the house of bondage."[38] The third stage would be the conquest of Canaan, which would be accomplished by *Havayah* through open miracles.[39]

Moses delivered the Lord's message to the Israelites, but they were so depressed with their lot that they hadn't the patience to listen to him.

MOSES AND AARON: SEPARATE ROLES

Moses was still insecure with his role in the redemption. In Exodus 6:10–12 we read:

> The Lord spoke to Moses, saying, "Go and tell Pharaoh king of Egypt to let the Israelites depart from his land." But Moses appealed to the Lord saying, "The Israelites would not listen to me;

---

36. Cf. M. Malbim, commentary on Exodus 6:6.
37. Ibid.
38. Ibid.
39. Ibid.

how then should Pharaoh heed me, a man of impeded speech." So the Lord spoke to Moses and Aaron in regard to the Israelites and Pharaoh king of Egypt, instructing them to deliver the Israelites from the land of Egypt.

The last verse here seems redundant. If we follow the sequence here carefully, however, we can deduce the following: The original intent was for Moses to speak to Pharaoh alone, but since he had spoken to the Israelites alone and they had no patience to listen to him, he was sure that Pharaoh would not listen either. Therefore, the text tells us, *Havayah* addressed both Moses and Aaron. Both of them were now to appear before Pharaoh.[40] It was a manifestation of Divine compassion on Moses' behalf

In Exodus 7:1–2 the roles of Moses and Aaron are spelled out. The text reads: "The Lord replied to Moses, 'See I make you a god to Pharaoh, and your brother Aaron shall be your prophet. You shall repeat all that I command you, and your brother Aaron shall speak to Pharaoh, to let the Israelites depart from his land.

Moses would receive the word of *Havayah* and assume the role of a god before Pharaoh. He would reveal the word of *Havayah* to Aaron who would assume the role of prophet and repeat to Pharaoh literally what Moses had told him.[41] An interesting comment is made by S. R. Hirsch who writes: "To a Pharaoh, Moses must finally have appeared as an incarnation of a god. To the heathen idea, the first attribute of deity is the fearsome power of God, inimical to the greatness of men, and we should not have been surprised if, after all the wonders Moses performed, Pharaoh laid himself at his feet and worshipped him as a god."[42]

The redemption would not come quickly. In Exodus 7:3–5 we read:

> But I will harden Pharaoh's heart, that I may multiply My signs and marvels in Egypt. When Pharaoh does not heed you, I will lay My

---

40. Cf. M. Malbim commentary on Exodus 6:12–13 and 7:28; also I. Abravanel on Exodus 6:12.
41. M. Malbim, on Exodus 7:2.
42. S. R. Hirsch, commentary on Exodus 7:1.

hand upon Egypt and deliver My ranks, My people the Israelites from the land of Egypt with extraordinary chastisements. And the Egyptians shall know that I am the Lord, when I stretch out My hand over Egypt and bring out the Israelites from their midst.

The signs and marvels that would be executed upon the Egyptians and finally, the redemption, would establish the fact that *Havayah* in His abundant compassion had intervened in the process of history on behalf of the Israelites.

THE SIGNIFICANCE OF THE PLAGUES

Moses and Aaron came before Pharaoh and did as *Havayah* commanded them. Aaron cast down his rod and it became a serpent. Pharaoh summoned his wise men, and they repeated the feat. Although Aaron subsequently caused his rod to swallow the other rods, Pharaoh was not impressed. He did not release the Israelites. *Havayah* then told Moses to go to Pharaoh in the morning and to confront him as he emerged from the Nile River and bring upon him the first of the ten plagues. And in Exodus 7:17 we read: "Thus says the Lord, 'By this you shall know that I am the Lord.' See, I shall strike the water in the Nile with the rod that is in my hand, and it will be turned into blood."

Let us understand the significance of the Divine name *Havayah* in this context. The Egyptians worshipped the Nile River as a god. By turning the Nile River into blood, Moses and Aaron would demonstrate to both Pharaoh and the masses of the Egyptian people the omnipotence of *Havayah* and His control over their gods. Moreover, the name *Havayah* represents the Divine attribute of compassion. It was compassion for Pharaoh that motivated the plague of blood, for Pharaoh deserved to be killed outright for his sins. Witnessing the control that *Havayah* had over his god should have motivated Pharaoh to repent his ways and immediately release the Israelites from bondage, but it didn't.[43]

---

43. Cf. H. Atar, *Or HaHayyim* on Exodus 7:17.

Pharaoh denied the existence of *Havayah*. But even if *Havayah* did exist, Pharaoh refused to accept the fact that He was concerned with mankind. Lastly, Pharaoh denied the ability of *Havayah* to perform the supernatural. The plagues were to demonstrate to Pharaoh that he was wrong on all three accounts.[44] The plague of blood was to prove the existence of the Supreme Being. This is implied in the words "by this you shall know that I am the Lord." The fact that the Lord had control over the god of the Egyptians (the Nile) proved that He exists.[45] The plague of wild beasts was to demonstrate that *Havayah* is concerned with what happens on Earth. This is implied in the words "that you may know that I the Lord am in the midst of the land."[46] The fact that the wild beasts did not appear in the section of the land where the Israelites lived proved Divine providence, namely, that the *Havayah* is concerned with His people.[47] It interesting to note that this plague as well as the plague of pestilence was not inflicted on Egypt by Moses and Aaron but by *Havayah* Himself. In Exodus 8:20 we read: "And the Lord did so. Large numbers of wild beasts invaded Pharaoh's palace and the houses of his courtiers; throughout the country of Egypt the land was ruined because of the wild beasts." Again, in Exodus 9:6 we read: "And the Lord did so the next day: all the livestock of the Egyptians died, but of the livestock of the Israelites not a beast died." Since these plagues were to demonstrate that the Supreme Being takes a personal, interest in his people, *Havayah* inflicted these plagues upon Egypt without an agent.[48] The plague of hail was to demonstrate that *Havayah* could perform the supernatural. This is implied in the words "that you may know that there is none like Me in all the world."[49] Perhaps it was the fact that this plague was a mixture of three substances that do not naturally

---

44. Cf. S. Laniado, *Keli Yakar*, Exodus 7:17 and I. Abravanel ad loc.

45. Cf. M. Malbim, commentary on Exodus 7:17, who also deals with three points. He differs from the others on the last of the three points that he considered being the unity of God.

46. Exodus 8:18. The full text reads: "But on that day I will set apart the region of Goshen, where My people dwell, so that no wild beasts shall be there, that you may know that I the Lord am in the midst of the land."

47. Cf. M. Malbim, op. cit., 8:18.

48. Ibid. 9:6.

49. Exodus 9:14.

combine—namely, hail, rain, and fire—was proof that *Havayah* could, indeed, perform the supernatural.[50]

It is important to take note of the fact that the first two plagues, i.e., blood and frogs, were preceded by a warning, while the third plague, i.e., lice, came with no warning at all. Pharaoh's magicians attempted to produce the lice, but they were unable to do so. And in Exodus 8:15 we read: "And the magicians said to Pharaoh, 'This is the finger of God!' But Pharaoh's heart stiffened and he would not heed them, as the Lord had spoken." With the exception of this instance, Pharaoh and the magicians never referred to The Supreme Being as *E-lohim*.[51] Why now? Perhaps it is because the magicians were telling Pharaoh that Moses and Aaron had not produced the plague of lice, that it had not come from the Supreme Being to induce him to release the Israelites. Had it been so, Moses and Aaron would have been told of the event, and they would have warned Pharaoh. Consequently, they reasoned, it was a natural occurrence due to the position of the stars under which the land of Egypt found itself at the time.[52]

Hail, the seventh plague, was preceded not only by a prediction of what was to happen but more importantly, by a strong word of advice. In Exodus 9:18 we read: "Therefore, order your livestock and everything you have in the open brought under shelter; every man and beast that is found outside, not having been brought indoors, shall perish when the hail comes down upon them." Those who feared God did so; others did not and were killed. Pharaoh was shocked. In Exodus 9:27–28 we read: "Thereupon Pharaoh sent for Moses and Aaron and said to them, 'I stand guilty this time. The Lord is the righteous one, and I and my people are the sinners. Plead with the Lord; there has been enough of God's thunder and hail. I will let you go; you need stay no longer.'"

Pharaoh did not consider it a sin to have refused to release the

---

50. Cf. Ibn Ezra, commentary on Exodus 9:14.
51. Cf. M. Malbim, commentary on Exodus 8:21. It should be noted that although Pharaoh did not refer to the God of the Israelites by the name *E-lohim*, he did use this term when referring to God in general terms such as in Exodus 8:21, "Go and sacrifice to your God [*E-lohekhem*] in the land."
52. Cf. Ibn Ezra and M. Malbim, commentaries on Exodus 8:15.

The God of Moses

Israelites from bondage. They were his slaves, and he intended that they remain so. What bothered him was the fact that he had been warned to order his people to stay indoors to protect them from the hail, and he hadn't heeded the warning. His stubbornness had resulted in the death of a multitude of Egyptians.[53] The fact that he mentioned the ineffable name of *Havayah* as "the righteous one" may indicate that he finally recognized that *Havayah* exists, and that He is a compassionate Supreme Being who is concerned with his people. Pharaoh's reference to the name *E-lohim* in his final remark ("there has been enough of God's thunder and hail") rather than *Havayah* was for one of two reasons. Either it was because he believed that there was a separate god of thunder and hail (perhaps the god of evil) or because he knew that the thunder and hail was a manifestation of Divine judgment against the Egyptians, which called for that name.

Pharaoh asked Moses to plead with *Havayah* to remove the hail. In Exodus 9:29 we read: "Moses said to him: 'As I go out of the city, I shall spread out my hands to the Lord; the thunder will cease and the hail will fall no more, so that you may know that the Earth is the Lord's.'" Moses knew very well that Pharaoh would renege on his promise. The sole purpose of his prayer to remove the hail was to demonstrate to Pharaoh the omnipotence of *Havayah*, that He is the Supreme Being of the universe.

Moses was instructed to appear before Pharaoh once again. In Exodus 10:1–2 we read:

> Then the Lord said to Moses, "Go to Pharaoh for I have hardened his heart and the hearts of his courtiers, in order that I may display My signs among them, and that you may recount in the hearing of your sons and of your sons' sons how I made a mockery of the Egyptians and how I displayed My signs among them—in order that you may know that I am the Lord."

There is a distinct difference in the meaning of the words "that I am the Lord" when spoken to the Israelites from what they meant when spoken to Pharaoh. Pharaoh had denied the existence of *Havayah*. Moses had

---

53. Cf. M. Malbim, Exodus 9:27.

to refute this. The Israelites, on the other hand, knew very well that *Havayah* exists. Moses wanted it to be recorded and passed down from generation to generation that the Israelites were redeemed from Egypt through open wonders and miracles, by supernatural Divine acts symbolized by the name *Havayah*. The names *E-lohim* and *Sha-dai* represent the Supreme Being who performs acts in conformity with nature.[54]

WHO ARE THE ONES TO GO

Appearing before Pharaoh, Moses announced that the eighth plague would be menacing locusts that would cover the surface of the land and devour the surviving remnant of the field that was left after the hail. They would fill his palace and the houses of his courtiers. With these words Moses left. The impending devastation terrified the courtiers. They turned to Pharaoh and advised him to release the Israelites. In Exodus 10:8–11 we read the following:

> So Moses and Aaron were brought back to Pharaoh and he said to them: "Go, worship the Lord your God! Who are the ones to go?" Moses replied, "We will all go, young and old: we will go with our sons and daughters, our flocks and herds, for we must observe the Lord's festival." But he said to them, "The Lord be with you the same as I mean to let you and your children go with you! Clearly evil is before you. No! You men go and worship the Lord, since that is what you want." And they were expelled from Pharaoh's presence.

It is important that we understand the meaning of this conversation and the significance of the name *Havayah* here. At the time, the religion of the Egyptians was polytheistic. Pharaoh believed in the existence of a god of good and a god of evil. The god of good was worshipped in joy. The worshippers would bring their families and worship with song and dance. The god of evil was worshipped and

---

54. Ibid., 10:1.

appeased with sacrificial offerings. Families were not brought lest they be harmed by his anger. This was the meaning of Pharaoh's question, "Who are the ones to go?" If they were to worship the god of good, they would need no offerings. If, on the other hand, they were to worship the god of evil, they should go without their families. Moses responded that they would go with their families as well as their flocks and herds. They were to worship *Havayah* who is One and is ultimately responsible for all things that occur in the universe, that which appears to us as good as well as that which appears to us as evil.[55] Moreover, they were to celebrate festivals to *Havayah*, before whom there are no second-class citizens. "We are all important: our wives, our sons, and our daughters," said Moses. "He wants us to appear before Him with all our possessions."[56] Pharaoh refused to accept this. Since Moses had said that they had to bring sacrifices to *Havayah*, Pharaoh insisted that they meant to worship the god of evil so he would not allow them to take their families with them.[57] Moses and Aaron were dismissed, and the plague of locusts came upon Egypt.

THE REMAINING PLAGUES

In Exodus 10:13 we read: "So Moses held out his rod over the land of Egypt, and the Lord drove an east wind over the land all that day and all night; and when morning came the east wind had brought the locusts." Later, in response to Moses' prayer *Havayah* brought a west wind to remove the locusts and hurl them into the sea. Clearly what is implied here is that the plague was a manifestation of Divine punishment.[58] Should not the name *E-lohim* have appeared here? Although an invasion by locusts is quite common in countries that are located to the southeast of Egypt, this time it was not natural. In point of fact it was

---

55. Ibid., 10:8–11.
56. Cf. S. R. Hirsch, commentary on Exodus 10:9.
57. See Exodus 8:22–23.
58. Cf. Rabbenu B'haye on Exodus 10:13.

a supernatural occurrence. It was a manifestation of Divine intervention in the process of history, and as such it called for the name *Havayah*.[59]

As was to be expected, Pharaoh refused to allow the Israelites to leave, and *Havayah* caused a plague of darkness upon the land of Egypt. The plague lasted for three days. It was so thick that the Egyptians were unable to see one another even at a short distance; only the Israelites enjoyed light in their homes. Again Pharaoh summoned Moses. He told him to take the Israelites, men, women, and children, and go out into the wilderness to worship *Havayah*. Only the flocks and herds should be left behind. Moses refused. He demanded that Pharaoh allow them to take their flocks and herds and, in addition, to supply them with livestock for sacrifice. *Havayah* stiffened Pharaoh's heart once more, and he refused to allow the Israelites to leave Egypt.

One more plague was to be brought upon the Egyptians, i.e., death of the firstborn son of every Egyptian family. Pharaoh was warned. In the middle of the night, *Havayah* struck down all the firstborn males in Egypt. Pharaoh arose because there was a loud cry in the land. He sent for Moses and Aaron and told them that the Israelites may leave with their families as well as their herds and flocks. How interesting that he added the words, "May you bring a blessing upon me also." In haste, the Israelites left Egypt. In Exodus 12:40–41 we read: "The time the Israelites remained in Egypt was four hundred and thirty years; at the end of the four hundred and thirtieth year, to the very day, all the ranks of the Lord departed from the land of Egypt." Who were the "ranks of the Lord" that left Egypt? Some say it was the Israelites themselves, "considered as a number of tribes, diverse in character and characteristics but with all their differences, united and assembled around the One Lord and Leader."[60] Others say that the phrase refers to the ministering angels of *Havayah*. When Israel was enslaved in Egypt, the *Shekhinah* ("Presence") was with them; and when they were redeemed, the *Shekhinah* was, so to speak, redeemed with them. This is the meaning of the Divine promise, "I will be with him in distress."[61]

---

59. Cf. M. Malbim, Exodus 10:13.
60. S. R. Hirsch, commentary on Exodus 12:40.
61. Psalm 91:15. Cf. *Mekhilta: Bo* 14.

THE EXODUS

The night of the redemption was a special night. In Exodus 12:42 we read: "That was for the Lord a night of vigil to bring them out of the land of Egypt; that same night is the Lord's, one of vigil for all the children of Israel throughout the generations." The Midrash points out that according to R. Joshua, Israel was redeemed in the month of Nissan and in the month of Nissan Israel is destined to be redeemed in the Messianic Era. R. Eliezer differs with him and opines that the future redemption will take place in the month of Tishre.[62] Our sages also point out that if Israel is worthy they are redeemed through open miracles; if not, through hidden miracles very much in conformity with nature. If the redemption takes place in the month of Nissan, it will be through open miracles; if it takes place in Tishre, it will be through hidden miracles.[63] The Israelites were aware of this tradition. Fully aware that they were unworthy, they inquired of Moses why they were being redeemed in Nissan. With this in mind, we can understand the meaning of the first part of the above verse. It was a night of vigil for *Havayah* to bring them out of the land of Egypt through miracles that were above the law of nature. It was His decision totally independent of the merit of the Israelites. The time and the character of the future redemption, however, are dependent upon the merit of Israel. This is the significance of the second half of the verse "one of vigil for all the children of Israel throughout the generations."[64]

One might have expected that the exodus of the Israelites from Egypt would be marked by great miracles wrought by *Havayah* with a strong hand and a crushing defeat of the Egyptians by the Israelites. Instead, Pharaoh willingly released the Israelites, in consequence of which the exodus was almost uneventful. What is the reason for this?

In Exodus 13:17–18 we read: "Now when Pharaoh let the people go, God did not lead them by way of the Philistines, although it was nearer; for God said, 'The people may have a change of heart when they see

---

62. *Mekhilta* op. cit.
63. Cf. M. Malbim, commentary on Exodus 12:42.
64. Ibid.

war, and return to Egypt.' So God led the people roundabout by way of the wilderness at the Red Sea." The fact that the name *E-lohim*, usually associated with natural events, appears in verses 17–19 rather than *Havayah*, the name that is usually associated with the supernatural and providential, already implies a less than wondrous exodus. But let us subject the event to more careful scrutiny.

The exodus came earlier than the destined time. The 400 years of enslavement that had been foretold to Abraham were not yet over.[65] The Israelites were still under Pharaoh's rule. Moses could not take them out of Egypt without Pharaoh's approval. It is for this reason that he commanded Pharaoh to declare the Israelites "free men" thus releasing them from his jurisdiction. Second, Jewish tradition teaches us that Divine intervention manifests itself in direct proportion to the worthiness of its recipients. Divine intervention on behalf of the Israelites to enable them to be victorious in a battle against a mighty nation would necessitate one of two alternatives. Either they had to be men of great courage, in which case *Havayah* would intercede on their behalf and endow them with supernatural power, or they had to be men of great faith. Regrettably, the Israelites lacked both of these qualities: they were fearful slaves and they had not shown the appropriate measure of faith.[66]

AT THE RED SEA

Despite the fact that the exodus itself was not marked by a resounding victory for the Israelites or a display of supernatural events, the Torah reveals to us that the journey of the Israelites through the wilderness was laden with miracles and wondrous events. Even their travels and encampments were under the providential hand of *Havayah*. As we read in Exodus 13:21–22: "The Lord went before them in a pillar of cloud by day, to guide them along the way, and in a pillar of fire by night, to give them light, that they might travel day and night. The pillar of

---

65. Ibid., Exodus 13:17.
66. Ibid.

cloud by day and the pillar of fire by night did not depart from before the people." From the very outset of their journey the Israelites were guided by day and by night.[67]

They had traveled for three days when it became evident that the Israelites had no intention of returning to Egypt. Pharaoh was informed of this, and he pursued them with an army of horsemen and chariots. The Israelites were encamped at the Red Sea.[68] When they saw the Egyptian army approaching, their reaction was swift. In Exodus 14:10 we read: "As Pharaoh drew near, the Israelites caught sight of the Egyptians advancing upon them. Greatly frightened, the Israelites cried out to the Lord." The Israelites felt that they were faced with a battle that, if fought by conventional means, i.e., military strategy, would result in a crushing defeat. It must have been eminently clear to them that only a miracle could save them from the well-equipped forces of Egypt. So they turned to *Havayah* in prayer with the hope that He would once again intervene in the process of history on their behalf and save them from defeat and annihilation. Panic-stricken by the impending disaster, they turned to Moses and faulted him for what had happened. It would seem that Moses was neither angry nor disturbed. Perhaps he felt that they had every right to complain.[69] Be that as it may, in Exodus 14:13–14 we read: "But Moses said to the people, 'Have no fear! Stand by, and witness the deliverance that the Lord will work for you today; for the Egyptians whom you see today, you will never see again. The Lord will battle for you; you hold your peace!'" It is important to understand the significance of the Divine name *Havayah* in this context. There is no question that Moses was informing the Israelites that something miraculous was about to happen. *Havayah* would intervene on their behalf; He would fight their battle; they would not have to fight at all.[70]

---

67. Cf. Rabbenu B'haye, and S. R. Hirsch on Exodus 13:21.

68. There is some question as to whether the body of water referred to here is what is known today as the Red Sea. Some prefer to translate "Sea of Reeds."

69. Cf. Nahmanides, commentary on Exodus 14:10, who opines that there were two factions among the Israelites: one group turned to the Lord in prayer while others complained and faulted Moses.

70. Let us recall the words of Moses in Exodus 15:3, in the song he sang after the splitting of the Red Sea: "The Lord, the Warrior—Lord is His name."

An event of this magnitude would be a sanctification of the Divine name of the highest order.

On the one side there was the Red Sea; on the other, the menacing Egyptian army. What were the Israelites to do? The charge to Moses came loud and clear: "Why do you cry out to Me? Tell the Israelites to go forward. And you lift up your rod and hold out your arm over the sea and split it, so that the Israelites may march into the sea on dry ground."[71] The Egyptians would not realize that the Israelites were in the sea. It would appear to them that they were merely retreating on dry land, so they would continue their pursuit. In Exodus 14:19–20 we read: "The angel of God who had been going ahead of the Israelite army, now moved and followed behind them; and the pillar of cloud shifted from in front of them and took up a place behind them, and it came between the army of the Egyptians and the army of Israel." The order was as follows: the army of the Israelites, the pillar of fire, the pillar of cloud, and the Egyptian army.[72] The pillar of fire enabled the Egyptians to see that the Israelites were marching forward, but the pillar of cloud prevented the Egyptians from recognizing that they were marching into the sea. Parenthetically, the fact that the angel[73] went behind the Israelites rather than ahead of them teaches a vital lesson: The sea is not to retreat before the angel of *E-lohim*; it is to retreat before human beings who put their trust in *E-lohim*.[74] It is important for us to note that it is the angel of *E-lohim*, not the angel of *Havayah*, that is spoken of in this context. It represents the Divine attribute of strict justice. Strict justice was decreed against the Egyptians at the Red Sea.

The waters of the Red Sea were split and a path of dry land was formed. The Israelites went into the sea on dry ground, and the Egyptians pursued them. In Exodus 14:24–25 we read:

---

71. Exodus 14:15–16.
72. Cf. Rabbenu B'haye, commentary on Exodus 14:20.
73. Cf. I. Abravanel, op. cit., Exodus 14:15, p. 120. According to many of the Bible commentators the angel of God here is the pillar of fire that accompanied the Israelites on their journey through the wilderness.
74. S. R. Hirsch, commentary on Exodus 14: 19.

> At the morning watch the Lord looked down upon the Egyptian army from a pillar of fire and cloud, and threw the Egyptian army into panic. He locked the wheels of their chariots so that they moved forward with difficulty. And the Egyptians said, "Let us flee from the Israelites, for the Lord is fighting for them against Egypt."

At this point the entire Egyptian army realized and admitted that *Havayah* had intervened on behalf of Israel, and they attempted to flee to the shore. Moses was told by *Havayah* once more to raise his arm over the sea. The waters returned to their original state, and the Egyptian army was drowned. A fitting conclusion to this event is found in Exodus 14:31 where we read: "And when Israel saw the wondrous power that the Lord had wielded against the Egyptians, the people feared the Lord: they had faith in the Lord and in his servant Moses." The event at the Red Sea strengthened the faith of the masses. Until then, their faith was based solely on the fear of punishment. The mighty power of *Havayah*, wielded against the Egyptian army, inspired within the hearts of the masses an eminently higher form of faith. It was a faith based not on fear but on awe. The great event affected Moses as well, and inspired him to offer a song of praise to *Haveyah* (Exodus 15:1–18). Several verses of this song are relevant for our studies.

THE SONG TO THE LORD

"The Lord is my strength and might; He is become my salvation. This is my God [*E-li*] and I will glorify Him, the God of my father and I will exalt Him" (15:2). Although Moses usually referred to the full name *Havayah*, which consists of the four letters *yud, he, vav, he*, in this verse he used only the first two letters of the name *(yud* and *he)*. We are well aware of the fact that compassion is among the Divine attributes to which the full name *Havayah* alludes. The two-letter name *(yud he)*, however, alludes to judgment,[75] as in the formula for an oath found in Exodus 17:16, "Hand upon the throne of the Lord" *(yud he)*. Perhaps

---

75. Cf. S. R. Hirsch, commentary on Exodus 15:2, which opines that the name also alludes to Divine might.

what is implied here is that Moses experienced the event at the Red Sea as a manifestation of both judgment and compassion. The judgment exacted upon the Egyptians was simultaneously experienced by the Israelites as Divine compassion. This is further evidenced in the second part of the verse where the Divine name *E-l* is found. For among several attributes this name represents is the attribute of compassion.[76]

"The Lord the Warrior, Lord is His name" (15:3). According to Rashi what is implied here is that the Supreme Being fights the battles of His people, not with weapons but with His name.[77] Additionally, Rashi writes: "He is a man of war, but His name is *Havayah*. Even when he battles against and avenges Himself against His enemies, He retains His attribute showing compassion to His creatures and feeding all the inhabitants of the world."[78] S. R. Hirsch adds: "The path that leads to the ultimate happy solution to the problem of life, can only lead via destruction of the bad and evil."[79]

"Your right hand, O Lord, glorious in power, Your right hand O Lord shatters the foe" (15:6). This verse is meant to be taken symbolically. Both the right hand and the left hand of *Havayah* represent power. The right hand represents the power He uses to benefit those who are threatened; the left hand symbolizes the power He uses to punish or destroy the wicked.[80] It was for the benefit of the Israelites that *Havayah* used the power of His right hand to destroy the Egyptians.

"Who is like You, O Lord, among the mighty, who is like You majestic in holiness, awesome in praises, working wonders" (15:11). Who are the mighty? According to some, they are the Heavenly angels;[81] others contend that the term refers to the powers of nature.[82] According to the latter interpretation, *Havayah* is unique among the mighty, i.e., the powers of nature, in that He performs supernatural acts. The supernatural power of *Havayah* inspires fear and awe in the hearts of those

---

76. Cf. *Mekhilta B'shalah 3* and M. Nahmanides, commentary on Exodus 15:2.
77. Cf. Rashi, on Exodus 15:3.
78. Ibid.
79. S. R. Hirsch, commentary on Exodus 15:3.
80. Ibid., Exodus 15:6
81. Cf. Nahmanides, commentary on Exodus 15:11.
82. M. Malbim, Exodus ad loc.

who witness it. They are awestruck to the extent that they fear that in enumerating His praises they will fall short, rendering their gesture inadequate.[83]

"The Lord will reign for ever and ever!" (15:18). *Havayah*, who has demonstrated His immanence in the world, will forever reign. As we have indicated many times, the name *Havayah* itself (i.e., past, present, and future) represents eternity. Clearly a testimony of faith, it is also a prayer for fulfillment.[84] But there is an even more significant lesson to be learned from this verse. *Havayah* is the eternal Ruler of the universe. Nothing happens in the universe contrary to His will. And though there are things that happen in the world that defy human understanding, such as the prospering of the wicked and the suffering of the righteous, we must have the faith to accept the fact that such matters fit in somehow in the greater plan that the Supreme Being has ordained for the world and man in particular.[85]

THE SPECIAL PROMISE

Moses and the Israelites traveled in the wilderness of Shur for three days. They thirsted for water but found none. They came to a place called Mara, where they found water but could not drink it because it was bitter. The people complained to Moses, and he cried out to *Havayah*. The water was made sweet, and the people were able to quench their thirst. Speaking in the name of *Havayah*, Moses made the people a promise. In Exodus 15:26 we read: "He said, 'If you will heed the voice of the Lord your God diligently, doing what is upright in His sight, giving ear to His commandments and keeping all His laws, then I will not bring upon you any of the diseases that I brought upon the Egyptians, for I the Lord am your healer." This is a remarkable promise, but it is of the utmost importance that we do not misconstrue the meaning. The promise clearly states that if the Israelites heed the laws

---

83. Cf. M. Nahmanides, ad loc.
84. Cf. Nahmanides, Exodus 15:18 and Rabbenu B'haye ad loc.
85. Cf. J. Z. Mecklenburg, *HaKetav V'haKabbalah* (New York: Ohm, 1946), Exodus 15:18.

of the Torah, *Havayah* will protect them from disease. This is generally interpreted to include any and every disease and illness that can come upon man. It is the reward promised for faithfully following all the *mitzvot* of the Torah.[86] But there are others who opine[87] that the diseases spoken of here are incurable by man. They are inflicted by *Havayah* upon man as punishment. The ten plagues brought upon the Egyptians is a case in point. There are other times, however, when disease comes as a warning from *Havayah* to the sinner that he must mend his ways. If he does, *Havayah* heals him. This is implied in the words "for I the Lord am your healer." I am He who performs supernatural acts, says *Havayah*. The *mitzvot* were given to enlighten man, to guide him in his interaction with his fellow man, and to prevent him from committing acts of ethical and moral depravity.[88] It is in keeping with the dictum that *Havayah* reveals the cure before He inflicts the disease.[89]

WHY DO YOU TEST THE LORD

In their journey through the wilderness, the people continually grumbled against Moses and Aaron. When they came to a place called "Sin," they complained about food, and *Havayah* gave them quail and manna to eat. They traveled from Sin and encamped at Rephidim where there was no water. Anticipating the worst, they complained to Moses again. In Exodus 17:2–3 we read:

> The people quarreled with Moses. "Give us water to drink," they said; and Moses replied to them, "Why do you quarrel with me? Why do you test the Lord?" But the people thirsted there for water; and the people grumbled against Moses and said, "Why did you bring us up from Egypt, to kill us and our children and livestock with thirst?"

---

86. Cf. Rabbenu B'haye, commentary on Exodus 15:26 and M. Nahmanides ad loc.
87. Cf. M. Malbim, commentary on Exodus 15:26.
88. Ibid.
89. *Megillah* 13b.

It seems that even before they thirsted for water they complained to Moses. Moses understood the significance of their complaint, and he snapped, "Why do you test the Lord?"

What is the meaning of the complaint of the Israelites and the significance of Moses' response? The Israelites had not doubted the power of *Havayah*; they had lost confidence in His concern for them. They knew that He was capable of the miraculous; what had to be demonstrated to them time and time again was that He was irrevocably concerned with their welfare. First, it was food; now it was water. It was Divine compassion, the providential hand of *Havayah*, that the Israelites seemed continually to put to the test.[90] In this regard, the insightful comment by S. R. Hirsch is noteworthy.

> The general ideas on nature, God and man were so completely opposite to the truths which were to be realized in Israel and through Israel; Nature and its laws were thought to be so completely absolute and above any other power whatsoever; the gods themselves to be similarly bound by these laws and Man to stand so powerless under the double ban of the blind powers of both Nature and gods, the step to Jewish conceptions of these matters was such a tremendous and overpowering contrast, that we really cannot wonder if these basic ideas . . . only became firmly established in the minds of the first People of God, very gradually, and that it required all the great and wonderful experiences of our history, which was then just at its commencement, to make these truths really and truly, and safely fixed in our consciousness.[91]

THE WAR WITH AMELEK

The Torah reports that the nation of Amalek attacked the Israelites at Rephidim. It is almost as if it was in response to their query, "Is the Lord present among us or not?" that *Havayah* set out to prove to the

---

90. Cf. S. R. Hirsch, commentary on Exodus 17:7.
91. Ibid.

Israelites that He was continually ready to come to their aid. Joshua was put in charge of the battle. In Exodus 17:9 we read: "Moses said to Joshua, 'Pick some men for us, and go out and do battle with Amalek. Tomorrow I will station myself on the top of the hill, with the rod of God in my hand.'" The rod is sometimes referred to as "the rod of Moses," other times as "the rod of Aaron," and here as "the rod of God." Perhaps it is because this was a time of war, and judgment was to be carried out against the Amalekites. As we already know, Divine judgment calls for the name *E-lohim*.

The Israelites were successful in the battle against Amalek. In Exodus 17:14–16 we read:

> Then the Lord said to Moses: Inscribe this in a document as a reminder, and read it aloud to Joshua: I will utterly blot out the memory of Amalek from under Heaven. And Moses built an altar and named it "The Lord is my banner." He said, "It means, 'hand upon the throne of the Lord.' The Lord will be at war with Amalek throughout the generations."

We are already familiar with the association of the name *Havayah* with victory in battle; it is certainly in place here. It is the memory of Amalek and its association with the throne of *Havayah* to which our attention is directed. S. R. Hirsch writes: "It is not Amalek who is so pernicious for the moral future of mankind but the glorifying of the memory of Amalek which is the danger."[92]

So long as war and war heroes are glorified in the annals of history, so long will each successive generation look up to these heroes with admiration. Their memory will awaken the desire to emulate them and thus acquire equal recognition and glory. Only when *Havayah* is recognized as the only true Creator of objective ethics and morality, only when the Torah that He has revealed to us becomes the sole criterion by which we judge the merit of the behavior of mankind, only then will the Amalek philosophy that reigns in the world today finally be

---

92. S. R. Hirsch, commentary on Exodus 17:14.

wiped out. Until then, *Havayah* will be at war with this notion in the hearts and minds of men. Indeed, the throne (*kes*)[93] of *Havayah* will not be full so long as the memory of Amalek lives.

MOSES AND JETHRO

In Exodus 18:1 we read: "Jethro priest of Midian, Moses' father-in-law, heard all that God had done for Moses and for Israel His people, how the Lord had brought Israel out from Egypt." *This is another instance when the names E-lohim and Havayah appear in the same verse. It demonstrates once again that the Divine names represent the multiple attributes of the One Supreme Being of the universe, and refutes once again the untenable position of the Bible critics who posit that the names are indicative of different documents.* The use of the two names is explained as follows: The Torah first mentions *E-lohim*, the name that was familiar to Jethro, and then states that *Havayah* brought the Israelites out of Egypt for that was the name that now came to be known through Moses and through which the signs were performed before Pharaoh.[94]

Jethro took Zipporah, Moses' wife, and Gershom and Eliezer, the two sons of Moses, and set out for the Israelite camp in the wilderness. When he arrived Moses greeted him warmly. He confirmed what Jethro had heard. In Exodus 18:8 we read: "Moses then recounted to his father-in-law everything that the Lord Had done to Pharaoh and to the Egyptians for Israel's sake, all the hardships that had befallen them on the way, and how the Lord had delivered them." In addition, Moses told him what had occurred after they left Egypt: the miracle at the Red Sea as well as the quail, the manna, and the battle against Amalek. These

---

93. The Hebrew word for throne is *kise*. The shortened form *kes* is not found anywhere else in the Bible. The Divine name *Havayah* is also shortened to *Y-ah*. What this is meant to teach us is that neither the name of the Lord nor His throne will be complete (so to speak) until the philosophy and the memory of Amalek is obliterated from society.

94. Cf. Nahmanides, commentary on Exodus 18:1.

had all been manifestations of Divine providence, the attribute that is represented by the name *Havayah*.

Jethro was thoroughly impressed with what *Havayah* had done for Israel, and he acknowledged it. In Exodus 18:10–11 we read: "And Jethro said, 'Blessed be the Lord who delivered you from the Egyptians and from Pharaoh, and who delivered the people from under the hand of the Egyptians. Now I know that the Lord is greater than all gods are: for it is in the thing wherein they acted presumptuously that punishment came upon them.'" What is the significance of Jethro's words? The nations of the world at the time believed that there is a First Cause whom they designated as the "god of gods," but they didn't believe in Divine providence. They had no tradition that this First Cause of the universe, referred to by Jethro by the name "Lord," takes note of the affairs of men. They were unaware that He rewards and punishes and even intervenes when he feels it to be appropriate in order to right the wrongs perpetrated by man against his fellow man. The term "blessed," when it refers to *Havayah*, designates His providential hand.[95] Jethro now acknowledged this. The words "greater than all gods" here means "greater than all the forces of nature." The Egyptians were judged measure for measure, i.e., they were punished in kind for the evil that they committed against the Israelites. *Havayah* superimposed His power over all the other powers of nature to inflict His punishment upon the Egyptians.[96]

The sages inform us that as a result of his newfound understanding of the Supreme Being of the universe, Jethro converted to the religion of Israel, and with great joy he offered sacrifices to God. In Exodus 18:12 we read: "And Jethro, Moses' father-in-law, brought a burnt offering and sacrifices for God; and Aaron came with all the elders of Israel to partake of the meal before God with Moses' father-in-law." The significance of the name *E-lohim* here is somewhat difficult. After all, Jethro had just converted; should he not have brought his sacrifices to *Havayah*? In point of fact, when it comes to sacrifices brought by Israel,

---

95. Cf. M. Malbim, commentary on Exodus 18:10.
96. Ibid.

the name *Havayah* is used exclusively. As S. R. Hirsch correctly points out, the fact that Aaron and the elders took part in the ritual clearly indicates that the offerings were brought to the One Supreme Being of the universe.[97] Perhaps the difficulty can be resolved in the following way. The great miracles performed by *Havayah* were for Israel, not for Jethro, who was not part of Israel at the time.[98] As such the Torah informs is that he offered his sacrifices to *E-lohim,* the Creator and Supreme Being of the universe.

Judging the people and solving their problems was Moses' daily routine. The people would bring their disputes to him, and he would make the teachings of *E-lohim* known to them. He was occupied with this task from morning till night. Rather surprised that Moses took such a heavy burden upon himself, Jethro inquired, "Why do you act alone, while all the people stand about you from morning until evening?"[99] Moses replied, "It is because the people come to me to inquire of God."[100] Jethro then offered some advice. In Exodus 18:19 we read: "Now listen to me. I will give you counsel and God be with you. You act for the people in behalf of God: you bring the disputes before God, and enjoin upon them the laws and the teachings, and make known to them the way they are to go and the practices they are to follow." Jethro further advised Moses to appoint judges over groups of thousands, hundreds, fifties, and tens of the people. It is important to note that, in their conversation, both Moses and Jethro continually referred to the Supreme Being as *E-lohim.* This is no more than logical since their conversation concerned the resolution of disputes among the people. Moses would bring these problems to *E-lohim* and seek justice.

---

97. S. R. Hirsch, commentary on Exodus 18:12.

98. In point of fact, Jethro was originally an idolator. He is referred to in Exodus 2:16 as the "priest" of Midian. Although when Moses came to Midian, Jethro had already rejected idolatry, he had not yet committed himself to the One true God. Cf. Rashi and *Sifte Hahamim* ad loc.

99. Exodus 18:14.

100. Ibid., 18:15.

THE ARRIVAL AT SINAI

In the third month after the Israelites had left Egypt, they arrived in the wilderness of Sinai and encamped there in front of the mountain. In Exodus 19:3 we read: "And Moses went up to God and the Lord called to him from the mountain saying, 'Thus shall you say to the house of Jacob and declare to the children of Israel.'" Here again, both Divine names, *E-lohim* and *Havayah*, appear in a single verse. Some Bible commentators contend that the words "went up to God" in this context mean that Moses went up *toward* the Glory of *E-lohim*, which abided upon the mountain but did not draw near to the pillar of cloud in which the Presence of *E-lohim* had descended.[101] Others contend that what is meant here is not physical but spiritual ascension. Moses withdrew to his tent and remained in temporary seclusion. He rose up to *E-lohim* the Judge and Lawgiver, not physically but intellectually and spiritually by preparing his soul to receive the Torah from the providential hand of *Havayah*. Then *Havayah* called to him and told him to ascend the mountain. There, He revealed to Moses the words he was to speak to the men and the women of Israel in the name of *Havayah*: "You have seen what I did to the Egyptians, how I bore you on eagles wings and brought you to Me. Now then if you will obey Me faithfully and keep My covenant, you shall be My treasured possession among all the peoples. Indeed, all the Earth is Mine, but you shall be to Me a kingdom of priests and a holy nation."[102]

The people responded with the words: "All that the Lord has spoken we will do,"[103] and Moses brought their words before *Havayah*. The people were told to purify themselves for two days in preparation for the revelation of the Torah. On the third day, *Havayah* would descend on Mount Sinai. In Exodus 19:17 we read that on the third day, "Moses led the people out of the camp toward God, and they took their places at the foot of the mountain." The words "toward God" imply that He was already there, and this prompted the Midrash to remark that the

---

101. Cf. Nahmanides, commentary on Exodus 19:3.
102. Exodus 19:4–6.
103. Exodus 19:8.

Divine Presence came forth to greet them as a groom comes forth to greet his bride.[104] Others insist that the term *E-lohim* in this context as in others does not refer to God but rather to a host of angels. A host of 600,000 angels came forth to greet the 600,000 Israelites.[105]

The Israelites surrounded the mountain and waited. In Exodus 19:19 we read: "The blare of the horn grew louder and louder. Moses spoke and God answered him loudly." What do the words "answered him loudly" mean here? It was on Mount Sinai that the Ten Commandments were revealed to Israel. The people heard only the first two commandments directly from *Havayah*; the others were heard from the mouth of Moses.[106] But how was the vast gathering of people able to hear Moses' voice? We have no choice but to assume that it was a profound miracle in accordance with natural law. *E-lohim*, the Creator of nature, superimposed His will over nature and gave Moses the ability to be heard in his natural voice by all.[107]

THE TEN COMMANDMENTS

The Ten Commandments are introduced with the words: "And God spoke all these words." This is followed by the first commandment, which reads: "I am the Lord your God who brought you out of Egypt, the house of bondage."[108] The commandments are ethical and moral laws. They are timeless. In this chapter, we shall discuss only those commandments that are relevant to our studies. It is most fitting that the commandments are introduced by the Divine name *E-lohim* that represents God, the Supreme Judge of the universe, from whom these laws derive. However, the fact that He has chosen to reveal them to humanity, is a manifestation of Divine providence and compassion; it calls for the name *Havayah*. Now one might rightfully inquire, "Why

---

104. *Mekhilta Yitro* 3.
105. Rabbenu B'haye, commentary on Exodus 19:17.
106. *Makkot* 24a.
107. Cf.. Rabbenu B'haye, commentary on Exodus 19:19.
108. Exodus 20:1, 2.

not refer to *Havayah* as the Creator of Heaven and Earth in this context? Is that not a greater accomplishment than redemption?" Perhaps the answer is that the redemption is something that our ancestors witnessed with their own eyes and handed down as a tradition through the generations. There can be no doubt about it; a parent does not lie to his child about such matters. The creation of the world, however, is a matter of faith. No human being has witnessed it nor can anyone testify to its truth.[109] It is interesting to note that some see in the words "I am the Lord your God" the principle of monotheism, namely, "the Lord and God are One."[110]

The second commandment reads: "You shall have no other gods beside Me."[111] This verse should not be misinterpreted. It does not imply that there are other gods but rather that there are objects that some people have deified and worship as gods. This is forbidden![112] The term *elohim* is generic. What is meant here is that to believe that there exists another god and to worship that god along with the One true God is forbidden.

The fourth commandment reads: "Remember the Sabbath day and keep it holy. Six days you shall labor and do all your work, but the seventh day is a Sabbath of the Lord your God. For in six days the Lord made Heaven and Earth and sea, and all that is in them, and He rested on the seventh day; therefore the Lord blessed the seventh day and hallowed it." Why does the name *Havayah* appear here? One would surely have expected *E-lohim* in this context since it is the name that represents the Supreme Being as Creator of Heaven and Earth and Ruler over nature. Perhaps the answer is that the subject here is the Sabbath not Creation, and the Sabbath is regarded as the wonderful gift given to mankind. It is a manifestation of Divine compassion. Consequently, the name *Havayah* is more appropriate.

---

109. Cf. Nahmanides, commentary on Exodus 20:2.
110. Rashi, Exodus 20:2.
111. Exodus 20:3.
112. Rashi, Exodus 20:3.

The God of Moses

THE EXPERIENCE OF REVELATION

In Exodus 20:15–17 we read the following:

> All the people witnessed the thunder and lightning, the blare of the horn and the mountain smoking; and when the people saw it they fell back and stood at a distance. "You speak to us," they said to Moses, "and we will obey; but let not God speak to us, lest we die." Moses answered the people, "Be not afraid; for God has come only to test you, and in order that the fear of Him may ever be with you, so that you do not go astray."

There is a difference of opinion among the Bible commentators as to when this conversation took place. Most commentators contend that it took place after the revelation of the Ten Commandments.[113] There is an opinion, however, that it took place before the revelation. Be that as it may, what was it that the people feared? The thunder and lightning, the likes of which they may never have experienced before, coupled with the anticipation of receiving the word of *E-lohim* directly, was too much for their bodies to bear, "and all the people who were in the camp trembled."[114] That which is accompanied by thunder and lightning and inspires fear and trembling is understood as coming from *E-lohim* the Supreme Judge of the world. So Moses reassured the people that their experience was not a death sentence but was merely meant to test them. Since they had thought that they were no less qualified than Moses to receive the word of *E-lohim*, they were put to the test. Others contend that the revelation was not to test them but rather to raise their status in the eyes of the nations of the world, for they would now be known among them as the nation to whom the Supreme Being had spoken directly.[115]

---

113. Cf. Rashi, Exodus 20:17; Ibn Ezra Exodus 20:16; and I. Abravanel, op. cit., Exodus 20:15, p. 194.
114. Exodus 19:16.
115. Cf. I. Abravanel, op. cit.

SOME OTHER INTERESTING LAWS

Much of Exodus 21 and 22 are devoted to the social laws. One of these is Exodus 21:12-13 which, reads: "He who fatally strikes a man shall be put to death. If he did not do it by design, but God delivered him into his hand, I will assign you a place to which he can flee." What is meant here by the words "God delivered him into his hand," and why is the appellative *E-lohim* chosen here rather than any other name? Verse 13 is a case of unintentional manslaughter; it is defined as an act that lies somewhere between carelessness and senselessness. God brought about this event to punish the victim for a sin that he had once committed, which had at the time gone unpunished. Needless to say, the one who committed this act of unintentional manslaughter was totally unaware of the fact that he was the medium through which Divine retribution was accomplished. It is difficult, perhaps totally incomprehensible to us, why the Supreme Being would choose to punish the victim through the hand of an innocent party. Perhaps this is why the name *E-lohim* is most appropriate in this verse. Strict Divine judgment is often unfathomable. It is perplexing, and at times anger provoking, but in the final analysis, it dare not be questioned.

In Exodus 22:19 we read: "Whoever sacrifices to a god other than the Lord alone shall be proscribed." Here again the name *elohim* does not refer to the Supreme Being of the universe. According to most authorities it refers to false gods, namely objects or stars that are worshipped as gods. We noted this in our discussion of the Ten Commandments. Some contend, however, that here the term refers specifically to angels,[116] for there are people who feel that if they bring sacrifices to the angels, it is as though they brought them to the Supreme Being Himself. Moreover, they feel that the angels will then be their intermediaries before *Havayah*.[117] Here, as in the second commandment, even if the individual wants merely to attribute some

---

116. Cf. Nahmanides, commentary on Exodus 22:19.
117. Ibid. For a more detailed discussion of what led people to this mistaken way of thinking see M. Maimonides, *Mishneh Torah*, trans. M. Hyamson (Jerusalem: Boys Town Jerusalem, 1965), "Laws Concerning Idolatry," chap. I.

Divine power to another being, angel or otherwise, he has committed a transgression for which he incurs the death penalty.

In Exodus 22:27 we read: "You shall not revile God, nor put a curse upon a chieftain of your people." Here we have a difference of opinion among the sages as to whether the name *E-lohim* refers to the Supreme Judge of the universe, or a human judge. In either case, faulting *E-lohim* when life turns sour or blaming the judge when his judgment is not favorable to us, is all too common a reaction. Minimally, such situations elicit a feeling of disappointment; maximally, however, they elicit harsh criticism, even vilification. When man is the object of such vilification, it is a sign of disrespect and improper behavior. When it is the Supreme Being who is involved, it is sacrilege.

After listing the three festivals: the Feast of Unleavened Bread, the Feast of the Harvest, and the Feast of Ingathering, we read in Exodus 23:17, "Three times a year, all your males shall appear before the Master, the Lord." What all three of these festivals have in common is their focus on the crops of the field. We are obligated to express our thanksgiving to *Havayah* for the success of our crops without which life cannot be sustained. True, He is the "Master" of the Earth; He is directly responsible for the success or failure of our crops, and as such a form of the Divine name *Adney* appears here. But the fact that He provides for the sustenance of His servants is a manifestation of His concern, and this calls for the name *Havayah* as well.[118] The latter point is confirmed in Exodus 23:25: "You shall serve the Lord your God and He will bless your bread and your water." Parenthetically, it should be noted that the idolater believes that to worship the idol is to ensure success in his endeavors. For example, the sun worshipper recognizes that the sun is indispensable to a successful crop. To counter such belief, the verse teaches that only through worship of *Havayah* who is concerned with His creations, will man's needs for physical sustenance be met.[119]

---

118. Cf. Nahmanides, commentary on Exodus 23:16.
119. Ibid., Exodus 23:25.

A STRANGE EVENT

Moses descended the mountain to the people and read them all the commands of *Havayah*, and he explained them.[120] The people accepted the laws without qualification. Moses then built an altar, and he instructed that sacrifices be offered to *Havayah*. He took of the blood and threw it toward the people as a sign of the covenant established between God and the people of Israel. What followed was a strange event. In Exodus 24: 9–11 we read: "Then Moses and Aaron, Nadav and Avihu, and seventy elders of Israel ascended; and they saw the God of Israel: under His feet there was the likeness of a brick of sapphire, like the very sky for purity. Yet, He did not send His hand to the nobles of the Israelites; they beheld God, and they ate and drank."

It is difficult for us to know precisely what is meant by the words "they saw the God of Israel." One thing is for certain, the Torah states specifically that no material form of the Supreme Being was witnessed at Sinai,[121] for mortal man cannot see the Divine Presence.[122] Perhaps what is meant here is an intellectual perception of the Supreme Being rather than a visual one, or as understood by S. R. Hirsch, "[These words] can only refer, not to God Himself, but to the phenomenon by which God announces His Presence."[123] Be that as it may, what these individuals were granted is the ability to perceive how the Supreme Being relates to the world on a level far above that for which they were prepared.[124]

The words "God of Israel" in this context indicate that it was through their act of accepting the Torah that *E-lohim*, the Supreme Judge and Lawgiver, became the God of Israel.[125] Some are of the opinion that the

---

120. Cf. S. R. Hirsch, commentary on Exodus 24:3.
121. Deuteronomy 4:12 and 15.
122. Exodus 33:20. There is an allusion to this point in Exodus 25:8 where we read: "And let them make Me a sanctuary that I may dwell among them." One might have expected the concluding phrase to be "that I may dwell in it." This could not be, however, for the Lord does not have a physical form that can be enclosed in a sanctuary.
123. Cf. S. R. Hirsch, commentary on Exodus 24:10.
124. Cf. M. Malbim, commentary on Exodus 24:11.
125. Ibid.

"nobles" referred to in the text were individuals who had prepared themselves to receive prophecy. Their perception, however, was limited to aspects of activities of *E-lohim* in nature.[126]

THE GLORY OF THE LORD

The Torah tells us that Moses remained on Mount Sinai for forty days and forty nights. During that period, he studied the Law under the guidance of what the Torah calls "the Glory of the Lord." What does this mean? In Exodus 24:16 we read: The Glory of the Lord abode on Mount Sinai, and the cloud hid it for six days." Unlike the appellative *Havayah* that represents the Divine attribute of compassion, the "Glory of the Lord" (*k'vod Havayah*), like the name *E-lohim*, represents the Divine attribute of strict justice.[127] Considering that Moses remained on the mountain to study the Law, the use of this phrase is very much in order. Interestingly, in Exodus 24:17 we read: "Now the Glory of the Lord appeared in the sight of the Israelites as a consuming fire on the top of the mountain." Surely the Torah does not mean to tell us that this was a visual experience, and that the Glory of *Havayah* is a consuming fire. It is rather to be taken as a simile. Just as the flame of a fire can be great or small depending upon the nature of the material that is being consumed, so, too, the level of understanding of Divinity depends upon the intellectual and spiritual level of the individual. This is to say that each individual among the people perceived the Supreme Being on his or her own level of intelligence and sophistication.[128]

AN INTERESTING NOTE

The law of Shabbat is repeated in Exodus 31: 12–17. The last verse offers the following rationale. "The Israelite people shall keep the

---

126. Ibid.
127. Cf. Rabbenu B'haye, commentary on Exodus 24:16.
128. Cf. J. Z. Mecklenburg, commentary on Exodus 24:17.

Shabbat, observing the Shabbat throughout the generations as a covenant for all time: it shall be a sign for all time between Me and the people of Israel. For in six days the Lord made Heaven and Earth, and with the seventh day He ceased to create and withdrew unto Himself." The choice of the name *Havayah* in this context is somewhat perplexing. Would not *E-lohim*, the name that depicts the Supreme Being as the Creator, have been more appropriate here? Probably not! Although Creation is mentioned as the rationale for Shabbat, the verse focuses primarily on Shabbat. It was a manifestation of Divine compassion that *Havayah* gave the Shabbat to the Jewish people to be observed throughout the generations.

THE GOLDEN CALF

Moses had tarried on the mountain for what seemed to the Israelites to be an exceedingly long period of time. In Exodus 32:1 we read:

> When the people saw that Moses was so long in coming down from the mountain, the people gathered against Aaron and said to him, "Come, make us a god [*elohim*] who shall go before us, for that man Moses, who brought us out from the land of Egypt—we cannot tell what has happened to him."

There is no question that the people sinned in their request, but the nature of the sin should not be misunderstood. They did not request of Aaron that he construct for them a material object that they could worship as God.[129] This was not idolatry, at least not in the ordinary sense of the term. The people panicked, and they wanted a replacement for Moses whom they feared had died on the mountain. The term *elohim* here, as in other places in the Torah, means "leader or judge." S. R. Hirsch explains:

---

129. Cf. commentaries of Nahmanides, H. ben Atar (Or HaHayyim), and Malbim on Exodus 32.

> They saw in Moses not the instrument of God's will . . . but a human being who . . . had become godlike. They thought his influence decided the will of God, and that it was his presence that insured for the protection of the Godhead. For them, it was not God who had brought them out of Egypt by means of Moses, but it was Moses who had been the means of making God accomplish that work of redemption.[130]

Seeing no other options, Aaron instructed the people to bring him their gold rings, which he took and made into a molten calf. Then the people exclaimed, "These are your gods O Israel, who brought you from the land of Egypt."[131] The term "these" refers to the Supreme Being and the golden calf. The people designated the golden calf, Moses' replacement, as a partner in redemption. Aaron became overwrought with what he saw. In Exodus 32:5 we read: "When Aaron saw this he built an altar before him; and Aaron made proclamation: 'Tomorrow shall be a feast to the Lord.'" Aaron had two purposes in mind. The first was a delay tactic: he hoped that by the next day Moses would have descended the mountain and the matter of his absence would no longer be an issue. The second was to refocus the people's attention. It was to be a day of feasting to *Havayah*, the One true Supreme Being of the universe. Perhaps that this would dissuade the people from their erroneous thinking and from their evil pursuit.[132] Much to Aaron's dismay, the plan did not work. The people brought sacrifices to the golden calf. They ate and drank and behaved wantonly.

The Lord appeared to Moses and informed him of the people's behavior. He revealed to Moses His plan to destroy them and make him the father of a new nation. Moses was devastated. This simply could not be! He appealed to Divine compassion. In Exodus 32:11 we read: "But Moses implored the Lord his God, saying, 'Let not Your anger O Lord, blaze forth against Your people, whom You delivered from the land of Egypt with great power and a mighty hand.'" He also made mention of

---

130. S. R. Hirsch, commentary on Exodus 32:1.
131. Exodus 32:4.
132. Cf. S. R. Hirsch, commentary on Exodus 32:5.

the merit of the patriarchs and the promise of *Havayah* to make their offspring as numerous as the stars of Heaven. Moses' efforts were successful. Indeed, it was *Havayah* who, in his abundant compassion, renounced the punishment that He had planned to bring upon His people.

Tablets in hand, Moses descended the mountain to enter the camp of the Israelites. In Exodus 32:16 the Torah makes an interesting comment: "The tablets were God's work, and the writing was God's writing, incised upon the tablets." One might have expected the name *Havayah*, indicative of Divine providence, to appear here. Yet, the name *E-lohim*, indicative of the Supreme Being as "Judge" and "Lawgiver" is also relevant. After all, the tablets and the writing that appeared on them were created by *E-lohim*. It is interesting to note that Moses hewed the second tablets from the rock.[133] As he drew near to the camp, Moses saw the calf and the dancing, and he became enraged. Our sages once remarked: "Hearing [about an event] is incomparable to seeing it [with one's own eyes]."[134] How true it was in this instance! He hurled the tablets from his hands and shattered them. Subsequently, he took the calf that the people had made, and he burned it. He ground it into powder, strewed it upon the waters, and he made those Israelites who were involved in this incident drink the waters. He then confronted Aaron for an explanation of what had led to this horrendous sin that had undermined the very basis of Torah.

Whatever the rationale may have been, the guilty parties had to be severely punished. In Exodus 32:26–27 we read:

> Moses stood up in the gate of the camp and said, "Whoever is for the Lord come here!" And all the Levites rallied to him. "Thus says the Lord, the God of Israel," said Moses. "Each of you put sword on thigh, go back and forth from gate to gate throughout the camp, and slay brother, neighbor and kin."

---

133. Cf. J. Z. Mecklenburg, commentary on Exodus 32:16. In Exodus 34:1 we read: "The Lord said to Moses: 'Carve two tablets of stone like the first, and I will inscribe upon the tablets the words that were on the first tablets, which you shattered.'"

134. *Mekhilta: Yitro* 19:9.

The God of Moses

Reference to the name *Havayah* has special significance here. It was not the Divine attribute of compassion represented by the name *Havayah* that Moses focused on here but rather the designation of the Supreme Being as the Eternal, and omnipotent Sovereign of the universe. Perhaps for shock value, he contrasted Him to the powerless, inanimate golden calf. "Who among you can say in all honesty that he had no share whatsoever in the sin of the golden calf?" asked Moses. "And from among those who can do so, who can claim total and unqualified allegiance to *Havayah* to the extent that he can do His bidding without question or hesitation and with no ulterior motive?" Only individuals of such high moral fiber would be protected from harm by *Havayah* and as such qualify for the dangerous task of circulating among the people and executing all those who had participated in the sin of the golden calf.[135] The entire tribe of Levi came forth. Moses informed them that what they had to do was not a personal vendetta but a punishment issued by *Havayah E-lohe Yisrael* ("the Lord and Judge of Israel").[136] In Exodus 32:28 we read: "The Levites did as Moses had bidden; and some three thousand of the people fell that day."

The courageous act of the Levites did not go unrewarded. In Exodus 32:29 we read: "And Moses said, 'Dedicate yourselves to the Lord this day—for each of you has been against son and brother—that He may bestow a blessing upon you today." The reward that *Havayah* had bestowed upon the Levites was in a very real sense the fulfillment of the rabbinic adage, "One mitzvah leads to another."[137] The Levites had come forth to fulfill the Divine charge without hesitation. In reward for their unqualified obedience, they and all their descendants were given the privilege of serving *Havayah* in His house of worship: first in the Tabernacle, and then in the Temple that stood in Jerusalem. The firstborn sons of Israel, who had been chosen for Divine service, had not stepped forth to declare their innocence of the sin of the golden calf,

---

135. Cf. I. Abravanel and N. Berlin (Haamek Davar) on Exodus 32:26.
136. Cf. Nahmanides, commentary on Exodus 32:27.
137. Mishnah: *Avot* 4:2.

nor had they claimed unqualified allegiance to *Havayah*. As a result, the holy calling was taken away from them and given to the Levites.[138]

The 3,000 men who were executed by the Levites had been properly forewarned of the sin they were about to commit and the acts that they committed had been properly witnessed.[139] Truthfully speaking, the entire nation was guilty for allowing this abomination to happen, even those who were not active participants. Consequently, in Exodus 32:30 we read: "The next day Moses said to the people, 'You have been guilty of a great sin. Yet I will go up to the Lord; perhaps I may win forgiveness for you.'" It was a grievous sin for which the people needed atonement, and Moses had to address the limitless compassion of *Havayah* to attain it. Alas, he found only limited success. For in Exodus 32:35 we read: "Then the Lord sent a plague upon the people for what they did with the calf that Aaron made." Those who could not be executed by the Levites, for they had not been forewarned nor were there any witnesses to their sin, did not escape justice. Only those who remained were forgiven.

AN UNACCEPTABLE CHANGE

The Lord (*Havayah*) informed Moses that the people of Israel were to continue their journey to the Promised Land. However, a change was to be initiated. In Exodus 33:2–15 we read:

> I will send an angel before you . . . But I will not go in your midst, since you are a stiffnecked people, lest I destroy you on the way. When the people heard this harsh word, they went into mourning and none put on his finery. The Lord said to Moses, "Say to the Israelites, 'You are a stiffnecked people. If I were to go in your midst for one moment, I would destroy you. Now, then, leave off your finery, and I will consider what to do to you . . .'" Moses said to the Lord, "See, you say to me, 'Lead this people forward,' but You have not made known to me whom You will send with

---

138. Cf. H. ben Atar (Or HaHayyim), commentary on Exodus 32:29.
139. *Yoma* 66b.

me ... Now, if I have truly gained Your favor, pray let me know Your ways, that I may know You and continue in Your favor" ... And He said, "My Presence will go in the lead and will lighten your burden." And he said to Him, "Unless Your Presence goes in the lead, do not make us leave this place" ... And the Lord said to Moses, "I will also do this thing that you have asked ..."

This conversation is most enigmatic, and it behooves us to attempt to understand the significance of what took place here. When the Israelites received the Torah at Sinai, *Havayah* designated them as a "kingdom of priests and a holy nation." Understandably, this designation came with a great responsibility. Of course, the reward for meeting this responsibility was the highest measure of Divine providence. The Supreme Being of the universe would protect Israel, His exclusive treasure, and watch over them more closely than over any other nation. This degree of providence is referred to as *P'ne Havayah* ("The Lord's Face or Presence"). It follows, of course, that to merit such providential exclusivity Israel's behavior as a nation would be subject to more careful scrutiny than that of any other nation. In punishment for the sin of the golden calf, *Havayah* threatened to withdraw this special measure of Divine providence. An angel would now accompany the nation of Israel to the Promised Land in His stead. In a sense, this change would be for their benefit. For the greater the measure of Divine providence, the greater the demand for perfection.[140] As it is stated in the Talmud in the name of R. Abba: "The Holy One blessed be He deals strictly with those round about Him even to a hair's breadth."[141] Another sin of such magnitude might incur the wrath of *E-lohim,* and they would be destroyed. On the other hand, the compassionate *Havayah* might save them once again. An angel is not endowed with such flexibility.

The words of *Havayah* plunged the Israelites into mourning, and Moses attempted to revoke the decree. As a concession, *Havayah* promised to endow the angel with the power to blend justice with mercy, thus tempering the Divine decree.[142] But Moses would not

---

140. Cf. Nahmanides, commentary on Exodus 32:34.
141. *Yevamot* 121b.
142. Cf. E. Ashkenazi, *Ma'ase Hashem* (Jerusalem, 1972), Ki Tisa 13.

relent. He insisted that Israel be accompanied directly by the "Divine Presence." Finally, *Havayah* acquiesced.[143]

LET ME BEHOLD YOUR GLORY

Seeing that this was an opportune time, Moses made two requests. In Exodus 33:13 we read: "Now if I have truly gained Your favor, pray let me know Your ways, that I may know You and continue in Your favor." In Exodus 33:18 we read: "He said, 'Oh, let me behold Your Glory!'" The response to the latter was negative, and in Exodus 33:20 we read: "But," He said, "you cannot see My face, for man may not see Me and live." Mortal man is incapable of perceiving the Divine essence. However, man *is* capable of knowing the *ways* of *Havayah*, i.e., His attributes. This answer is given in Exodus 33:19: "And He answered, 'I will make all My goodness pass before you as I proclaim the name Lord before you: I will be gracious to whom I will be gracious, and show compassion to whom I will show compassion." *Havayah* promised to show Moses the nature of creation. As Maimonides explains: "I mean to imply that God promised to make him comprehend the nature of all things, their relation to each other, and the way they are governed by God both in reference to the universe as a whole and to each creature in particular.[144] Specifically, Maimonides refers to the Divine attributes which are revealed to Moses in Exodus 33:6,7.

How does Moses react to this revelation? His immediate response is to bow in homage. He then puts forth a request. In Exodus 34:9 we read: "If I have gained Your favor, O Master, pray, let the Master go in our midst. Stiffnecked though this people be, pardon our iniquity and our sin, and take us for Your own." The name *Adney* (Master) appears here twice. It does not appear anywhere else in this *Sidrah*. As we have learned, this name represents the Supreme Being as "Master" of the universe. In a posture of total humility Moses addressed *Havayah* and implored Him to withdraw the angel and lead them personally to the

---

143. Nahmanides, op.cit., Exodus 33:14.
144. M. Maimonides, *Guide of the Perplexed*, Part I, chap. 54, p. 193.

Promised Land.[145] With great insight, Nahmanides explains the significance of this request.

> God is to go in their midst because they are a stiffnecked people, for now that the Holy One blessed be He became reconciled with them, His Presence among those that are stiffnecked would be better than that of the angel. For He will want to increase their blessings more, since they are His people and His inheritance. And just as at the time of anger it was better for them that He send before them an angel . . . so at the time of good will it is better for them that the Divine Glory go with them, because they are a stiffnecked people, and He would more readily show grace and mercy upon His servants.[146]

The Lord accepted Moses' request, and He made a covenant with the nation concerning the future. In Exodus 34:10 we read: "He said: 'I hereby make a covenant. Before all your people I will work such wonders as have not been wrought on all the Earth or in any nation, and all the people who are with you shall see how awesome are the Lord's deeds which I will perform for you.'"[147] The promise was reinstated and the Divine Presence rested amidst the people and with it the special measure of providence that they had previously merited. Most appropriately, the Supreme Being is referred to here as *Havayah*. *Havayah* would drive the idolatrous Canaanite nations out of the land, but the Israelites were charged to destroy all signs of idolatry. They were warned not to make any treaties with these nations lest they be tempted by their idolatrous practices.

THE DEMAND FOR EXCLUSIVITY

In Exodus 34:14 we read: "For you must not worship any other god, because the Lord whose name is Exclusive, is a God demanding

---

145. Cf. Y. Z. Mecklenburg, op. cit., Exodus 34:9.
146. Nahmanides, commentary on Exodus 34:9.
147. Cf. M. Malbim, commentary on Exodus 34:10.

exclusive rights." The point is made quite succinctly in the second commandment of the Decalogue (Exodus 20:3), which reads: "You shall have no other god before My Presence." Let us note that Divine exclusivity is mentioned only with regard to the sin of idolatry. It stands to reason. As S. R. Hirsch explains:

> If God is God then everything except Him is "no-god," everything besides Him is only His creation... Before His Presence... there can be no other god... The placing of another god at the side of God means doing away altogether with the real idea of God.[148]

The Divine name that appears in the biblical text is *E-l*. It is symbolic of Divine power, and it reminds us that the punishment for the sin of idolatry is a severe one.

THE THREE DIVINE NAMES

In Exodus 34:23 we read: "Three times a year, all your males shall appear before the Master, Lord, God of Israel." On the festival of *Pesah* we appear before the *Adon* (Master) of the universe, for we commemorate our redemption from human bondage to serve Him. On *Shavuot* we appear before *Havayah* (Lord) the Eternal Supreme Being of the universe in commemoration of the revelation of the Torah, a manifestation of eternal truth, to the Jewish people. On Sukkot we appear before *E-lohe Yisrael* (God of Israel), for this festival reminds us of His special concern for Israel in their journey to the Promised Land.

BEZALEL, THE ARCHITECT

Bezalel the son of Uri had already been chosen by *Havayah* to be in charge of the construction of the Tabernacle. He was a man of great skills who had been endowed by the Supreme Being with a unique

---

148. S. R. Hirsch, commentary on Exodus 20:3.

ability. In Exodus 31:3 we read: "I have endowed him with the spirit of God in wisdom, in understanding and in knowledge in every kind of craft." What does the "spirit of God" mean here? The Talmud explains: "Rabbi Judah said in the name of Rav: 'Bezalel knew how to combine the letters by which the Heavens and Earth were created.'"[149] It was *E-lohim*, the name that symbolizes the Supreme Being as "Creator," who inspired Bezalel with a measure of the wisdom, understanding and knowledge with which He created the universe. For it is written: "The Lord by *wisdom* founded the Earth; by *understanding* He established the Heavens" (Proverbs 3:19), and it is also written: "By His *knowledge* the depths were broken up" (Proverbs 3:20).

THE DIETARY LAWS

The Jewish dietary laws are listed in the book of Leviticus. What is the rationale for these laws? It is to attain a measure of holiness. In Leviticus 11:44 we read: "For I the Lord am your God: you shall sanctify yourselves and be holy for I am holy." In Jewish thinking, there are two aspects to holiness: separateness, and exaltedness beyond the natural realm. *Havayah* is separate from all other existing things in the universe; He is unique beyond human comprehension. At the same time, He is exalted in rank above all other existing things.

The Lord charges man: "Just as I am separate so must you be separate; just as I am exalted so must you be exalted."[150] If you make yourselves holy in this world, I will treat you as holy above and in the world to come.[151] Parenthetically, it is interesting to note that whenever the term *Kadosh* ("Holy") is adjoined to the name *Havayah* it is written in full form (plene), i.e., with a *vav*. Whenever it relates to man, however, it is written in shortened form (defective), i.e., without the *vav*. This is not merely coincidental; it is to teach us that man can only

---

149. *Berakhot* 55a.
150. Cf. *Sifra* on Leviticus 11:44 and M. Malbim ad loc.
151. Cf. Rashi, commentary on Exodus 11:44.

hope to attain a spark of the Divine, at best. Absolute holiness applies only to the Supreme Being.[152]

ILLICIT SEXUALITY

The laws of forbidden sexual relations are also discussed in the book of Leviticus. They are introduced in Leviticus 18:2 with the following statement: "Speak to the Israelite people and say to them: 'I the Lord am your God.'" These few words convey a vital message. Three aspects of Divinity are alluded to here: compassion, creation, and providence. They all apply to the moral laws that are to follow. *Havayah* in His limitless compassion created the first woman as a "helpmate" to Adam, specifically, to teach him morality. As *E-lohim*, He created the laws of nature. He differentiated one species from another, and He set the laws of human reproduction and sexuality to ensure the proper development of mankind. Lastly, as *E-lohe Yisrael* ("the God of Israel"), He revealed to His people special marital laws in order to produce and to preserve generations of righteous people.[153] It is interesting to note that the marital laws are followed with the same charge with which they are introduced. Thus in Leviticus 19:2 we read: "You shall be holy, for I, the Lord your God am holy."[154] In Leviticus 20:7 we are again given the rationale: "You shall sanctify yourselves and be holy, for I the Lord am your God,"[155] which is followed once again by marital laws.

THE LAW OF *MOLEKH*

Following the first section of the laws of forbidden sexual relations we are introduced to the law of *Molekh*. In Leviticus 18:21 we read: "Do not allow any of your offspring to be passed through to *Molekh*, and do not profane the name of your God: I am the Lord." The ritual was as

---

152. D. Z. Hoffmann, commentary on Leviticus 11:44.
153. Cf. D. Z. Hoffmann, commentary on Leviticus 18:2.
154. Cf. Rashi and Or HaHayyim on Leviticus 19:2.
155. Cf. O. Seforno, commentary on Leviticus 20:7.

follows: Two blazing fires were built. The father would take his child and hand him over to the priests of *Molekh*. The priests would then hand the child back to his father. The father would pass the child through the fire.[156] The ritual was based on the notion that by sacrificing one child to this force called *Molekh*,[157] the rest of the family would be spared. There is a difference of opinion in the Talmud as to whether or not the *Molekh* ritual fits the definition of idolatry.[158] Be that as it may, the biblical verse indicates that the ritual is a desecration of God's name. The use of the Divine name *Havayah* in the concluding phrase focuses on the Divine attribute of compassion. It makes the unequivocal statement that *Havayah* despises rituals that demand human sacrifice.[159]

THE DIVINE PROMISE

In Leviticus 20:26, the concluding verse of the laws of holiness (the dietary and marital laws), the rationale of which we have spoken is spelled out precisely. The last half of the verse reads: "You shall be holy to Me, for I, the Lord am holy, and I have set you apart from other peoples to be Mine."

Leviticus 26:3–43 is called the *Tokhahah* ("Rebuke"). In actuality, both the reward for obedience to the law and the punishment for disobedience are enumerated.[160] Perhaps the most encouraging of the rewards is the one mentioned in Leviticus 26:11–12. It reads: "I will establish My abode in your midst, and I will not spurn you. I will be ever present in your midst: I will be your God and you shall be My people."

---

156. Cf. Rabbenu B'haye and Nahmanides on Leviticus 18:21. Most commentators were of the opinion that the child was burned alive. Cf. S. R. Hirsch ad loc. who disagrees.

157. According to S. R. Hirsch (Ibid.), *Molekh* was not an idol per se but rather a concept. He writes: "We think we find in it the heathen idea of irrevocable fate, luck, which rules the world, on which even the gods have no power to change, to whose decisions they themselves cannot but submit."

158. Cf. *Sanhedrin* 64a.

159. Cf. D. Z. Hoffmann, commentary on Leviticus 18:21.

160. The rewards and punishment are also listed in Deuteronomy 28.

If you commit yourselves to the law and follow it, I will be with you, says *E-lohim*. As you move from place to place, I will accompany you. I will be continuously involved in your destiny, keeping you from committing any sin, which would otherwise cause Me to withdraw My Presence.[161] As *E-lohim*, I will exercise My power of severe judgment upon the nations that choose to harm you.

THE LAW OF THE FRINGES

The law of *tsitsit* ("fringes") is found in Numbers 15:37–41. It reads:

> The Lord spoke to Moses saying: Speak to the Israelite people and instruct them to make for themselves fringes on the corners of their garments throughout the generations . . . That shall be your fringe; look at it and recall all the commandments of the Lord and observe them, so that you do not follow your heart and eyes in your lustful urge . . . I the Lord am your God who brought you out of the land of Egypt to be your God: I the Lord am your God.

The last verse is particularly significant. I have manifested My special providence on your behalf by redeeming you from exile in the land of Egypt, says *Havayah*. Alas, your sins will be the cause of your exile once again, but this is not an indication that I have abandoned you. The bond between us will never be broken. You will always be under My special protection. Nevertheless, I am *E-lohim*; the Supreme Judge of the universe. I reward the righteous, but I also punish the wicked who disobey My commandments.[162]

THE REBELLION OF KORAH

In the forty-year journey in the wilderness to the Promised Land there were many instances when Moses was confronted by unwarranted

---

161. Cf. D. Z. Hoffmann, Leviticus 26:12.
162. M. Malbim, commentary on Numbers 15:41.

complaints, but none of them challenged the validity of the mission of the man himself, i.e., his "chosenness" by the Lord. The rebellion of Korah, Datan, and Aviram did just that. Mark the words of Korah in Numbers 16:3, "You have gone too far! For all the community are holy, all of them, and the Lord is in their midst. Why then do you raise yourselves above the Lord's congregation." Datan and Aviram were summoned to appear before Moses, but they refused. Note their response: "Is it not enough that you brought us from a land flowing with milk and honey to have us die in the wilderness, that you would also lord it over us?" (16:13). How does Moses react to this audacious challenge? In Numbers 16:28–29 we read:

> And Moses said: "By this you shall know that it was the Lord who sent me to do all these things; that they are not of my own devising; if these men die as all men do, if their lot be the common fate of all mankind, it was not the Lord who sent me. But if the Lord brings about something unheard of, so that the ground opens its mouth wide and swallows them up with all that belongs to them, and they go down alive into the grave, you shall know that these men have spurned the Lord."

The rebels themselves recognized that *Havayah* was in their midst. They knew that the redemption from Egypt was a miraculous event. They knew that *Havayah* had intervened in the process of history so that the fate of His people Israel went contrary to the natural course of events. What Korah, Datan, and Aviram tried to do was to implant within the minds of the masses the seeds of doubt as to the authenticity of Moses' claim to leadership. What had to be demonstrated to the people was that *Havayah*, who had redeemed them from Egypt, had also appointed Moses to lead them out of Egypt to the Promised Land. It would not be enough for the rebels to die by Divine decree; they had to die an unnatural death. The words of S. R. Hirsch here are enlightening: "If their downfall is brought about by something new that just proclaims God as the Lord, in Whose Name I [Moses] acted, then you will know that these people in denying that I [Moses] was carrying out God's commission, altogether denied the free-willed Rule of God and His work."[163]

Moses' request was fulfilled, and his mission was thus confirmed. It seems that it was not enough for the masses, for they now accused Moses of bringing death upon the community. This angered *Havayah*, and He threatened to annihilate the sinners. In punishment, a plague broke out among the people in which 14,700 of them died. It was also established that the sacred duties that were to be assumed by the tribe of Levi and the children of Aaron would be so by Divine authority.[164]

If the people had now accepted the authority of Moses and Aaron, it was short lived. For when they came to a place called Kadesh and they thirsted for water, they complained once more against them. In Numbers 20:3–5 we read: "The people quarreled with Moses, saying, 'If only we had perished when our brothers perished before the Lord. Why have you brought the Lord's congregation into this wilderness for us and our beasts to die there? Why did you make us leave Egypt to bring us to this wretched place . . . There is not even water to drink.'" The "brothers" to whom the people had referred were those of the generation that had been redeemed from Egypt but who were denied entry to the Promised Land. The providential hand of *Havayah* had not forsaken them till the end. Those people had died a peaceful and natural death in the wilderness by Divine decree; but we are to die of thirst, they intimated, a painful and unnatural death. By referring to themselves as "the Lord's congregation," they implied that it was the will of *Havayah* that they be brought to the Promised Land to live there in peace and in happiness.[165] Notwithstanding their arrogance and self-centeredness, Moses drew water from a rock and the people were able to quench their thirst.

---

163. S. R. Hirsch, commentary on Numbers 16:30.
164. Cf. Numbers 17:16–24 for the details. What was established by this event is put quite succinctly by S. R. Hirsch as follows: "The Levites and Aaronides are not superior to the rest of the Israelites but are only always to be in the van, leading spiritual and general development of life which all the other brother tribes are called on to follow and attain the same spiritual level" (Numbers 17:17).
165. Cf. S. R. Hirsch, commentary on Numbers 20:3–4.

The God of Moses

SUCCESS IN BATTLE

In their journey to the Promised Land, the Israelites had to pass through several kingdoms. From Kadesh they had to pass through Edom, and Moses sent messengers to the king of Edom to get permission to pass peacefully through his land. The message said that they would not spoil the fields or vineyards; they would not even drink water from the wells. Edom refused. He went out against the Israelites with a strongly armed force, and Israel turned away from them. The Cannanite king of Arad heard that the Israelites were coming his way, so he came out against them with a large army. He engaged them in battle, and he took some of them captive. The Israelites vowed that if the *Havayah*, in His abundant compassion, would deliver Edom into their hands they would destroy their cities. Much to their good fortune, Israel was victorious. So it was with Sihon, king of the Amorites and Og, king of Bashan.

BALAAM AND HIS MISSION

When Balak, king of Moav, heard what had happened to the Amorites, he became uneasy. He sent messengers to Balaam, son of Beor, requesting that he come and put a curse upon the Israelites. In Numbers 22:7–9 we read:

> The elders of Moav and the elders of Midian, versed in divination, set out. They came to Balaam and gave him Balak's message. He [Balaam] said to them, "Spend the night here, and I shall reply to you as the Lord may instruct me." So the Moabite dignitaries stayed with Balaam. God came to Balaam and said, "What do these people want of you?"

It is interesting to note that Balaam, who was a prophet of the nations, informed the messengers that he must commune with *Havayah*, but it is *E-lohim* not *Havayah* who appeared to Balaam. This happened again in 22:18–20 and in 23:3–4. Our Rabbis explain that a prophetic revelation introduced by the name *Havayah* is on a higher level than one introduced by the name *E-lohim*.[166] Perhaps the Torah wishes to hint at Balaam's self-centeredness and arrogance. He felt that he merited the highest degree of prophecy and boasted of this to his visitors. The Torah indicates to us that in point of fact, he merited and received a much lower degree of prophecy than what he expected.

E-lohim commanded Balaam not to go with the messengers to curse Israel, and Balaam obeyed. But the messengers returned with a promise of great reward, so Balaam once more put forth his request to *Havayah*. Again, it was *E-lohim* who answered Balaam. He allowed Balaam to go with the messengers, but limited what he would be permitted to speak. Balaam went with the messengers, and in Numbers 22:22 we read: "But God was incensed at his going; so an angel of the Lord placed himself in his way as an adversary..." What was the problem? Had Balaam not been given permission to go? Yes, but he could speak only the words that *E-lohim* would put in his mouth. He was not given permission to curse the Israelites. Despite the charge given to him by *E-lohim*, Balaam saddled his ass and went with the messengers with the full intention of cursing Israel. The angel of *Havayah*, by name a merciful angel, was sent to prevent Balaam from disobedience, clearly a manifestation of Divine compassion.[167] Considering Balaam's intentions, perhaps the angel was sent to prevent him from going altogether. Is this not implied in the words "placed himself in his way"? The point is further confirmed in Numbers 22:23–27 where we read:

> When the ass caught sight of the angel of the Lord standing in the way, with his drawn sword in his hand. The ass swerved from the road and went into the fields, and Balaam beat the ass to turn her back onto the road. The angel of the Lord then stationed himself in a lane between the vineyards, with a fence on either side. The ass, seeing the angel of the Lord, pressed herself against the wall and squeezed Balaam's foot against the wall . . . Once more the angel of the Lord moved forward and stationed himself on a spot so narrow that there was no room to swerve right or left.

---

166. Cf. N. Z. Berlin, *HaAmek Davar*, commentary on Numbers 22:8.
167. Cf. Rashi, commentary on Numbers 22:22.

The angel tried to stop Balaam from going any further. Again, the fact that the angel is called "the angel of the Lord" indicates that the gesture is a manifestation of Divine compassion. Perhaps to emphasize the fact that it was Divine compassion that interceded on Balaam's behalf, the angel is referred to four times by this name. Seeing that the angel was unsuccessful, however, *Havayah* Himself entered the scene. In Numbers 22:28 we read: "Then the Lord opened the ass's mouth, and she said to Balaam, 'What have I done to you that you have beaten me these three times?'" Some contend that this entire event took place in a dream.[168] If what occurred is taken literally, however, it is clearly in the realm of the supernatural.

Balaam saw the angel. Sensing that what had happened was a sign that he had done wrong, Balaam was willing to return home. This was not the will of *Havayah*, however, and so the angel tells Balaam to continue on to Balak. He was to speak only the words that the angel put in his mouth, compassionate words that came directly from *Havayah*. Thus in Numbers 23:5 we read: "And the Lord put a word in Balaam's mouth and said, 'Return to Balak and speak thus . . .'" Again in 23:16 we read: "The Lord manifested Himself to Balaam and put a word in his mouth saying, 'Return to Balak and speak thus.'" Among the words that Balaam was to speak is reference to the special measure of providence accorded to the nation of Israel represented by the name *Havayah*. Thus in Numbers 23:21 we read: "No harm is in sight for Jacob, no woe in view for Israel. The Lord their God is with them, and their King's acclaim in their midst."

Balak made another attempt to induce Balaam to curse Israel, and in Numbers 23:27–28 we read: "Then Balak said to Balaam, 'Come now, I will take you to another place. Perhaps God will deem it right that you damn them for me there. Balak took Balaam to the peak of Peor, which overlooks the wasteland.'" What did Balak have in mind by going to this place? Peor was a pit of depravity. S. R. Hirsch explains:

> And he took him to the point where he could look down over the "waste of deified shamelessness," for that is Peor, a cult which turns

---

168. Cf. M. Malbim, commentary on Numbers 22:22.

the most animal side of human functions toward the gods, and says to man: "Why do you dream of decency and modesty and a higher calling, your own alimentary system shows you that you are no better and designed to no higher calling than an animal."[169]

Was Balak able to see into the future and predict that Israel, too, would fall prey to Peor, as some suggest?[170] Perhaps by taking Balaam to this depraved place, Balak turned his focus to the issue of morality, hoping that in this realm even Israel was vulnerable. Surely they were deserving of punishment by *E-lohim*, as a manifestation of strict Divine judgment.

Again Balak failed to gain his objective for by now Balaam had come to realize that he had no alternative but to bless the people of Israel. In Numbers 24:1 we read: "Now Balaam, seeing that it pleased the Lord to bless Israel, did not, as on previous occasions, go in search of omens, but turned his face toward the wilderness." Balaam had seen the light. Israel had been blessed with special providential care, and neither he nor any other human being could prevail against providence. In Numbers 24:3–5 a humble Balaam spoke out:

> Taking up his theme he said: "Word of Balaam son of Beor, word of the man whose eye is true. Word of him who hears God's [*E-l*] speech, who beholds visions from the Almighty, prostrate but with eyes unveiled: 'How fair are your tents O Jacob, your dwellings, O Israel.'"

Balaam heard the word of *E-l*, the all-powerful One, of *Sha-dai*, who sets limits to His creations and has now expanded Balaam's limited prophetic ability, thus enabling him to perceive the true qualities of Israel.

---

169. S.R. Hirsch, commentary on Numbers 23:28.
170. Cf. Rashi, commentary on Numbers 23:28.

A SPECIAL APPEAL

The long journey to the Promised Land was coming to an end. *Havayah* told Moses to ascend the heights of Mount Avarim and view the land that was given to Israel for he would not enter therein. In Numbers 27:15–16 we then read: "Moses spoke to the Lord saying, 'Let the Lord, Source of the spirits of all flesh, appoint someone over the community.'" This is the second of only two references to the Supreme Being as "Source of the spirits of all flesh."[171] What is the meaning of this appellative and its relevance to the matter of leadership?

Having been informed of his impending demise, Moses knew that the people needed a leader who would be sensitive to the nature, the character, the temperament, indeed, the "spirit" of each individual. *Havayah* is responsible for placing the spirit (soul) in the body of every living being. It is clearly a manifestation of Divine compassion. He protects it and strengthens it for the duration of its existence in the human body. As such Moses appealed to the "Source of the spirits" to indicate his hope that the soul of the new leader would be protected and strengthened during his tenure by its "Source," *Havayah*, the Supreme Being of the universe. Indeed, it is *Havayah* who would select the best replacement for Moses.[172]

MOSES BIDS FAREWELL

For the most part, the book of Deuteronomy consists of Moses' last words to the nation of Israel. To a great extent, these words are recollections of events in the history of the past generation in their forty-year journey through the wilderness from the time they left Mount Horev (Sinai). Early in his speech, Moses made reference to the

---

171. The first reference is found regarding the Korah rebellion. When the Lord wanted to wipe out the entire community of Israel, Moses and Aaron appealed for forgiveness, and the text in Numbers 17:22 tells us, "But they fell on their faces and said, 'Source of the spirits of all flesh! When one man sins, will You be wrathful with the whole community.'"

172. Cf. M. Malbim and S. R. Hirsch commentaries on Numbers 27:16.

growth of the nation, and in Deuteronomy 1:10-11 we read: "The Lord your God has multiplied you until you are today as numerous as the stars in the sky. May the Lord, the God of your fathers, increase your numbers a thousand fold, and bless you as He promised you." In 210 years, the Israelites grew from a family of seventy that Jacob had brought with him to Egypt to well over a million people at the time of the redemption. *Havayah*, who superimposed His will over the law of nature, performed this miracle on behalf of the nation of Israel. Moses predicted that Israel would continue to be blessed with rapid growth when they entered the Promised Land as well.[173] It is interesting to note that the phrase "the Lord your God" (*Havayah E-lohekha*), a phrase that appears in the Ten Commandments, appears consistently in Deuteronomy. Perhaps the implication is that the Supreme Being, who made Himself known to Israel in the Ten Commandments as "the Lord your God who brought out of the land of Egypt, the house of bondage," will continue His miracles in behalf of Israel when they enter the Promised Land.

MOSES' PERSONAL APPEAL

After the victory of the Israelites over the armies of Sihon king of the Amorites and Og king of Bashan, Moses made a personal appeal to *Havayah* to be allowed to enter the Promised Land. In Deuteronomy 3:23-25 we read:

> I pleaded with the Lord at that time, saying, "O Master Lord,[174] You who let your servant see the first works of Your greatness and Your mighty hand, You whose powerful deeds no god in Heaven or on Earth can equal! Let me, I pray, cross over and see the good land on the other side of the Jordan, that good hill country and the Lebanon."

---

173. Cf. M. Malbim, commentary on Deuteronomy 1:11.

174. In the chapter on the names of the Lord, we have discussed the special pronunciation of these names when they appear together. I have translated the text as it is written. The Hebrew transliteration is as it is to be pronounced.

The God of Moses

On what basis did Moses appeal to the Supreme Being in this supplication? According to some, Moses knew that if he were to appeal to *E-lohim* and be judged by strict Divine justice, he would not be permitted to enter the land. He, therefore, appealed to *Havayah*. He wanted to be granted permission to enter the land as an unearned, perhaps even an unwarranted, Divine gesture. Some would consider such a gesture a manifestation of compassionate judgment (*Rahamim B'Din*).[175] Others take a different approach. The order of Divine names here is *Adney Havayah*. When they are juxtaposed in the text, however, they are read *Adney E-lohim*. Our sages commented that this teaches us that Moses first appealed to the Supreme Being in the name of justice; if he did not deserve to enter the land on that basis, he prayed that compassion override strict justice to allow him to enter the land.[176] It is also noted that by addressing the Supreme Being with both names, "Moses declares beforehand how without discontent he will not complain if God's decision finds it right to deny him his last and warmest wish."[177] It is interesting to note that in this instance the "greatness" of *Havayah*, at least according to one commentator, consists not in His omnipotence but in His kindness. His "mighty hand" does not manifest itself by destroying the evildoer but rather by allowing compassion to override strict justice.[178]

THE SIN OF IDOLATRY

Idolatry was rampant in biblical times, and the temptation to become involved in idol worship must have been overwhelming. In the forty-year journey to the Promised Land, Moses consistently warned the people not to fall prey to this abomination, for to do so would be to incur severe punishment. In Deuteronomy 4:23–24 we read:

---

175. Cf. Rashi, commentary on Deuteronomy 3:23–24. Cf. *Sifte HaHamim*. The fact that the name *Havayah* has the vocalization of the name *E-lohim* when it appears together with the name *Adney* gives credence to Rashi's comment here.
176. Cf. Nahmanides, commentary on Deuteronomy 3:23.
177. S. R. Hirsch, commentary on Deuteronomy 3:24.
178. Cf. Rashi, commentary on Deuteronomy 3:24.

> Take care, then, not to forget the covenant that the Lord your God [*Havayah E-lohekhem*] concluded with you and make for yourselves a sculptured image in any likeness, against which the Lord has enjoined you. For the Lord your God is a consuming fire, a God [*E-l*] demanding exclusive rights.

Three Divine names are mentioned here: *Havayah, E-lohim,* and *E-l*. The covenant referred to is the one made at Sinai[179] in which the nation faithfully committed itself to *Havayah* and accepted upon itself unqualified adherence to the Ten Commandments in which the law prohibiting idolatry is included.[180] It was a covenant made between Israel and *Havayah E-lohekhem* that implied strict compliance by the nation, and was subject to strict Divine judgment. In turn, *Havayah* would make the people of Israel His exclusive treasure and grant them a special measure of providence. The severity of Moses' warning against idolatry is seen in verse 24 where the Supreme Being is compared to a consuming fire and is vividly depicted as the all powerful *E-l* who demands exclusive rights. Indeed, just as a fire consumes everything in its path, so will the all-powerful *E-l* punish all those in Israel who practice idolatry, says the Torah.

The punishment for idolatry will be exile. Should the time come that Israel acts wickedly and begins to practice idolatry, says Moses, they will be exiled from the land to a place where they will serve man made idols of wood and stone. But what if they regret their impropriety, if they search for *Havayah* and repent in sincerity? In Deuteronomy 4:29–31 we read: "But if you search there for the Lord your God, you will find Him, if only you seek Him with all your heart and all your soul—when you are in distress because all these things have befallen you and, in the end, return to the Lord your God and obey Him. For the Lord your God is a compassionate God [*E-l*]: He will not fail you nor will He let you perish; He will not forget the covenant, which He made under oath with your fathers." If the people are sincere in their attempted return to *Havayah, He* will accept them and forgive them because He is a

---

179. Exodus 24:7–8.
180. Cf. D. Z. Hoffmann, commentary on Deuteronomy 4:13,

The God of Moses

compassionate Being. His ways are such that He will never give up hope for their return. The Talmud teaches the following:

> Even in the World to Come, Israel will be redeemed only through repentance, compassion and the merit of the Patriarchs . . ." And you shall return to the Lord your God," this is repentance, "For the Lord your God is compassionate," this is compassion, "And He will not forget the covenant with your fathers," this is the merit of the Patriarchs.[181]

TEMPERING JUSTICE WITH COMPASSION

The Supreme Being is not merely *E-l,* the manifestation of power and strict judgment, He is *E-l Rahum;* He tempers justice with mercy.[182] "Inquire about bygone ages," says Moses. Has any other nation experienced the miracles that have been wrought in behalf of Israel? Has any other nation heard the voice of God speaking from out of a fire and survived? Has any other nation experienced redemption through the mighty hand of God? Finally, says Moses, "It has been clearly demonstrated to you that the Lord alone is God; there is none beside Him" (Deuteronomy 4:35). *Havayah* who performs the supernatural is identical with *E-lohim* who spoke and created the universe. You know from your own experience, says Moses, that there is only *One* God! Even more. Perhaps the most well-known verse in the Torah is Deuteronomy 6:4, which reads: "Hear O Israel! the Lord our God, the Lord is One." Compassion, depicted in the name *Havayah,* and strict justice: depleted in the name *E-lohim,* are both attributes of the One and only Supreme Being of the universe who tempers justice with compassion in His judgment of mankind.[183] Ethical monotheism is the great contribution of the Jewish people to the world. In merit of this contribution our sages commented: "The Holy One blessed be He said

---

181. Jerusalem Talmud, *Taanit* 1:1.
182. Cf. D. Z. Hoffmann, commentary on Deuteronomy 4:31.
183. Cf. S. R. Hirsch, commentary on Deuteronomy 6:4.

to Israel: 'You have made Me a unique entity in the world, and I shall make you a unique entity in the world.'"[184]

In Deuteronomy 7:9 we read: "Know, therefore, that only the Lord your God is God, the faithful God [*E-l*] who keeps His gracious covenant to the thousandth generation of those who love Him and keep His commandments, but who instantly requites with destruction those who reject Him. . . ." For emphasis, Moses repeats the fact that the God who brought Israel out of Egypt, is none other than the God who created Heaven and Earth. But a new point is added here: He is faithful to the thousandth generation to those who obey His laws. He made a covenant with the patriarchs that their children would inherit the Promised Land of Canaan. He did not forget that covenant, but He also remembers the wickedness of man to the thousandth generation.[185] It is because of His faithfulness to the righteous even to the thousandth generation that the wicked at times go unpunished. For the sages tell us that the Holy One blessed be He is long-suffering. Not only do the righteous benefit from this attribute; the wicked do as well. But why should the wicked benefit? Our sages tell us that it is for one of three reasons: they might repent; they might have done some good in their lives for which they deserve reward; righteous offspring might descend from them.[186]

Another facet of the special measure of providence that would be afforded to Israel if they faithfully follow the commandments concerns their physical well-being. In Deuteronomy 7:15 we read: "The Lord will ward off from you all sickness; He will not bring upon you any of the dreadful diseases of Egypt, about which you know, but will inflict them upon all your enemies." The sages differ in their thinking as to precisely what diseases the text refers to here.[187] But whether these diseases are the result of natural phenomena or Divine punishment, they will not affect Israel.

An important principle in the ways of *Havayah* is found in Deuter-

---

184. *Berakhot* 6a.
185. Cf. Nahmanides, commentary on Deuteronomy 7:9.
186. Ibid.
187. Cf. Rabbenu B'haye, J. Mecklenburg, and M. Malbim, on Deuteronomy 7:15 for their differing approaches.

onomy 8:5 where we read: "Bear in mind that the Lord your God disciplines you just as a man disciplines his son." Just as a father has only his son's welfare in mind when he disciplines him, so is it with *Havayah*. Again the text explains: "God with His management is like a father to us, and all the joy and trouble He sends to us aim at nothing else than our betterment and moral ennoblement."[188]

FORGIVE YOUR PEOPLE

Moses reminds the people that when they had committed the sin of the golden calf, he had pleaded with *E-lohim* on their behalf. The text of the prayer is found in Deuteronomy 9:25–27 and reads:

> When I lay prostrate before the Lord—those forty days and forty nights—because the Lord was determined to destroy you, I prayed to the Lord and said, "O Master Lord,[189] do not annihilate your very own people, whom You redeemed in Your majesty and whom You freed from Egypt with a mighty hand. Give thought to Your servants, Abraham, Isaac, and Jacob, and pay no heed to the stubbornness of this people, its wickedness and its sinfulness."

What does this prayer teach us about the Supreme Being of the universe? We have already dwelled sufficiently on the significance of the juxtaposition of the two Divine names *Adney Havayah* in Moses' personal prayer to enter the Promised Land (Deuteronomy 3:23). Let us add the following note. One must approach the Supreme Being with the utmost humility. The greater the individual, the more humble he must be before his Master, for greatness engenders self-pride and self-pride tends to build egocentric thinking. The name *Adney* (Master) implies that man is the servant of the Divine. As such it expresses man's total commitment to the Divine will. The name *Havayah* in this context

---

188. S. R. Hirsch, commentary on Deuteronomy 8:5.
189. As in Deuteronomy 3:24, I have written the English as it appears in the text and the Hebrew as it is pronounced.

symbolizes "the whole depth of God's way of government."[190] In essence, what we have here is an affirmation of Divine justice. Truthfully speaking, however, were man to appeal to Divine justice in his personal requests, he would never prevail.[191] His moral weakness all too often leads him astray. King Solomon put it simply: For there is not one good man on Earth who does what is best and doesn't err."[192] Moses petitioned *Havayah* for compassion. To reinforce his plea, he referred to *zekhut avot* ("the merit of the Patriarchs"), which for all intents and purposes is an appeal to Divine faithfulness.

What does *Havayah* want of Israel? Only that they follow His commandments, says Moses, that they love Him and worship Him. In two verses Moses then enumerates nine Divine attributes.[193] In Deuteronomy 10:17–18 we read: "For the Lord your God is a God of gods and Master of masters, the great, the mighty, and the awesome God (*E-l*), who shows no favor and takes no bribe, but upholds the cause of the fatherless and the widow, and befriends the stranger, providing him with food and clothing."[194] *Havayah* whom you have taken to be your *E-lohim* is in control of all the forces of nature (God of gods), and all the rulers of men must submit to His rule (Master of masters). He is the all-powerful God (*E-l*) from whom all power in the universe emanates.[195] He is *great* in His loving-kindness, *mighty* in His judgment, and *awesome* in His compassion.[196] He *shows no favor* to ancestry, social position, or intellectual superiority but punishes them if they commit even minor transgressions of the Torah.[197] He takes no

---

190. Ibid. 9:26.

191. Let us recall the words of Rashi on Genesis 1:1: "At first God intended to create it [the world) to be placed under the attribute of strict justice, but He realized that the world could not thus endure and therefore gave precedence to Divine mercy allaying it with Divine justice."

192. Ecclesiastes 7:20.

193. According to Rabbenu B'haye, Moses alluded to the thirteen Divine attributes that are found in Exodus 33:6.

194. There are different interpretations as to the meaning of the Divine attributes enumerated here. Those we have chosen to mention will be appropriately annotated.

195. Cf. S. R. Hirsch, commentary on Deuteronomy 10:17.

196. Cf. Rabbenu B'haye, commentary on Deuteronomy ad loc.

197. Cf. S. R. Hirsch, op. cit.

bribe from the righteous. To allow a sin committed by the righteous to go unpunished because of the multiplicity of *mitzvot* that they have fulfilled would be unjust; it would be considered a bribe.[198]

GOD'S HIDDEN COUNTENANCE

The time of Moses' death was drawing near, and *Havayah* revealed to him the sad tidings that the people would not long endure in the Promised Land. They would go astray after the alien gods in their midst, and they would break the covenant that He had made with them. In Deuteronomy 31:17–18 we read the result:

> Then My anger will flare up against them, and I will abandon them and hide My countenance from them. They shall be ready prey; and many evils and troubles shall befall them. And they shall say on that day, "Surely it is because my God is not in our midst that this evil has befallen us." Yet I will keep My countenance hidden on that day, because of all the evil they have done in turning to other gods.

We have mentioned more than once in this chapter that as the chosen people, the special "treasure" of *Havayah*, the Jewish people have been granted the highest measure of Divine providence, but we must keep in mind that it was with the proviso that they remain true to the tenets of the Torah and observe the 613 commandments. If they relinquish their commitment to the commandments or fall prey to idolatry, *Havayah* will remove that special measure of providence, and they will be left to the law of nature and the whims of the nations of the world. If they repent, that special measure of providence will be restored; if they do not repent, it will be removed permanently. This is what is meant by the words "I will hide My countenance from them."[199]

In a short yet magnificent poem, in which he called Heaven and Earth to witness against the people of Israel, Moses briefly reviewed the wonders that *Havayah* had performed on their behalf. He chastised the

---

198. Nahmanides, commentary on Deuteronomy 10:17.
199. Cf. S. R. Hirsch, commentary on Deuteronomy 31:17,18.

people for their sins in the past and warned them of the severe punishment that awaits them if they sin in the future. Nevertheless, in the end, when all the might of Israel is gone, says Moses, the Lord will vindicate His people and take revenge for His servants." Let us examine one verse of this magnificent poem.

In Deuteronomy 32:4 we read: "The Rock!—His deeds are perfect, yea, all His ways are just; a faithful God, never false, True and upright is He." We have already discussed the meaning of the Divine appellative *HaTzur* ("The Rock,")[200] but let us add one more significant point here. The Supreme Being is called *HaTzur* because He is omnipotent: His strength or power is unlimited. Despite His power, however, He deals with humanity with the utmost of sensitivity and kindness. This is an aspect of His perfection.[201] He is a just God. Not only are His "ends" just, but the means to attain these ends are just and proper.[202] *HaTsur* is faithful in His relationship with mankind, which manifests itself in the fact that He does not fail to reward the righteous in the World to Come for their good deeds.[203] Neither is He false. For He punishes the wicked in this world for their wickedness.[204]

---

200. Cf. Chapter One.
201. Cf. Rabbenu B'haye, commentary on Deuteronomy 32:4.
202. S. R. Hirsch, commentary on Deuteronomy 32:4.
203. Rashi, commentary on Deuteronomy 32:4.
204. Ibid. Cf. also *Taanit* 11a.

6

THE MEANING AND SIGNIFICANCE OF PROVIDENCE

In the preceding chapters we have discussed the Divine names most commonly referred to in the Torah, and we have indicated their significance as appellatives in the context of the verses in which they appear. In this chapter we will examine some aspects of Divine providence, i.e., the record of Divine concern for the welfare of man and the preservation of the world. We will cull this information mainly from the Book of Psalms as interpreted by our sages from ancient to modern times. Unlike in previous chapters, the material here will be topical rather than sequential, and we will not always focus on the Divine names.

Let us begin with a definition of terms. What do we mean by Divine providence, and and how does Divine providence manifest itself in the world?

Divine providence means Divine concern; it is a manifestation of God's compassion for his creations. As we have already pointed out, Judaism teaches that God created the world and is very much concerned with its destiny. Divine providence falls into two categories: *hashgahah k'lalit,* i.e., general concern for the preservation of the species and *hashgahah p'ratit*, i.e., specific concern for the preservation of each and every member of the species. According to Maimonides, Judaism teaches that with regard to all creatures with the exception of man, God's concern manifests itself merely in the preservation of the species. With man, however, providence is extended to each and every human being.[1] What this means is that what happens to the individual members of all animal and plant species is left to chance. God is concerned with the future of the cat family but what happens to each and every cat in this world is of no concern to Him. On the other hand, what happens to every human being, namely, the good as well as the evil he experiences in his life, is the result of Divine justice. Consequently, while it is completely by chance that a ship carrying 100 head of cattle sinks into the sea, the fact that a particular person who was on that ship was drowned is due to Divine will, and is in full accordance with Divine justice.[2]

Maimonides makes another important point of which we must take note. Divine providence manifested upon man is directly related to human perfection. As such, writes Maimonides, "The relation of Divine providence is not the same to all men; the greater the human perfection a person has attained, the greater the benefit he derives from Divine providence."[3] It follows, therefore, that God more carefully monitors the righteous and the intellectually superior, so to speak, than the rest of society. Perhaps this is because such individuals can and do assume a greater responsibility for the welfare of society than the average person.

Divine providence poses a dilemma. The Talmud teaches: "Everything is in the hand of Heaven with the exception of the fear of Heaven."[4] Similarly in the name of R. Hanina, "No man bruises his finger here on Earth unless it was so decreed against him in Heaven."[5] Now at first blush this principle is comforting. After all, what could be

---

1. M. Maimonides, *Guide of the Perplexed* (New York: Hebrew Publishing Company), Part III, chapter xvii, p. 74.
2. Ibid., p. 75.
3. Ibid., chap. xviii, p. 80.
4. *Berakhot* 33b.
5. *Hullin* 7b.

better for man than to have his destiny left in God's hands? More careful consideration, however, presents the following difficulty. If everything is determined by God (Heaven), retribution is meaningless at best and terribly unjust at worst. If God has predetermined man's response to every situation he will face in life so that he is compelled to act in a particular way, of what purpose is the law? It would be meaningless to charge man to obey the law when he has already been programmed by God either to obey or disobey. Moreover, if man has no choice he should neither be rewarded nor punished for his behavior. Considering that man has been given the Torah, and he has been charged to commit to the Torah as a way of life, we must postulate that the Creator has endowed man with free will. For good or for bad, man makes his own decisions and, at least to some extent, he is in control of his destiny.[6] Forcefully, Eliezer Berkovits writes:

> If God did not respect man's freedom to choose his course in personal responsibility, not only would the moral good and evil be abolished from the Earth, but also man himself would go with them. For freedom and responsibility is the essence of man. Without them man is not human. If there is to be man, he must be allowed to make his choice in freedom.[7]

In point of fact, the Torah indicates very clearly that man has free will. In Deuteronomy 30:15–16, 19 we read: "See I set before you this day life and prosperity, death and adversity. For I command you this day to love the Lord your God, to walk in His ways, and to keep His commandments, His laws and His norms, that you may thrive and increase . . . *Choose life*—if you and your offspring would live . . ."

Man would not have been charged to choose life had he not been endowed with free will. There is no force on Earth or in Heaven that compels man to make a particular choice, says Nahmanides.[8] An

---

6. We shall leave the matter of how to reconcile man's free will with God's omniscience for another time.

7. Eliezer Berkovits, Faith *after the Holocaust* (New York: Ktav, 1973), p. 105.

8. Cf. M. Nahmanides in his commentary on Deuteronomy 30:15; also Rabbenu B'haye ad loc. who makes the same point.

interesting comment is made in the Talmud that indicates the extent of man's freedom of choice.

> R. Huna said: From the Pentateuch, the Prophets, and the Writings it may be shown that one is allowed to follow the road he wishes to pursue. From the Pentateuch, as it is written, "And God said to Balaam, 'Do not go with them.'" And then it is written ["If these men have come to invite you"] "you may go with them" . . . From the Writings, as it is written, "If he is of the scorners, He will [be allowed] to speak scorn and [if] of the meek, he will show forth grace."[9]

Clearly, even if man chooses to act contrary to a command revealed to him by God directly, as in the case of Balaam, he is not held back. Understandably, he may be punished for doing so, but he is free to make his own choice.

There is another difficulty presented by the principle of providence that should be of concern to us. We have already pointed out that one of the Divine attributes is "long suffering." God does not exact retribution immediately; He awaits man's return; perchance he will repent his sins. If he truly regrets his sins and returns to God sincerely, his sins are forgiven; his slate is clean, and for all intents and purposes, he begins his life anew. This Divine gift to man is called *Teshuvah* (literally, "return"). The prophet spelled it out quite clearly: "Let the wicked give up his ways, the sinful man his plans; let him turn back to the Lord, and He will pardon him; to our God, for He freely forgives."[10] In point of fact, God wants the wicked to return to Him and be forgiven. Again, the prophet spells it out clearly: "Say to them: As I live—declares the Lord God—it is not My desire that the wicked shall die, but that the wicked turn from his [evil] ways and live. Turn back, turn back from your evil ways, that you may not die O House of Israel."[11] Our sages took this statement one step further. On the verse "Surely He

---

9. *Makkot* 10b.
10. Isaiah 55:7.
11. Ezekiel 33:11.

scorns the scorners, but He gives grace to the lowly"[12] the sages commented: "If one comes to cleanse himself, he is helped."[13] One of the beautiful prayers of the *Ne'elah* service for Yom Kippur begins with the words, "You give [Your] hand to the transgressors and Your right hand is stretched forth to receive the repentant." One who attempts to repent his sin but for some reason is having difficulty, such a person is helped by God to complete the gesture.

All this is understandable and certainly acceptable when dealing with the righteous. Their sins are few in number, and they deserve to be given the opportunity to repent. When the wicked are also given this opportunity, however, we cannot help but voice objection. After all, while God waits for the wicked to repent, the innocent are being abused, maimed, and killed. Is this just? We would prefer that God not be long-suffering with the wicked, but that they be punished immediately. Now while this might be preferable, it would clearly be unjust. There must be parity in God's system of justice. Every human being must be treated equally. Note the words of Eliezer Berkovits:

> While God waits for the sinner to turn to Him, there is oppression, persecution and violence among men. Yet, there seems to be no alternative. If man is to be, God must be long suffering with him; He must suffer man . . . While God tolerates the sinner He must abandon the victim . . . This is the ultimate tragedy of existence . . . It is the tragic paradox of faith that God's direct concern for the wrongdoer should be directly responsible for so much pain and sorrow on Earth.[14]

We cannot resolve this paradox of faith. We must accept it as a "given" and link it with all the other aspects of life that are incomprehensible. We must accept God's judgment as binding and His system of justice as proper. Our thinking must reflect the words of Isaiah, who said, "For My thoughts are not your thoughts, neither are your ways My ways, declares the Lord."

---

12. Proverbs 3:34.
13. *Shabbat* 104a.
14. Eliezer Berkovits, op. cit., p. 106.

I

Let us now address some of the references to providence in the books of the Prophets and the Writings.

I NATURE

1. "The Heavens declare the glory of God, the sky proclaims His handiwork" (Psalm 19:2).

To contemplate the vastness of the universe, and to study the information we already have concerning the multiplicity of systems that operate in our solar system alone, is to be awe-stricken. The more one studies these sophisticated systems and the more familiar one becomes with their operation, the more one is convinced of the existence of God, the Creator who set things into motion and governs their operation continuously. This irrefutable truth inspires a feeling of reverence and love of God.[15] The term "Heaven" in the above verse is inclusive of everything in the universe with the exception of the planet Earth.[16] The Heavens testify to God's concern with the world in the past. The sky, the source of rain, assures man that God is concerned with the world and the welfare of its inhabitants in the present.[17] This concern is a manifestation of Divine providence.

---

15. Cf. M. Malbim, commentary on Psalm 19:2. An interesting comment is made by Bachya Ibn Pakuda in *Duties of the Heart* (New York: Feldheim, 1970), *Shaar HaBehinah*, p. 167 who writes: "Wonderful it is that among the great works of the Creator, which the human eye beholds, the Heavens are always present. For wherever on Earth a man stands he sees above his head a hemisphere of firmament encompassing the Earth. And when he contemplates it thoughtfully, he will realize that the one who created it by His will is infinite in power, wisdom and greatness. For the sight of any example of architecture of the ancients arouses in us wonder at their ability to make anything like it . . . Now if such very small and petty work . . . looms so large in our sight, how exceedingly indeed should we marvel at the infinite greatness of Him who created the Heavens and the Earth."

16. Cf. S. R. Hirsch, *Torah Commentary* (London: Isaac Levy, 1959), Genesis 1:1.

17. Ibid.

The Meaning and Significance of Providence

2. *"Whatever the Lord desires he does in Heaven and Earth, in the seas and all the depths" (Psalm 135:6).*

3. *"[He is the] Maker of Heaven and Earth, the sea and all that is in them; who keeps faith forever"(Psalm 146:6).*

God created Heaven and Earth and all that exists in Heaven and on Earth: the host of angels in Heaven and all forms of life that exist on the Earth as well as that, which exists in the oceans and the seas. What's more, He is in complete control over all.[18] Although God had designated the Heavens to be His realm, so to speak, and the Earth to be the realm of man,[19] when He revealed the Torah He nullified that decree. For in Exodus 19:20 we read: "The Lord came down upon Mount Sinai . . . and Moses went up." Indeed, whatever the Lord desires he does.[20] As the Creator of all, God shows His faithfulness to all. In the words of S. R. Hirsch: "He alone is the One who has always proven to be dependable and faithful, for there are no limits to His essence and to His power.[21]

4. *"By the word of the Lord the Heavens were made, by the breath of His mouth all their host" (Psalm 33:6).*

The Lord created the Heavens and the Earth by willing them into existence. He exerted no physical effort in creation. Echoing the words of the Psalmist, the Midrash comments: "Neither with toil nor with strain did the Holy One blessed be He create the world, but by His word." The Heavens and everything in the Heavens—i.e., the sun, the moon, the stars, and the planets—were created all at once on the first day of creation. Although the Earth was created on the first day, its multiple components were created on the subsequent six days that followed.[22] As we have already indicated, by definition the term

---

18. Cf. Ibn Ezra and Radak commentaries on Psalm 146:6.
19. Cf. Psalm 115:16.
20. Cf. *Shemot Rabbah* 12:4.
21. S. R. Hirsch commentary, ad loc.
22. M. Malbim, commentary on Psalm 33:6.

shamayim ("Heavens") includes all things in the universe with the exception of the Earth.[23] The fact that the Divine name *Havayah* appears here rather than *E-lohim* indicates that the natural laws that operate in the Heavens (universe) are to some extent governed by man's behavior on Earth.[24]

5. *"For He spoke and it was; He commanded and it endured"* (Psalm 33:9).

The most obvious and perhaps the greatest manifestation of Divine providence is the creation of the world. The world was created by the word of God. Man cannot in any way alter the nature of God's creations. So they were created and so they will remain forever.[25] The endurance and the viability of the Earth are totally dependent on God's providential hand. He alone created the law of nature by which the Earth is governed and sustained. He alone brings the rains in their season, and He alone prevents these rains from overrunning the Earth and destroying everything in its path. "One mere signal from Him would suffice to bring to a standstill all that world order which He Himself has instituted and upon the stability of which men base all their hopes and plans."[26] The Earth's total dependency on God should humble man. It should inspire him to fear God and obey Him lest He relinquish His providential hand and the Earth is destroyed.[27]

6. *"He heaps up the oceans waters like a mound, stores the deep in vaults"* (Psalm 33:7).

Originally, the oceans covered the land. Had the planet Earth remained in that condition, there could be no land life. In Genesis 1:9 we read: "God said: 'Let the water below the sky be gathered into one area, that

---

23. Cf. S. R. Hirsch, commentary on Genesis 1:1.
24. Ibid., Genesis 2:4.
25. Cf. Radak, commentary on Psalms 33:9.
26. S. R. Hirsch, commentary, ad loc.
27. Cf. M. Malbim, commentary, ad loc.

The Meaning and Significance of Providence

the dry land may appear." God gathered the waters into heaps, so to speak, enabling the land to appear. Eventually the land would dry up and be ready to sustain life: plants, animals, and finally man, who was the next step in the Divine plan of creation.

7. *"[He] Who stills the raging seas, the raging waves, and tumultuous peoples" (Psalm 65:8).*

Although it is within the nature of the seas to rage, God at times sees fit to still the raging waters clearly establishing His total control of nature. What is interesting is that in this verse we are also told that God stills tumultuous peoples. The implication of the parallelism is clear: what God does in nature is to a great extent connected with human behavior. We certainly know this to true with regard to rain. In its season and in moderation, rain is a blessing; out of season and in overabundance it can be a curse.[28]

8. *"It is I who made the Earth, and the men and the beasts who are on the Earth, by My great might and My outstretched arm; and I gave it to whomever I deem proper" (Jeremiah 27:5).*

Since I created the Earth and everything upon it, mineral, animal, and man, it is all Mine, says God. The creation was accomplished through My great might, but I maintain the Earth through My outstretched arm that is continuously functioning on the Earth since the beginning of time.[29] The Earth and the animals are programmed to fulfill the Divine will, but man has been endowed with free will. Of his own volition, he must fulfill what has been ordained for him by God.

---

28. Note Deuteronomy 11:13–14: "If, then, you obey the commandments that I enjoin upon you this day . . . I will grant the rain for your land in season, the early rain and the late . . ."

29. Cf. M. Malbim, commentary on Jeremiah 27:5. Undoubtedly, Rashi had this verse in mind when on the opening verse in Genesis I he commented: "All the Earth belongs to the Holy One, blessed be He. He created it and gave it to whom He pleased."

9. *"I form the light and create darkness; I make peace and create evil; I am the Lord that does all these things" (Isaiah 45:7).*

God created physical light and darkness on the first day of creation. In Genesis 1:5 we read: "And God called the light day, and the darkness He called night. And there was evening and there was morning, a first day." The Talmud teaches: "Whatever the All-Merciful does is for good."[30] Everything that has been created has a specific function and a specific purpose in the world. Even darkness has its function and purpose in the world. It is the mother of life for it is the environment in which life begins. Plant life begins in the darkness of the soil; animal and human life begin in the darkness of the womb. But what is the meaning of peace in the context of this verse? In Job 25:2 we read: "Dominion and dread are His; He imposes peace in His heights." Peace means harmony. God creates harmony among the multiplicity of angels and elements in Heaven. In recognition of this, we petition God: "May He who makes peace [harmony] in His heights make peace [harmony] for us and all Israel." The term "evil" in this context may denote suffering and refer to Divine punishment of the wicked. For this, too, is a manifestation of Divine providence. All of the above taken into consideration, we can understand why the Divine name "Lord" appears here.

10. *"He makes clouds rise from the end of the Earth; He makes lightning for the rain; He releases the wind from His vaults" (Psalm 135:7).*

11. *"Sing to the Lord a song of praise, chant a hymn with a lyre to our God, who covers the Heavens with clouds, provides rain for the Earth, makes mountains put forth grass . . . He lays down snow like fleece, scatters frost like ashes. He tosses down hail like crumbs . . . He issues a command—it melts them; He breathes—the waters flow" (Psalm 147:8, 16–18).*

The omnipotence of God is clearly demonstrated by the rain cycle. And whether the rains are rains of blessing that bring successful crops or

---

30. *Berakhot* 60b.

rains of curse that bring punishing floods and devastation,[31] they are also testimony to God's concern for man, His providential hand in the world. For it is quite obvious that God's purpose is not merely the preservation of the environment, as important as that might be. Water is life! Without water, man cannot endure. Water rights figure heavily in treaties between nations in whose territory this precious commodity is scarce. The fact that every culture and religion has its prayers for rain is testimony to the fact that rain is an absolute necessity for man's survival. But man must earn the blessing of rain. Note the words of S. R. Hirsch: "Even as all other creatures receive their nourishment and joy of life from God's own order of nature, so man, too, may look to Divine providence for his own sustenance. While other creatures receive such gifts from God unconditionally, however, man must first show himself to be worthy of salvation."[32] The consistent natural process that transforms water into snow, or frost or hail and back into water, is an example of how God works within the realm of nature. It demonstrates nature's conformity with God's will and serves as a lesson to man that he must conform to the Divine will as well.

13. *"He reckoned the numbers of the stars; to each He gave its name" (Psalm 147:4).*

Names have meaning. Each star has its function in the universe. This, too, is a manifestation of the providential hand of God in nature. God, who created the stars, gave each of them an appropriate name in accordance with its function on Earth.[33] They are beloved to God, and that is why he counts them. The nation of Israel is as beloved to God as the stars, and He counts them as well. Indeed, in Exodus 1:1 we read: "These are the names of the sons of Israel who came to Egypt with Jacob, each coming with his household."[34]

---

31. In *Taanit* 2b we read: "Should Nisan terminate and then rain fall it is a sign of [God's] anger."
32. S. R. Hirsch, *The Psalms* (New York: Feldheim, 1966), Psalm 147:15.
33. Cf. Radak, commentary on Psalms 147:4.
34. *Shemot Rabbah* 1:2.

14. "The eyes of all look to you expectantly, and You give them their food when it is due. You give it open-handedly, feeding every creature to its heart's content" (Psalm 145:15, 16).

15. "All of them look to you to give them food when it is due. When You give it to them, they gather it up; when You open Your hand, they are well satisfied" (Psalm 104: 27, 28).

16. "You make the grass grow for the cattle and herbage for man's labor that he may get food out of the Earth—wine that cheers the hearts of men, oil that makes the face shine, and bread that sustains man's life" (Psalm 104:14–15).

All creatures, those on land as well as those in the sea, look expectantly to God upon whom they rely for food. Some need vegetation, others need meat. It is not nature that is their benefactor; it is the Almighty. Their very lives are dependent upon Him. At times they will receive enough to sustain them but no more. Other times, He gives open-handedly, and they have more than enough to be fully sated. We have no way of knowing the considerations taken into account with regard to the sustenance of animals, but we do believe that man's sustenance is dependent in some way upon his behavior. Moreover, S. R. Hirsch writes: "Man owes his daily sustenance not to accident . . . he owes it to the rule of God Himself which freely commands the forces of nature and society and leads both to fulfill His purposes."[35] The recurring theme "the Earth with its components that operate by the law of nature was not created for its own sake but for man's benefit and his moral training" appears here once more. Note the words of Bahya Ibn Pakuda: "When this will have become clear to a human being, and his recognition of the verity of God's loving-kindness will have become strong, he will put his trust in Him, give himself up completely to Him, leave the guidance of his life to him, never suspect the justice of his sentence nor get angry at what He has chosen for him . . ."[36]

---

35. S. R. Hirsch, op. cit., Psalm 136:1.
36. Bahaya Ibn Pakuda, op. cit., *Shaar HaBitahon*, p. 301.

The Meaning and Significance of Providence

17. *"You take care of the Earth and irrigate it; You enrich it greatly with the channel of God full of water; you provide grain for men; for so do You prepare it. Saturating its furrows, leveling its ridges, You soften it with showers, You bless its growth. You crown the year with Your bounty; fatness is distilled in Your paths; the pasturelands distill it; the hills are girded with joy. The meadows are clothed with flocks, the valleys mantled with grain; they raise a shout, they break into song"* (Psalm 65:10–14).

How beautifully the Psalmist describes the wonders of God as He works through nature. Here again, the verse focuses on the fact that the flourishing of nature is not an end in itself but serves frequently as a means through which God rewards or punishes man. S. R. Hirsch writes: "If the flourishing and blossoming of the soil were an end in itself, then God would never permit drought to strike or crops to fail, and the Earth would be in full flower eternally. But the growth of the fruit of the soil has its purpose to advance the moral training of mankind."[37]

18. *"You alone are the Lord. You made the Heavens, the highest Heavens, and all their host, the Earth and everything upon it, the seas and everything in them. You keep them all alive and the host of Heaven worship You"* (Nehemiah 9:6).

This verse is a fitting summary and conclusion to our discussion of Divine providence in nature. The creation of the universe is a manifestation of unbounded Divine compassion. The nourishment and preservation of the universe from the time it was created until now is clear testimony to Divine providence. An interesting point is emphasized in the Talmud: "Rav Judah said in Rav's name: 'Of all that the Holy One blessed be He created in His world, He did not create a single thing without purpose.'"[38] Of course, it stands to reason that God does not perform purposeless acts. Everything that has been created has a purpose in the world. The challenge to man is to discover the purpose

---

37. S. R. Hirsch, commentary on Psalm 65:10.
38. *Shabbat* 77b.

and function of all things and in this way benefit from his discoveries. There is another point of interest here that is worth noting. In response to creation the prophet tells us that the "host of Heaven" worship the Lord. Is this meant to be taken literally or symbolically? According to our sages, the components of the universe, i.e., the sun, the moon, the stars, and the planets are animate and intellectual.[39] They are capable of comprehending things, and they have an influence on what happens in the world. When Nehemiah wrote, "the host of Heaven worship You," he meant his words to be taken literally. When the Psalmist wrote, "The Heavens declare the glory of God, the sky proclaims His handiwork" (Psalm 19:2), he meant his words to be taken literally. Maimonides writes: "It is a great error to think that this is merely a figure of speech for the verbs *l'saper* ("to declare") and *l'hagid* ("to proclaim") when joined together . . . are only used of intellectual beings."[40] Of course, we are not privy to how this form of worship manifests itself, but we must accept it as a fact.

II DIVINE JUDGMENT

1. *"The Lord looks down from Heaven; He sees all mankind. From His dwelling place He gazes on all the inhabitants of the Earth—He who fashions their hearts for one another, who discerns all their doings"* (Psalms 33: 13–15).

2. *"It is He who judges the world with righteousness, rules the nations with equity"* (Psalm 9:9).

Although the Lord's dwelling place is in Heaven, so to speak, Judaism teaches that He is intimately concerned with what takes place on Earth.[41] He has a general plan that focuses on the preservation of the Earth and the multiplicity of species that inhabit the Earth. Set from the beginning, the sages refer to this plan as *hashgahah klalit*. With regard

---

39. Cf. M. Maimonides, op. cit., Part II, chap. v, p. 34.
40. Ibid.
41. Mezudot David, commentary on Psalm 33:13

to man, however, God is concerned not only with the species but with the individual members of mankind as well, rewarding or punishing each and every human being according to his behavior. Our sages refer to this concern as *hashgahah pratit*. God's concern for man is directed from His dwelling place.[42] Though He resides, as it were, in the Heavens, He knows what transpires on the Earth, says the Psalmist.[43] No one can escape Divine scrutiny. Having created man, God knows the abilities and the limitations of each and every human being, and He sets goals for him accordingly. He expects every human being to fulfill these goals to the best of his ability, and He judges every human being in terms of how well he has fulfilled them.[44] Of particular importance is the promise that He will fight the battle of the oppressed and judge the oppressors with equity.[45]

3. *"He guards the steps of His faithful, but the wicked perish in darkness for not by strength shall man prevail" (I Samuel 2:9).*

Experience teaches us that some people are stricken by plagues or other mishaps in nature while the rest of humanity escape that fate. We must be careful not to attribute this to physical strengths or weaknesses. What happens to man depends on the level of perfection he has attained. Our tradition teaches us that the greater the perfection the greater the protection or Divine providence." Moreover, when the time of retribution comes, the strength of the wicked will not save them.[47]

4. *"The Lord tries the righteous man; but loathes the wicked one who loves injustice" (Psalm 11:5).*

At times, the Lord conceals His providential acts from the righteous man; He may even afflict him with suffering and have him witness what

---

42. M. Malbim, commentary ad loc.
43. Ibn Ezra and Mezudot David commentaries on Psalm 33:13.
44. S. R. Hirsch op. cit., Psalm 33:13.
45. Cf. M. Malbim, commentary on Psalm 9:9.
46. See note 66.
47. Mezudot David, commentary on I Samuel 2:9.

appears to be the good fortune of the wicked. But this is to test his sincerity. Will he remain righteous or will he falter in adversity? Others maintain that it is a manifestation of Divine compassion. The Lord only tests the righteous for He knows that they will prevail.[48] In point of fact, if the righteous experienced only reward and the wicked only punishment, righteousness would not result from a sense of duty or devotion to the Supreme Being; it would be a matter of good practical judgment. There are times when a wicked person is spared from punishment because it would do him no good; it would not lead to repentance. In the final analysis, however, "the books must be balanced." Whether in this world or the next, the righteous receive their reward and the wicked their punishment. Indeed, the Talmud teaches: "The Holy One blessed be He brings suffering to the righteous in this world in order that they may inherit the future world."[49] The rationale for such suffering is as follows: Let them experience some suffering in this world in punishment for the few sins that they have committed (for no one is so perfect that he has never sinned) so that they can enter the next world with a clean slate. Such concern for the righteous of the world is, indeed, a manifestation of Divine providence of the highest order.

5. *"God [E-lohim] vindicates the righteous; God [E-l] makes His indignation felt each day" (Psalm 7:12)."*

It is of *E-lohim,* the Judge of the world, that the Psalmist speaks here. The vindication of the righteous is not a manifestation of Divine compassion, which would have called for the name *Havayah,* but of justice. The punishment of the wicked is also a manifestation of justice, powerful Divine retribution. This is indicated by the name *E-l.* What's more, since the Supreme Being has implanted a conscience within the heart of every human being, the wicked are ridden with guilt, They feel Divine indignation every day of their lives.[50]

---

48. Bereshit Rabbah 32:2.
49. *Kiddushin* 40b.
50. Cf. S. R. Hirsch, commentary on Psalm 7:12

The Meaning and Significance of Providence

6. *"For the Lord cherishes the ways of the righteous, but the way of the wicked is doomed" (Psalm 1:6)*

Havayah loves the ways of the righteous for they are in pursuit of the goals that He has ordained for them. Divine providence will, therefore, facilitate the attainment of these goals. The ways of the wicked, on the other hand, are contrary to the Divine will; they need no special Divine attention to thwart their fulfillment. They are doomed to failure from the beginning.[51] Moreover, Divine providence will secure the righteous in their ways so that they do not falter while the wicked will be deprived of providence and left to fend for themselves in the world.[52]

7. *"The eyes of the Lord are on the righteous, His ears attentive to their cry. The face of the Lord is set against evil doers to erase their names from the Earth" (Psalm 34:16-17).*

Havayah perceives the deeds of the righteous for what they are. He rewards them by giving them all that they need for their welfare, regardless of whether they asked for it or not. And when, out of need, they offer prayers to Him, He hears them and reacts accordingly. This is another example of the principle put forth by Maimonides that providence is in proportion to man's perfection.[53]

8. *"He, who fashions the hearts of them all, who discerns all their doings" (Psalm 33:15).*

It is no more than logical to assume that God, who designed and created man, knows everything about him. Though man is free to make his own decisions in life, God knows the way man's mind works; He is privy to man's innermost thoughts and aspirations. Man can hide nothing from God.[54] Others understand the opening words to mean "He who fashions their hearts for one another."[55] God has fashioned man to live

---

51. S. R. Hirsch, op. cit., Psalm 1:6.
52. Cf. Mezudot David commentary, ad loc.
53. Cf. M. Maimonides, op. cit., Part III, chap. xviii, p. 81.
54. Radak, commentary on Psalm 33:15.
55. S. R. Hirsch translation.

in society. Man must be concerned not merely with his own welfare but with the welfare of his fellow man as well. Man's merit in God's eyes is measured by how well he lives up to the purpose for which he was created, and his concern for his fellow man ranks high in that evaluation.[56]

III DIVINE COMPASSION

1. *"For the Lord is good; His steadfast love is eternal; His faithfulness is for all generations"* (Psalm 100:5).

2. *"The Lord is good to all, and His mercy is upon all His works"* (Psalm 145:9).

As a manifestation of Divine compassion, God is good to all people. At times, even the wicked enjoy God's favor. With regard to the latter, God exerts His influence upon them in order to bring them to repent their ways. Nonetheless there is a difference. The Talmud offers the following analogy: "This may be compared to a man who has an orchard. When he irrigates it, he irrigates the whole, but when he prunes, he prunes only the best."[57] While it is true that God cares for all people, the righteous are cared for with greater concern. But Divine compassion is not limited to man. He is merciful to all living creatures by ensuring the preservation of the species.[58] A beautiful thought was expressed by S. R. Hirsch in this regard when he wrote: "Every living thing was given the first and most precious possession through its creation, when it was given life, and anything that preserves and enhances that life is an extension and enhancement of this first great good."[59] Unlike man's love, the Lord's love is unwavering. It is eternal, and it inspires His mercy.

---

56. S. R. Hirsch, commentary ad loc.
57. *Sanhedrin* 39b.
58. M. Malbim, commentary on Psalm 145:9.
59. S. R. Hirsch, commentary ad loc. Most people are too blind intellectually to recognize the benefits God grants to His creatures. See Bahya Ibn Pekuda, *Duties of the*

3. *"Truly then the eye of the Lord is on those who fear Him, who wait for His faithful care to save them from death, to sustain them in famine"* (Psalm 33:18–19).

Divine providence manifests itself upon the righteous whose life style is in strict accordance with the Torah. They entrust their fate to God without reservation. Because they fear God and anticipate His faithful care, He comes to their aid in difficult times. It is a manifestation of "measure for measure" retribution.[60] In point of fact, the precedent was already set in the time of the Exodus from Egypt. He saved the Israelites from being killed by the Egyptians and He sustained them through their wanderings in the wilderness.[61] One should not take the examples given by the Psalmist to be limited to those situations exclusively, however.

4. *"As a father has compassion for his children, so the Lord has compassion for those who fear Him"* (Psalm 103:13).

The analogy is a poignant one. A father has compassion for his child. Yet, he doesn't want to spoil him by giving him everything he wants. He loves his child, and shows compassion to him whenever the opportunity presents itself. But he also knows that what the child desires is not always the best thing for him. At times, it may be necessary to deny the child what he wants. It may make him angry and frustrate him, but ultimately it is for the child's benefit. We must accept this principle with regard to God's way with the world. Though it may be painful in the short term, even incomprehensible to our limited minds, it is ultimately for the general welfare of the world. As our sages remarked: "Whatever the All-Merciful does is for good." It is important to recognize, however, that this statement does not imply that God *feels* compassion towards mankind, for it is inappropriate to attribute emotions to God. In the words of Maimonides: "Such instances do not imply that God is

---

Heart (New York: Feldheim, 1970), *Shaar HaBehinah*, p. 125, who lists three reasons for this.

60. Cf. Sanhedrin 90a: "In all measures [of punishment or reward) taken by the Holy One, blessed be He, the Divine act befits the [human] deed."

influenced by a feeling of mercy, but that acts similar to those which a father performs for his son, out of pity, mercy, and real affection, emanate from God solely for the benefit of His pious men, and are by no means the result of any impression or change [produced in God]."[62] There is another facet to the father–child analogy. A devoted father does what he can to effect a proper marriage for his children; God does even more. The Talmud teaches: "Forty days before the creation of a child, a Heavenly voice issues forth and proclaims: 'The daughter of A is for B . . .'"[63]

5. *"The father of orphans, the champion of widows [is] God in His holy habitation"* (Psalm 68:6).

6. *"The Lord watches over the stranger; He gives courage to the orphan and widow, but makes the path of the wicked torturous"* (Psalm 146:9).

God is far removed from the world in which we live; yet, in many ways, He is ever so close. While He is concerned with each and every human being, He pays particular attention to orphans and widows who all too often are bereft of the concern of others.[64] He will give them the courage to endure their misfortune and rise above it.[65] His essence transcends the universe, but His attributes are clearly immanent. In the words of S. R. Hirsch: "He seems exalted in His unattainable greatness . . . [He] is still . . . the Father and Defender of the most forsaken of His creatures."[66] In the Talmud we find the following note: "Rabbi Johanan said: In every passage where you find the greatness of God mentioned, there you also find His humility . . . It is . . . stated in the Writings, 'Sing to God chant hymns to His name, extol Him who rides the

---

62. M. Maimonides, op. cit., Part I, chap. 54, p. 195.
63. *Sotah* 2a. Some opine that this refers to first marriages only. Be that as it may, whether or not they find their destined mate is dependent on many variables.
64. Ibn Ezra, commentary on Psalm 146:9.
65. Cf. S. R. Hirsch, commentary ad loc.
66. S. R. Hirsch, commentary on Psalm 68:6.

clouds' . . . and it is written afterwards, 'the father of the fatherless, the champion of the widows.'"[67]

7. "The Lord makes poor and makes rich; He casts down, He also lifts high" (I Samuel 2:7).

8. "It is God who gives judgment; He brings down one man, He lifts up another. There is a cup in the Lord's hand with wine that has ceased to ferment but it is full of mixture; from this He pours; all the wicked of the Earth drink, draining it to the very dregs" (Psalm 75:8,9).

Contrary to what one may think, poverty and wealth are not in man's hands; they are in the hands of God. Wealth is not a permanent state of affairs. With little more than a blink of an eye many a rich man has been transformed into a pauper, and many paupers have become rich men overnight, to be sure. It is not unusual for God to take the wealth from the wicked and distribute it among the righteous poor.[68] The Midrash teaches: "He makes ladders in Heaven raising one and lowering another, enriching one and impoverishing another."[69] The destiny of man is not simply a matter of reward or punishment. God is not merely a Judge; He is the teacher of mankind. In determining man's lot, God takes into account the future needs of every individual as well as his past and present deeds. The "wine" that is in the Lord's hand is fully fermented and mixed, indicating that what is meted out to man is given to him with careful deliberation and with compassion. Note the words of S. R. Hirsch: ". . . it is full of mixture mixed precisely in those proportions that it should have . . . undiluted good fortune does not agree with the average man . . . for each person there is designed a specific mixture that corresponds to his own particular requirements."[70]

---

67. *Megillah* 31a.
68. Cf. *Yalkut Shimoni*, Part II, no. 85.
69. Midrash *Tanhuma: Vayishlah* 10.
70. S. R. Hirsch, commentary on Psalm 75:9.

9. *"It is I, I—who for My own sake—wipe your transgressions away and remember your sins no more" (Psalm 43:25).*

God forgave the sins of Israel in the past, and He will continue to forgive them in the present as well as in the future, says the Psalmist. How different Divine compassion is from human compassion. Man is indeed capable of forgiving, but to forgive and not to remember or hold any ill feelings is compassion of such magnitude that it can only be attributed to God. It should be clearly understood, however, that it is not always man's righteousness that earns him forgiveness. At times, God forgives simply to safeguard His name. Were He to annihilate Israel in punishment for their sins, His name would be profaned in the eyes of the nations.[71]

10. *"He has not dealt with us according to our sins, nor has He requited us according to our iniquities. For as the Heavens are high above the Earth so great is His loving-kindness toward those who fear Him" (Psalm 103:10, 11).*

He is a forgiving God, whether the sin is the result of error or weakness. But there are times when, like a father that must punish his children in order to teach them right from wrong, God must punish us for our sins. Yet, even in those instances, the punishment is always relatively mild measured against the severity of the sin and as such it is a manifestation of loving-kindness rather than anger.[72] This Divine loving-kindness had an overwhelming effect upon the Jewish people to the extent that it has strengthened their commitment to God and to Torah.[73] The Heaven and Earth analogy is not meant to be taken simply in terms of spatial distance. It is the powerful influence of Heaven upon the Earth that is implied here as well. S. R. Hirsch writes: "The Earth is dependent upon all the extraterrestrial world and the overpowering influence of the latter has a . . . refining . . . effect upon everything that is part of

---

71. Cf. Radak and Mezudot David commentaries on Psalm 43:25.
72. Cf. M. Malbim, commentary on Psalm 103:10.
73. Cf. S. R. Hirsch, commentary ad loc.

the Earth."[74] The influence of Divine loving-kindness upon the Jewish people is compared to the influence of the Heavens upon the Earth.

11. "He raises the poor from the dust, lifts up the needy from the refuse heap to set them with the great, with the great men of His people" (Psalm 113:7, 8).

In the Talmud we read: "All is in the hands of Heaven with the exception of the fear of Heaven."[75] As we have already stated, there is no permanence to man's condition on Earth. It can change overnight. The poor can be lifted out of their state of poverty. The needy, who in their condition are defenseless and must subordinate themselves to the will of others, can suddenly be endowed with both the will, and the ability to actualize qualities they never knew they had, enabling them to be on a par with those whom they once served. This is the power of Divine providence. Neither economic nor sociological conditions can thwart the will of God. Indeed, nothing is beyond His jurisdiction or His ability.

12. "He sets the childless woman among her household as a happy mother of children" (Psalm 113:9).

God, the creator of the universe, can and does superimpose His will over nature to perform miracles. Among the most wonderful of such miracles is the granting of a child to the woman who is barren by nature. What better example can one find than Sarah and Rebecca, the two matriarchs of our people. Motherhood is a unique phenomenon. Resigned to a childless marriage, many barren women find other ways to fulfill the void in their lives, but deep in their hearts they know that nothing can really take the place of motherhood, the source of a woman's true happiness. When God opens a mother's womb and grants her a child, she assumes her most significant role in life. She becomes "a happy mother of children."

---

74. Ibid.
75. *Berakhot* 33b.

13. *"The Lord protects the unaware [simple]; I had been brought low but He grants me new life" (Psalm 116:6).*

The Talmud teaches: "One must not rely on miracles."[76] Man must take the initiative in resolving his problems. Knowing what to do and what not to do in a given situation, how to act and how to react, when to get involved and when to refrain from getting involved, is what differentiates the naïve child from the mature, experienced adult. Most adults are capable of making their own decisions in life and know enough to consult with others when the situation requires a more expert opinion. But life is fraught with potential dangers. Some situations pose dangers of which we are unaware; others pose dangers over which we have no control. Should we refrain from socializing with people because of the fear of contracting a communicable disease? Should we refrain from crossing the street for fear of being hit by a car; never go swimming out of fear of drowning? What are the parameters? Jewish law teaches that in terms of risk one may follow the practices of the majority of society and rely on Divine providence for protection.[77] "The Lord protects the unaware."

14. *"The steps of a man are made firm by the Lord, when He delights in his way. Though he stumbles, he does not fall down, for the Lord gives him support" (Psalm 37:23–24).*

15. *"The Lord supports all who stumble, and makes all who are bent stand straight" (Psalm 145:14).*

There are times when even the righteous stumble as they ascend the path of righteousness. After all, was it not King Solomon who said: "For there is not one good man on Earth who does what is best and doesn't

---

76. *Pesahim* 64b.
77. Cf. M. Feinstein, *Iggrot Moshe: Yoreh De'ah* (New York: Balshon, 1973), II, no. 49, who rules that it is permissible to take any risk that falls into the category of "the multitude has trodden thereupon" in which case one may rely on the principle "The Lord protects the unaware [simple]."

err."⁷⁸ Though the righteous may stumble, they do not fall down totally; the Lord supports them, enabling them to continue their ascension to righteousness.⁷⁹ What is of the utmost importance is to see things in their true perspective. One is about to fail either in his faith in God or in his commitment to Torah. Suddenly he sees things from a new perspective. He perceives the error in his thinking, and he remains secure in his faith and in his commitment to *mitzvot*. This, too, must be understood as a manifestation of Divine providence.⁸⁰ From another perspective, the Talmud teaches: "No man bruises his finger here on Earth unless it was so decreed against him in Heaven, for it is written, 'The steps of a man are made firm by the Lord.'"⁸¹ Nothing that happens to man is merely by chance; everything he encounters has been decreed by the Lord.

16. *"The ear that hears, the eye that sees—the Lord made them both"* (Proverbs 20:12).

17. *"Shall He who implants the ear not hear, He who forms the eye not see?"* (Psalm 94:9).

In terms of intellect, the ears and the eyes are man's most important senses. In the beginning, his eyes are most important. For he begins to learn by seeing things. Later, his ears take on importance, for he learns by listening to the teachings of his parents. Still later in life, when he begins to read, his eyes become his most important entrées to knowledge.⁸² Is it logical to believe that the Lord, who conceived and created these magnificent organs of sight and hearing with which He has endowed man, is Himself unable to see and to hear? In His own unique way, the Lord perceives all.⁸³ Note the words of R. Judah Halevi: "The religious person never acts, speaks or thinks without

---

78. Ecclesiastes 7:20.
79. Cf. M. Malbim, commentary on Psalm 37:23, 24.
80. Cf. S. R. Hirsch, commentary on Psalm 145:14.
81. *Hullin* 7b.
82. Cf. Ralbag and Malbim commentaries on Proverbs 20:12.
83. Cf. S. R. Hirsch, commentary ad loc.

believing that he is observed by eyes which see and take note, which reward and punish and call to account for everything objectionable in word and deed."[84]

18. *"For the Lord grants wisdom; out of His mouth comes knowledge and discernment" (Proverbs 2:6).*

Wisdom, knowledge, and discernment are powers with which God has endowed man. They have made it possible for him to progress from generation to generation in his mastery of the secrets of the universe. Much to his credit, man has progressed at an astounding pace. When Solomon became the King of Israel the Lord appeared to him in a dream and asked him, "What shall I grant you?"[85] Solomon asked for wisdom. The Lord then responded: "I now do as you have spoken. I grant you a wise and discerning mind; there has never been one like you before nor will anyone like you arise again."[86] To have blessed man with the ability to master the universe is perhaps the greatest of all manifestations of Divine compassion and providence.[87]

IV PRAYER

1. *"The Lord is near to all who call Him, to all who call Him with sincerity. He fulfills the wishes of those who fear Him; He hears their cry and delivers them" (Psalm 145:18, 19).*

God transcends the universe, but He is immanent in the universe as well, for He offers a listening ear to the prayer of every human being.[88]

---

84. Judah Halevi, *The Kuzari* (New York: Pardes, 1946), pp. 127–128.
85. I Kings 3:5.
86. I Kings 3:12.
87. Cf. Bahya Ibn Pekuda, *Duties of the Heart*, (New York: Feldheim, 1970), Introduction, p. 15, who writes: "The noblest of the gifts which God bestowed on His human creatures, next to having created them with mature faculties of perception and comprehension, is wisdom."
88. It is important to recognize the phrase "God is near" does not imply physical proximity. Note the words of Maimonides: "The Supreme [God] is incorporeal, and

The Meaning and Significance of Providence

In Exodus 25:8 we read: "And let them make Me a sanctuary that I may dwell among them."[89] The prophet made this clear in his statement: "Holy, holy, holy is the Lord of Hosts: the whole Earth is full of His glory."[90] This is a paradox with which the believer must live. Indeed, God listens to every prayer, but there is one proviso—the prayer must be offered in sincerity. The nationality, race, or religion of the supplicant is irrelevant.[91] What is relevant is his motivation. Is his prayer a one-time appeal to God who never meant anything to him when things went well but to whom he now turns as a last resort simply because all else has failed? Some refer to such a gesture as "foxhole religion."[92] On the other hand, his appeal might be an expression of total dependency, a manifestation of his lifelong commitment to God to whom he offers prayers of thanksgiving in good times, when he experiences Divine beneficence, and prayers of petition in times of trouble or distress.[93] Motivation makes the difference. Note the words of Bahya Ibn Pekuda: "Repentance is only withheld from the sinner by his own evil mind and deceitful heart. But if he sincerely wishes to draw near to God, the gate of repentance is not closed to him and no hindrance exists to prevent his attaining his aim. On the contrary, God opens the gate of rectitude for him . . . and instructs him in the good way."[94]

---

consequently He does not approach or draw near a thing, nor can ought approach or touch Him; for when a being is without corporeality, it cannot occupy space, and all idea of approach . . . or proximity is inapplicable to such a being" (*Guide of the Perplexed*, Part I, chap. xviii, p. 71).

89. According to Jewish mystical thinking, the lowest of the ten *sefirot* ("Divine emanations") is called *Shekhinah* ("Divine Presence"). It is the facet of Divinity that is said to relate directly to the world. Perhaps in that sense we can speak of God as "dwelling" in this world.

90. Isaiah 6:3.

91. Radak, commentary on Psalm 145:18.

92. Nevertheless, it should be noted that even when the appeal to God derives from a life-threatening situation, as long as the supplicant has had a true change of heart his prayers are accepted. See commentary of S. R. Hirsch on Psalm 145:19.

93. Cf. S. R. Hirsch, commentary ad loc.

94. Bahya Ibn Pekuda, op. cit., *Shaar HaTeshuvah*, chap. 10, p. 175.

2. *"Call upon Me in time of trouble; I will rescue you and you shall honor Me"* (Psalm 50:15).

3. *"Cast your burden on the Lord and He will sustain you; He will never let the righteous man collapse"* (Psalm 55:23).

God gives man permission to call upon Him in prayer. He promises Man that if he does, he will be rescued. Still more, God tells man that he should not regard the right to pray simply as an accommodation to human frailty. On the contrary, to turn to God for help is the ultimate expression of praise for it recognizes Divine omnipotence. When man confronts God and appeals for help in time of travail, he honors God.[95] And when man's prayers are answered and he is redeemed from trouble, God is honored still more. For man will proclaim before all that his prayers were answered through Divine compassion.[96] When he is sincere, man can bring his troubles to God with confidence that his burden will be eased. Indeed, God will not forsake the righteous.[97]

4. *"In my time of trouble I call You, for You will answer me"* (Psalm 86:7).

5. *"When he calls on Me, I will answer him; I will be with him in distress; I will rescue him and make him honored; I will let him live to a ripe old age, and show him My salvation"* (Psalm 91:15).

Our sage remarked: "God yearns for the prayers of the righteous."[98] He does not shield man from the vicissitudes of life. He allows him to experience the world to his fullest capacity. When he encounters evil, anticipates danger, or is faced with a difficulty beyond his control, he can turn to God for guidance with the reassurance that his prayers will be heard and answered. Understandably, the answer may not always please him. Due to his limited understanding, he is often unable to

---

95. Cf. Rashi, commentary on Psalm 50:15
96. Mezudot David, commentary ad loc.
97. Mezudot David, commentary on Psalm 55:23.
98. *Yevamot* 64a.

fathom God's ways. Nonetheless, he must accept on principle that in the final analysis God's way is the best way.

6. *"The Lord is far from the wicked, but He hears the prayers of the righteous" (Proverbs 15:29).*

7. *"The sacrifice of the wicked is an abomination to the Lord, but the prayer of the upright pleases Him" (Proverbs 15:8).*

We have already presented the position of Maimonides that Divine providence operates in accordance with man's deeds.[99] The closer man is to God in terms of the fulfillment of his Divinely endowed potential and his observance of the laws of the Torah, the closer God is to him in terms of providence. A person is not expected to do more than what is in his capacity to do in the realm of Torah, but if he simply neglects what he is capable of doing, he is regarded as wicked, and providence will be withdrawn from him.[100] Some interpret, "The Lord is far from [the world] [because of] the wicked." At times, God "hides His face" [*hester panim*], so to speak, from the world, because of the wicked; i.e., He relinquishes His providential hand and allows nature to take its course, come what may. The prayers of the righteous in behalf of the world are most effective in such a situation, however. When God hears their sincere prayers, He reinstitutes providence in the world.[101] In the days of the Temple in Jerusalem, it was not the sacrifice but the sincerity with which it was brought that was of the essence. The prophets admonished the people severely for bringing sacrifices that were not accompanied by sincere repentance. The prayers of the righteous are always sincere;

---

99. M. Malbim, commentary on Proverbs 15:29. There is a difference of opinion on this matter among the sages. According to Maimonides Divine providence operates in man according to his intellect. The greater the intellect the greater the Divine providence. Cf. M. Maimonides, op. cit., Part III, chap. xvii, p. 78.

100. Cf. Bahya Ibn Pakuda, op. cit., *Shaar Heshbon HaNefesh*, chap. 3, p. 251.

101. Cf. J. Azubiv, *Tokhahot Mussar* (Livorno, 1871), Proverbs 15:29. Cf. *Sukkah* 14a: "Why are the prayers of the righteous likened to a pitchfork? To teach you that just as a pitchfork turns the corn from place to place in the barn, so the prayers of the righteous turn the mind of the Holy One blessed be He from the attribute of harshness to that of mercy."

they are accepted even without sacrifices.[102] According to the Midrash, the "wicked" here are the false prophets of the nations of the world; the "righteous" are the true prophets of Israel.[103]

5. *"He has turned to the prayer of the solitary, and has not spurned their prayer"* (Psalm 102:18).

This verse has been taken to apply to the individual as well as the nation of Israel as a collective. History will testify to the fact that Israel stands alone among the nations of the world. The words of Balaam in Numbers 23:9 ring clear today: "As I see them from the mountain tops, gaze on them from the heights, there is a people that dwells apart, not reckoned among the nations." The nation of Israel has but one friend: The Holy One blessed be He. He listens to their prayers and answers them; He will not spurn them. The same is true of the individual who despite well-meaning friends feels alone in his suffering. When he turns to God he finds a listening ear, ready to hear his outcry in pain and anxious to ease his suffering.

V ISRAEL

1. *"For the Lord has chosen Jacob for Himself, Israel, as His treasured possession"* (Psalm 135:4).

The Jewish people as a nation has been chosen by the Lord to teach the world ethics and morality. They are referred to here as "Jacob," for this name includes the entire nation, the most as well as the least accomplished individuals among them. The name "Israel" refers to the most noteworthy among the nation. The noteworthy among the nation are the Lord's most precious possession, and, to reiterate, they are subject to a special measure of Divine providence.[104] The Lord chose the Jewish people from among the nations of the world because they are

---

102. M. Malbim, commentary on Proverbs 15:8.
103. *Bereshit Rabbah* 52:7.
104. Cf. M. Malbim, commentary on Psalm 135:4.

the weakest. Their survival in a world that has made every effort to annihilate them is testimony to both the existence and the omnipotence of the Lord.[105]

2. *"Say then: Thus said the Lord God: I have indeed removed them from among the nations and have scattered them among the countries, and I have been to them a diminished sanctuary in the countries whither they have gone. Yet say: Thus said the Lord God: I will gather you from the peoples and assemble you out of the countries where you have been scattered, and I will give you the land of Israel"* (Ezekiel 11:16–17).

Though the people of Israel were exiled from their land in punishment for their sins, they have not lost favor in God's eyes. Although they no longer have the Sanctuary that stood in Jerusalem to which to come with their troubled hearts, God will be with them in their synagogues, the "diminished sanctuaries," in the countries of their exile. One should not take the importance of the "diminished sanctuary" lightly. The Midrash tells us that when one prays in the synagogue in this world, it is as if he prays in the Holy Temple that stood in Jerusalem.[106] In the synagogue, the Lord will hear their prayers, and as a result He will save them from their enemies.[107] In the Lord's time [according to some, it has already arrived], they will eventually be restored to their homeland, a true manifestation of Divine providence.

3. *"For I have spread you abroad as the four winds of the Heavens"* (Zechariah 2:10).

The love that God has for the people of Israel is unparalleled. They are compared to the winds that sustain the system that nourishes the world. The Talmud teaches the following: "What does this verse indicate? Were it to mean that Israel was to be scattered to the four corners of the world as *the four winds,* the verse would have said *to the four winds.* It can only mean that just as the world cannot exist without winds so the

---

105. Cf. S. R. Hirsch, commentary ad be.
106. Cf. *Yalkut Shimoni*, Part II, 5659; also Berakhot 10a.
107. Radak, commentary on Ezekiel 11:16.

world cannot exist without Israel."[108] But why is this true? Perhaps it is because God designated Israel as the conscience of the world. It exists and has been preserved through the centuries in order to teach mankind by example how to live by Divine ethics. This too is a manifestation of Divine providence.

4. *"The Lord will give strength to His people; the Lord will bless His people with peace" (Psalm 29:11).*

In the Messianic Era, the Lord will humble Israel's enemies. He will give strength to His people so that no nation will ever again dare to wage war against them. As a result, Israel will live in eternal peace, a blessing from which the world at large will benefit as well. As the prophet foretold: "Nation shall not take up sword against nation; they shall never again know war" (Isaiah 2:4). This blessing from God is perhaps the greatest manifestation of Divine providence revealed in Scripture.[109] In point of fact, the land of Israel itself is treated in a very special way as a manifestation of Divine providence. For the Talmud teaches: "The land Israel was created first and then the rest of the world . . . The land of Israel is watered by the Holy One blessed be He, and the rest of the world is watered by a messenger . . . the land of Israel is watered by the rain and the rest of the world by the residue . . . the land of Israel is watered first and then the rest of the world."[110]

---

108. *Avodah Zara* 10b.
109. Cf. *Megillah* 18a where peace is called the "Lord's blessing."
110. *Taanit* 10a.

7

WHEN GOD RELATES TO MAN

Were it not for the fact that God relates to man, all that we profess to know about the Supreme Being of the universe would be nothing more than conjecture. How fortunate is man that in the early history of the world God chose to relate to him and make known His will through the unique medium of prophecy. How fortunate we are that our ancestors, the patriarchs and the prophets of Israel, have been the recipients of Divine messages attained through prophecy. How fortunate we are that the Torah, the greatest prophecy of all time, was revealed to Moses our teacher at Mount Sinai to be the way of life of the Jewish people for all time.

Prophecy is a dialogue between man and God where God takes the initiative, in contradistinction from prayer, which is a dialogue between God and man where man takes the initiative. How does one qualify for prophecy? Maimonides teaches that prophecy rests only upon people who are wise, of strong moral fiber, physically fit, and in control of their passions. "When one abundantly endowed with these qualities . . ." writes Maimonides, "zealously training himself not to have a single thought of the vanities of the age . . . but keeping his mind concentrated on higher things . . . and contemplating the wisdom of God as displayed in His creatures, on such a man the spirit will descend."[1] However, unless these qualities are combined with the highest excellence of his imaginative faculty, i.e., the ability "to retain impressions by the senses, to combine them and chiefly to form images,"[2] he will not prophesy. It is important that we understand what Maimonides means here. He does not mean to imply that if a person has all these qualifications he will be able to prophesy at will. Since prophecy derives from God, the prophet can only prophesy when the "spirit of God" comes upon him. This will never occur if the prophet is melancholy or indolent. He must be cheerful and joyous before he can even anticipate that prophecy will come upon him.[3] It should also be understood that, for whatever reason, God might choose to withhold prophecy from an individual even if he has the qualifications.[4]

What is the purpose or function of prophecy? Maimonides teaches that prophecy is a gift bestowed by God upon man for his benefit, i.e., so that he can develop his mind and increase his knowledge concerning matters Divine; or for the benefit of the inhabitants of a particular city or kingdom, i.e., to restrain them from evil courses that they are pursuing. In such a case, he is given a sign to authenticate his prophecy. It should be noted, however, that Maimonides insists that a sign authenticates a prophet only when his contemporaries recognize him as a wise, ethical, and moral person who is indeed worthy of prophecy. If an individual is not properly prepared, says Maimonides, he cannot be a prophet. Nevertheless, an individual who preaches God's message and brings a sign should be accepted as a wise man, and the people of the

---

1. M. Maimonides, *Mishneh Torah: Foundations of the Torah* 7:1.
2. M. Maimonides, *Guide of the Perplexed* (New York: Hebrew Publishing Company), Part II, p. 174.
3. M. Maimonides, *Mishneh Torah*, op. cit., 7:4.
4. Cf. M. Maimonides, Guide *of the Perplexed*, op. cit., p. 162: "For we believe that even if one has the capacity for prophecy, and has duly prepared himself, it may yet happen that he does not actually prophesy. It is in that case, the will of God [that withholds from him the use of the faculty]."

community that he addresses should listen to him.⁵ The sign that the prophet brings need not involve a change in nature. It would be sufficient if he were to predict an event in the future and it came true.⁶ This is implied in the following verses: "And should you ask yourselves, 'How can we know that the oracle was not spoken by the Lord?' If the prophet speaks in the name of the Lord and the word does not come true, that word was not spoken by the Lord; the prophet has uttered it presumptuously: do not stand in dread of him."⁷

There is an exception to the above rule, however. If a prophet predicts a calamity such as a famine or a war and it does not materialize, he is not automatically discredited and branded a false prophet. As we have already learned, God is long-suffering; His compassion abounds in the world. He may have intervened in the historical process, averting or deferring the tragedy.⁸ On the other hand, Maimonides writes: "If the prophet, in the name of God, assures good fortune, declaring that a definitive event would come to pass, and the benefit promised has not been realized, he is unquestionably a false prophet; for no blessing decreed by the Almighty, even if promised conditionally, is ever revoked."

According to Maimonides there are eleven degrees of prophecy.⁹

1. The first degree is inspiration, where an individual is inspired by what is termed *Ruah haKodesh* ("the Holy Spirit") to do courageous acts, e.g., to save a person from death or to bring happiness to a large number of people. The individual is not encouraged to speak on a particular subject, only to act. All the judges of Israel possessed this quality. Maimonides adds: "Just as not all who have a true dream are prophets, so it cannot be said of everyone who has assisted in a certain undertaking . . . that

---

5. M. Maimonides, *Mishneh Torah*, op. cit., 7:7.
6. Ibid., 10:1.
7. Deuteronomy 18:21–22.
8. M. Maimonides, *Mishneh Torah*, op. cit., 10:4.
9. Cf. M. Maimonides, *Guide of the Perplexed*, op. cit., pp. 206–214. The first and second of these degrees are not actual prophecy.

the spirit of the Lord came upon him or that the Lord was with him or that he performed his actions by the Holy Spirit."[10]

2. The second degree is where an individual feels that something descended upon him and encouraged him to speak. He composes hymns, exhorts his fellow man, and discusses political or theological problems. He does this while fully awake. Such an individual is said to speak by the Holy Spirit. David composed the Psalms by the Holy Spirit, and Solomon, his three works, namely, Proverbs, Ecclesiastes, and Song of Songs. According to the Talmud, the book of Esther was written in this way.[11] The seventy elders of Israel[12] as well as Eldad and Medad[13] possessed this degree. Balaam spoke by the Holy Spirit.[14]

3. The third is the lowest degree of actual prophecy. It comes in a dream. The prophet usually introduces his prophecy with the words, "And the word of the Lord came to me." In a dream by night, he sees an allegory and its interpretation. Most of the allegories of the prophet Zechariah are of this category.

4. The fourth degree is where the prophet hears spoken words in a dream but does not see the speaker. This was the case with the prophet Samuel when he first began to prophesy.

5. The fifth degree is where a person in his dream addresses the prophet. This was the case in some of the prophecies of Ezekiel.

6. The sixth degree is where the prophet is addressed in his dream by an angel. All of the prophets were on this level at some time in their ministry.

7. The seventh degree is where it appears to the prophet that God is speaking to him in a dream. Isaiah, for example, writes: "And I saw the Lord, and I heard the voice of the Lord saying, 'whom shall I send, and who will go for us?'"[15]

8. The eighth degree is the first level of visions. The prophet sees

---

10. Ibid., pp. 207–208.
11. *Megillah* 7a.
12. Cf. Numbers 11:25.
13. Ibid., v. 26.
14. Cf. Ibid., 23:5.
15. Isaiah 6:1,8.

allegorical figures in a prophetic vision by day, but he hears nothing. Abraham had such a vision at the "covenant between the pieces."[16]

9. The ninth degree is where the prophet hears words in a vision by day as when Abraham was promised by God that his heir would be his son rather than his servant Eliezer.[17]
10. The tenth degree is where the prophet sees a man speaking to him in a vision by day. Abraham saw such a vision in the plain of Mamre[18] and Joshua in Jericho.[19]
11. The eleventh degree is where the prophet sees an angel who speaks to him in a vision by day. This occurred to Abraham at the sacrifice of Isaac.[20] With the exception of Moses, this level was the highest degree of prophecy that a prophet could attain.

Unlike prophecies that occur in dreams, Maimonides felt that it was improbable that a prophet would perceive God speaking to him in a vision. He based his theory on the verse, "In a *vision* I will make Myself known, in a *dream* I will speak to him."[21] Speaking is connected to the dream whereas the influence or action of the intellect (implied in the words "make Myself known") is connected to the vision.

Forty-eight men and seven women prophesied in Israel. The first prophet of the Jewish people was Abraham.[22] God revealed many things to Abraham, perhaps the most significant of which is the future of his descendants. He informed Abraham that his seed would be enslaved in a strange land for 400 years, after which they would be redeemed.[23] Jacob was a prophet as well. Before he died, he called his

---

16. Genesis 15:9,10.
17. Genesis 15:4.
18. Genesis 18:1
19. Joshua 5:13.
20. Genesis 22:15.
21. Numbers 12:6.
22. In Genesis 20:7 we find: "But you must restore the man's [Abraham] wife—since he is a prophet, he will intercede for you—to save your life."
23. Genesis 15:12.

sons together and revealed what would occur in the "end of days."[24] As mentioned above, the prophetic message was communicated in allegorical form to the prophets with the exception of Moses. The allegory did not need prolonged study or analysis, however; the prophet understood its interpretation immediately.[25] There were many prophets in Israel of whom we know nothing, for only those prophecies that were relevant to future generations in terms of a law or a lesson that they taught were preserved.[26] It is interesting to note that at least one prophet emerged from every tribe in Israel.

The prophets were not gods nor were they angels. In many ways they were ordinary people. They lived and died like ordinary people. They ate and drank, married, and had families. They were prone to the same sicknesses and diseases as their fellow man. They were not shielded by God from harm or given special protection against violence. They often put their lives on the line by challenging the established authority (the king) in order to deliver God's message. The great prophet Jeremiah, for example, was falsely accused by one of the priests, resulting in his imprisonment. It should be understood that the prophets had no special power to perform miracles. God performed miracles through the prophet, and that was for only one purpose—to authenticate the prophet's mission.[27] Neither were the prophets able to predict the future. God revealed events to them that would take place in the future but only when such an event was relevant to their mission.[28] Note the following: "It is not what the prophet predicts that stamps him as a prophet, but his ability to announce events in the name of God, by Divine order. Thus it is the origin of his message not its content which

---

24. Genesis 49:1.
25. M Maimonides, *Mishneh Torah*, op. cit., 7:3.
26. *Megillah* 14a and Rashi ad loc.
27. With regard to this point Maimonides makes an important clarification. In his *Mishneh Torah*, op. cit., 8:2 he writes: "It must be said that in every prophet who rises up after Moses, our Master, we do not believe because of the sign alone, as to say, 'If he delivers a sign we will listen to all his prophesying'; but because of the commandment that Moses commanded in the Torah and said, if he does give a sign, 'To him you shall listen'" (Deuteronomy 18:15).
28. Cf. Saadya Gaon, *The Book of Beliefs and Opinions*, trans. S. Rosenblatt (New Haven: Yale University Press, 1948), p. 149–150.

elevates it above the achievements of the human intellect."[29] It should be noted, however, that according to Maimonides if a prophet comes and seeks to deny the prophecies of Moses, he should not be accepted. He writes:

> The Torah accordingly ordains that even if the sign or wonder takes place, you are not to listen to the words of such a prophet since he shows a sign and wonder in order to deny what you saw with your own eyes [the revelation at Sinai]. Since we only accept signs [as a prophet's credentials] because we are so bidden in the commandment given by Moses, how shall we, on the strength of such a sign, accept a man as a prophet who seeks to repudiate Moses' prophecy for the truth of which we have evidence of our own eyes and ears?[30]

Let us elaborate on this a bit. The Torah clearly states that the *mitzvot* are timeless; they will always be relevant.[31] It is, therefore, incumbent upon every generation to commit itself to the fulfillment of the commandments. It is forbidden for any prophet to found a new religion based on a new set of laws or even to suggest that a particular law in the Torah be emended. He may neither add to nor subtract from the Torah. Neither may he offer an interpretation of any of the *mitzvot* that is not in line with what was transmitted to Israel by Moses our teacher. A prophet who preaches any of the above is regarded as a false prophet; he is to be put to death.[32] However, if an individual who has already been established as a prophet comes and tells us on one specific occasion to transgress a particular commandment, even several commandments, we must obey him. The single exception to this ruling is the commandment against idolatry.[33]

How did the prophet himself know that his prophecy was an

---

29. J. Breuer, *Fundamentals of Judaism* (New York: Philip Feldheim, 1949), p. 258.
30. M. Maimonides, *Mishneh Torah*, op. cit., 8:3.
31. "All this word which I command you, you shall observe to do; you shall not add to it nor take away from it" (Deuteronomy 13:1). We also find: "but the things that are revealed belong to us and to our children forever, that we may do all the words of this law" (Deuteronomy 30:12).
32. Cf. M Maimonides, *Mishneh Torah*, op. cit., 9:1.
33. Ibid., 9:3. As an example, Maimonides cites the case of the prophet Elijah who

authentic revelation from God? The prophet knew that what he had perceived was a message that came from God because a sign such as a pillar of fire, a cloud, or a light that did not come from an ordinary light source accompanied the encounter.[34] The sign would appear to him at the beginning and would remain there until the end.[35] Could the prophet not have been deluded? I. Epstein writes: "One of the best proofs that the prophets were not victims of self-illusion is provided by the harmony and agreement among all the prophets in regard to themselves and their mission."[36] Also to be considered is their humility. They felt that they were not qualified to assume the responsibility that came with prophecy. Not infrequently do we find that they pleaded with God not to be sent on their mission. Note the words of Moses: "Please, O Lord, I have never been a man of words either in times past or now that You have spoken to Your servant; I am slow of speech and slow of tongue."[37] The prophet Amos said to Amaziah, the priest: "I am not a prophet and I am not a prophet's disciple. I am a cattle breeder . . . but the Lord took me away from following the flock, and the Lord said to me, 'Go, prophesy to My people Israel.'"[38]

The greatest of all prophets was Moses. Of him the Torah testifies, "Never again did there arise in Israel a prophet like Moses, whom the Lord singled out face to face."[39] Moses was differentiated from the

---

offered sacrifices outside the Temple, which was forbidden. This was an extenuating circumstance that was necessary to discredit the false prophets of Baal.

34. For an excellent discussion on the authenticity of prophecy see E. Berkovits, *God, Man and History* (New York: Jonathan David, 1959) chap. iii, pp. 18–25.

35. Saadya Gaon, op. cit., p. 151.

36. I. Epstein, *The Faith of Judaism* (London: Soncino Press, 1954), p. 125. His words are based on a statement by Judah Halevi in his monumental work *The Kuzari*, Part IV, #3.

37. Exodus 4:10.

38. Amos 7:14–15.

39. Deuteronomy 34:10. The precise meaning of the expression "face to face" is not clear. In the Talmud we find: "The Holy One blessed be He said to Moses: Moses, I and you will propound views [lit. 'faces'] on the law," also "The Holy One said to Moses: Just as I have turned a cheerful face upon you, so should you turn upon Israel a cheerful face" (*Berakhot* 63b). For a discussion on the "rays of light" that issued forth from Moses' face, see Walter Orenstein, *Etched in Stone* (New York: Bash Publications, 1989), pp. 124–134.

other prophets in several ways. He needed no special preparation for prophecy. During the encounter, he was awake and fully cognizant of what was happening.[40] That which was revealed to him was in its true form whereas communication with all the other prophets was in either a dream or a vision.[41] This latter point is confirmed in the biblical text: "If there be among you a prophet, I, the Lord, will make Myself known to him in a vision, in a dream will I speak to him."[42] God spoke to Moses "face to face"[43] and "mouth to mouth,"[44] which Maimonides explains to mean that Moses perceived the Divine message clearly without riddles or parables.[45] When prophecy came upon the other prophets they were terrified and became weak. Not so Moses; he was strong enough to tolerate the encounter with God while remaining in his normal state.

Moses needed no authentication. Miracles were performed by God through Moses when they were needed by the people. For example, when the Egyptians were in pursuit of the Israelites at the Red Sea, God divided the waters through Moses. When the people needed food, He provided the manna through Moses. When the Israelites thirsted, He provided the water through Moses. Maimonides writes: "Israel did not believe in Moses, our teacher, on account of the signs [miracles] he brought. For when one's faith is founded on signs, a lurking doubt always remains in the mind that these miracles have been performed with the aid of occult arts and witchcraft."[46] According to Maimonides, the sole proof of the authenticity of Moses' prophetic mission is the revelation of the Torah at Sinai. This is confirmed in the following biblical text: "And the Lord said to Moses, 'I will come to you in a thick cloud, in order that the people may hear when I speak with you and so trust you thereafter."[47]

The last of the prophets of Israel were Haggai, Zechariah, and

---

40. M. Maimonides, *Mishneh Torah*, op. cit., 7:6.
41. Ibid. 7:2,3.
42. Numbers 12:6.
43. Exodus 33:11.
44. Numbers 12:8.
45. M. Maimonides, *Mishneh Torah*, op. cit., 7:6.
46. Ibid., 8:1.
47. Exodus 19:9.

Malachi. For all intents and purposes the age of prophecy came to a close with the destruction of the First Temple in 586 B.C.E., for the Holy Spirit rested on man only in the land of Israel. The few prophets who did prophesy in the exile had already begun to prophesy in the land of Israel.[48] Prophecy was indeed a unique and wonderful phenomenon in Israel. Heinrich Graetz, the noted historian, was so impressed with the prophets and prophecy that he wrote:

> It is, however, undeniable that the human mind can without help from the senses cast a far seeing glance into the enigmatic concatenation of events and the complex play of force. By means of an undisclosed faculty of the soul, man has discovered truths that are not within the reach of the senses. A soul devoted to mundane matters and to selfishness can never attain to this degree of perfection. But should not a soul which is untouched by selfishness, undisturbed by low desires and passions, unsoiled by profanity and the stains of everyday life—a soul which is completely merged in the Deity and in a longing for moral superiority—should not such a soul be capable of beholding a revelation of religious and moral truths?

A few excerpts from the writings of the prophets should suffice to demonstrate the profundity of their ideas and the beauty of their words. Let us begin with Isaiah.

ISAIAH

Isaiah began his ministry in 736 B.C.E., the year of the death of King Uzziah. In his day, he witnessed among the masses of the people the oppression of the poor, the unyielding pursuit of pleasure, and the spread of idolatrous practices. He knew that the day of reckoning was not too far on the horizon. In many of his prophecies he stressed the gloom of what he called "The Day of the Lord." All this notwithstand-

---

48. *Moed Katan* 25a.

ing, he also prophesied the glory that would return to Israel and the peace that would come to the world in the Messianic Era. The following verses are from Isaiah 2:2–4.

> And it shall come to pass in the last days that the Mount of the Lord's House shall stand firm above the mountains and tower above the hills; and all the nations shall flow unto it with joy.
>
> And the many peoples shall go and shall say, "Come let us go up to the Mount of the Lord, to the House of the God of Jacob; that He may instruct us in His ways, and that we may walk in His paths." For instruction shall come forth from Zion, the word of the Lord from Jerusalem.
>
> Thus He will judge among the nations and arbitrate for the many peoples, and they shall beat their swords into plowshares and their spears into pruning hooks: Nations shall not take up sword against nation; they shall never again know war.

It is quite clear from the biblical commentators that the prophet makes reference here to the Messianic Era.[49] In contradistinction from the attitude the nations of the world had toward Israel and its beliefs in Isaiah's time [for that matter in our own time as well], in the Messianic Era all the nations of the world will look with reverence to Israel, and they will look with great joy to the Temple that will stand firm on Mount Moriah in Jerusalem. Indeed, they will gather together to worship at this mountain, which will at that time be regarded as the most significant of all the mountains of the world.[50] The inhabitants of one nation will say to those of the other, "Let us go up to the Mount of the Lord so that He may teach us through His Torah scholars[51] the fundamental principles of His Law. We ourselves will strive to discover the details."[52] For Zion will be the center for religious instruction for

---

49. Cf. Radak, commentary on Isaiah 2:2.
50. Cf. Rashi ad loc.
51. Cf. Radak, commentary to Isaiah 2:3, who opined that the teaching will be done by the King Messiah.
52. Cf. M. Malbim, commentary on Isaiah 2:3.

the entire world, and, as in days of old, Jerusalem will be the gathering place for the prophets and the home of prophecy. The King Messiah will judge and resolve difficulties that arise between nations so that war will become obsolete.[53] The implements formerly used for the destruction of human life will no longer be necessary. They will be converted into farm implements to sustain life.

JEREMIAH

Let us now turn to the prophecy of Jeremiah, who began his ministry in the year 626 B.C.E. Jeremiah loved his people dearly. He anticipated the multifaceted catastrophe that was about to befall the people of Judea: the destruction of the Temple and the city of Jerusalem, and the exile of the Jews to Babylonia. But Jeremiah was not to be remembered as a prophet of doom. He saw beyond the catastrophic events of the immediate future and prophesied the return of the Jews to Judea and the restoration of the kingdom to its former glory. In Jeremiah 31:14–19 we read:

> Thus said the Lord: A cry was heard in Ramah, wailing and bitter weeping: Rachel weeping for her children. She refused to be comforted for her children who are gone.
>
> Thus said the Lord: Restrain your voice from weeping, your eyes from shedding tears; for there is reward for your labor—declares the Lord. They shall return from the enemy's land.
>
> And there is hope for your future—declares the Lord. Your children shall return to their country.
>
> I can hear Ephraim lamenting: You have chastised me, and I am chastised. Like a calf that has not been broken. Receive me back, let me return, for You O Lord, are my God.

---

53. Cf. Mezudot David, commentary on Isaiah 2:4.

When Man Relates to God

Now that I have turned back, I am filled with remorse; I am ashamed and humiliated, for I bear the disgrace of my youth.

Is Ephraim a dear son to Me? [Is he] a child that is dandled? Whenever I have turned against him, My thoughts would dwell on him still. That is why My heart yearns for him; I will receive him back in love declares the Lord.

A voice is heard in Heaven. It comes from the northern border of the land of Benjamin. It is the voice of Rahel who weeps for her children, the descendants of the ten tribes of Israel (called here Ephraim) who were in exile. She refuses to be comforted for none of her children were left in the land.54 "Do not despair," says the Lord, "your children shall return to their homeland." The commentaries bring an interesting Midrash to explain the return of the people to the land of Israel.

When King Manashe who ruled in Judea from 692–638 B.C.E. placed an image of Ishtar, the Assyrian goddess of love and fertility, in the Temple, our matriarch Rahel came before God and said: "Is it not true that You are more merciful than man? I had mercy on my sister Leah and saved her from embarrassment by giving her the signs that Jacob and I had arranged so that my father Laban could not substitute Leah for me on my wedding night. I appeal to You to be merciful to Your children Israel and forgive them their sin." The Lord responded to her plea, and He informed her that in reward for the mercy she showed for her sister, the people would return to their homeland [55]

"I hear Ephraim's lament," said the Lord. What was that lament? The people argued that there are two ways to bring the masses to repentance. Inflicting suffering upon them is one way; it can bring on repentance through fear. Another way is the performance of miracles and wonders; it can bring on repentance through love. God chose the former, but it was not effective. Let Him demonstrate the latter, i.e., His

---

54. Ibid., Jeremiah 31:14. Another view is that the return of the Judeans to their land was in merit of the fact that they did not fail to observe the *mitzvot* in their exile.
55. Ibid., 31:15.

miracles and wonders, and the people will repent out of love and knowledge of God.[56]

The Lord responded to the thinking of the people as follows:[57] There is a difference as well between a (mature) beloved son and a dandled son. The former has many good qualities and is beloved by his father because of them. They work in his behalf so that his father loves him despite his sins. The latter is a young son. His father still plays with him. He is still too young to show any special qualities. Though he sins, his father so delights in him that he looks away from his sins.

There is a difference between the earlier generation for which the Lord had performed miracles and wonders and the present generation. In Egypt, the Israelites had no special good qualities but they were like the dandled son to God, and He forgave their sins. In the wilderness and in the early years of the Jewish State, when among them were prophets and sages, Israel was like a beloved son. When they sinned, God remembered the righteous among them and forgave them. At this point in time, says the Lord, when I turn against them, I remember the good among them. My heart yearns for them, and I forgive them like a young, immature son in whom I delight.[58]

EZEKIEL

We now turn to the prophet Ezekiel who lived during the destruction of Jerusalem and the Babylonian Exile. Together with King Jehoiachin, Ezekiel was taken to Babylonia in 586 B.C.E. As he himself testifies, his first prophecy took place five years after the Exile. The people were depressed and discouraged. They despaired of the restoration of the kingdom of Judea. Ezekiel preached not only the return of the people to their homeland but also their self-renewal to a purer state of morality. One of the best-known prophecies of Ezekiel is the vision of "The Valley

---

56. Cf. M. Malbim, commentary on Jeremiah 31:17.
57. We shall follow the interpretation of Malbim here.
58. M. Malbim, op. cit., verses 18,19.

of Dry Bones." We have selected this vision to represent his work. In Ezekiel 37:1–14 we read:

> The hand of the Lord came upon me. He took me out by the spirit of the Lord and set me down in the valley. It was full of bones. He led me all around them; there were very many of them spread over the valley, and they were very dry. He said to me, "O mortal, can these bones live again?"
>
> I replied, "O Lord God, only You know." And He said to me, "Prophesy over these bones and say to them: O dry bones hear the word of the Lord! Thus said the Lord God to these bones: I will cause breath to enter you and you shall live again. I will lay sinews upon you, and cover you with flesh, and form skin over you. And I will put breath into you, and you shall live again. And you shall know that I am the Lord!"
>
> I prophesied as I had been commanded. And when I was prophesying, suddenly there was a sound of rattling, and the bones came together, bone to matching bone. I looked, and there were sinews on them, and flesh had grown, and skin had formed over them; but there was no breath in them. Then he said to me, "Prophesy to the breath, prophesy, O mortal! Say to the breath: 'Thus said the Lord God: Come, O breath, from the four winds and breathe into these slain, that they may live again.'" I prophesied as He commanded me. The breath entered them, and they came to life and stood up on their feet, a vast multitude.
>
> And He said to me: O mortal, these bones are the whole House of Israel. They say, "Our bones are dried up, our hope is gone; we are doomed." Prophesy, therefore, and say to them: Thus said the Lord your God: I am going to open your graves and lift you out of your graves, O My people, and bring you to the land of Israel. You shall know O My people that I am the Lord when I have opened your graves and lifted you out of your graves. I will put My breath into you and you shall live again, and I will set you upon your own soil. Then you shall know that I the Lord have spoken and have acted—declares the Lord.

In the Talmud we find the following comment:

> R. Eliezer said: The dead whom Ezekiel resurrected stood up, uttered song and immediately died. R. Judah said: It was truth; it was a parable. R. Nehemiah said to him: If truth, why a parable; and if a parable, why truth? But [say thus]: In the truth there was but a parable. R. Eliezer the son of R. Jose the Galilean said: The dead whom Ezekiel revived went up to Palestine, married wives and begat sons and daughters. R. Judah b. Bathyra rose up and said: I am one of their descendants, and these are the *tefillen*, which my grandfather left me [as an heirloom] from them. Now who were they whom Ezekiel revived? Rav said: They were the Ephraimites who counted [the years] to the end [of the Egyptian bondage], but erred therein[59] . . . Samuel said: They were those who denied resurrection.[60]

There is a clear difference of opinion among the sages as to the interpretation of this vision. Some see it as a parable that alludes to the revival of the nation of Israel.[61] This would be quite apropos considering that Ezekiel was the first prophet of the Exile and the return of the Jews to their homeland was uppermost in his mind as well as the minds of all the Jews in the Exile.

In the vision, the Lord brought Ezekiel into a valley filled with dry bones. He told him to prophesy to these bones, which represented the nation of Israel. Having been exiled to Babylonia, with both the Temple and the city of Jerusalem in ruins, the hope of the people for the restoration of the kingdom of Judea had virtually dried up. God had not forsaken them, said the prophet. Just as in this vision the dry bones were able to live again so, too, would the nation of Israel be restored once more to their former glory. Tell them that I shall open their graves and lift them out of these graves, said the Lord God. I shall return them to their homeland and restore their kingdom.[62] Others opine that the

---

59. They erred in counting the 400 years foretold by God to Abraham (Genesis 15:13). As a result, they left Egypt thirty years before the rest of Israel.

60. *Sanhedrin* 92b.

61. Cf. Rashi and Maharsha on Sanhedrin 92b.

62. Depending upon the meaning of the parable, this refers either to the restoration

vision is to be taken literally, and what Ezekiel witnessed was the miracle of the resurrection of the dead.

Let us recall the significance of the juxtaposition of the Divine names "Lord God" and determine their implication here. The name "Lord" is the Tetragrammaton that denotes the personal character of the Supreme Being, the attribute of mercy that manifests itself in Divine providence. The name "God" depicts the Supreme Being as the totality of all forces in control of the universe; what is referred to as the attribute of strict justice. Perhaps the implication is that God tempers justice with mercy in His judgment of mankind. The destruction of Jerusalem and the exile of the Judeans to Babylonia was a well-deserved punishment, albeit a manifestation of strict Divine justice. But the Lord is also abundant in compassion. As a manifestation of His compassion He will return His people to their homeland, says the prophet, and restore the kingdom of Judea.

Let us now turn to the second interpretation. Death, even when it comes in tired old age, is a devastating Divine decree. Alas, in this world man has no choice but to accept it. The Divine promise to resurrect the dead in the Messianic Era, however, tempers that decree somewhat. Thus justice is tempered with mercy. The limited resurrection witnessed by Ezekiel was a forerunner, and in a sense a confirmation, of the resurrection that will take place in the Messianic Era. Be that as it may, the Jew looks forward to the day when he will no longer be obsessed by the anticipation of death, when the words of the prophet Isaiah will at last be realized, for "He will destroy death forever. My Lord God will wipe the tears from all faces and will put an end to the reproach of His people over all the Earth—for it is the Lord who has spoken" (Isaiah 25:8).

---

of the kingdom of Israel in the Second Temple period or the resurrection of the dead in the Messianic Era.

8

WHEN MAN RELATES TO GOD

The angel who is appointed over the prayers takes all the prayers that were offered in all the synagogues and makes of them crowns Which he places on the head of the Holy One blessed be He.
                                                               Exodus Rabbah 21

To the Jew, God is no stranger. By nature of his religion, a Jew has an intimate relationship with God that begins when he is very young. This relationship is initiated when as a child he is told that there is a God who created the beautiful world into which he was born, and that he must express his thanks to this God for granting him the blessing of life. Even before he is able to comprehend the meaning of what he is saying, he is told that upon awakening each morning he is to recite the following prayer: "I thank You living and everlasting King, that You have restored my soul to me—how great is Your faithfulness." Once he has mastered this little prayer, he adds: "The beginning of wisdom is the fear of the Lord; a good understanding to all that fulfill them [the commandments]. His praise endures forever. Blessed be the name of His glorious kingdom forever and ever." With the obligation to recite these words a new phenomenon has entered the life of the child; he has become involved with *mitzvot*. He learns that the fulfillment of *mitzvot* will bring him wisdom and understanding. With these simple gestures, a dialogue between the Jew and his God is set into motion; a relationship is established through prayer and *mitzvot* that he will nurture and that will nurture him throughout his life.

As the child matures and becomes capable of understanding more and more about God, he is taught of God's concern for the world, and how this concern impacts on man. The little prayer service with which he began his interaction with God is amplified quantitatively and qualitatively. By the time he has reached the age of Bar Mitzvah, he has learned to recite the entire Daily and Sabbath services with facility, and he has put into practice many of the 613 *mitzvot*. Hopefully, he has also gained some understanding of the sophisticated precepts and concepts inherent in the prayers. All things being equal, by this time he has established in his mind a kind of "comradery" with God. This will bring him great satisfaction and happiness when he experiences Divine beneficence on a personal level. It will bring him consolation in times of personal tragedy, and hope in times of personal suffering and adversity.

I. RELATING THROUGH PRAYER

Let us pose the following questions: How does the Jew express his feelings to God when he experiences Divine immanence? How does he confront God when he experiences Divine hiddenness, what appears to him to be deliberate Divine disconcern? Lastly, how does he address the Holy One blessed be He in terms of his personal needs and the needs of the Jewish community? The answer can be found in an analysis of the prayer service.

There are three major themes in every service: praise, petition,[1] and thanksgiving. We will discuss each separately.

---

1. Prayers of petition are, for the most part, omitted in the Shabbat and Festival services.

When Man Relates to God

Praise

Prayer is a dialogue between God and man in which man is the initiator and the sole speaker. Praise is one facet of that dialogue. Perhaps the most well-known expressions of praise to God are the *Kaddish*, a litany recited to divide sections of the service, and the *Amidah*, the prayer par excellence of every service. Many will ask: By what right does man initiate a dialogue with God? Do we dare confront God with our meager words of praise? One recalls the admonition in the Talmud: "R. Jose said: May my portion be of those who complete the entire Hallel every day. But that is not so, for a Master said: He who reads Hallel every day blasphemes and reproaches [the Divine name]. We refer to the 'verses of song.'"[2] Most assuredly there is a place for praise of God in our daily prayers, but it must be limited to that which our sages have ordained. Be that as it may, it is quite clear that praise needs a precedent. Our sages found such a precedent in the Bible. Note the following discussion in the Talmud:

> R. Simlai expounded: A man should always recount the praise of the Holy One, blessed be He and then pray. From where do we know this? From Moses, for it is written: "I pleaded with the Lord at that time," and it goes on, "O Lord God, You who let Your servant see the first works of Your greatness and Your mighty hand, You whose powerful deeds no god in Heaven or on Earth can equal" and afterwards is written, "Let me, I pray cross over and see the good land, etc."[3]

Moses' request to cross over and see the land that was promised to the Jewish people was preceded by words of praise. This is our precedent.

It has also been asked: "Why does man praise God? Surely God has no need or desire for praise. Besides, God's greatness so far exceeds anything man can put into words that were it not for the statement of R. Simlai, one might have said that the very notion of man praising God

---

2. *Shabbat* 118b.
3. *Berakhot* 32a.

is hubris of the highest order. The Talmud records the following incident.

> A certain [reader] went down in the presence of R. Hanina and said: O God the great, mighty, terrible, majestic, powerful, awful strong, fearless, sure, and honored. He [R. Hanina] waited till he had finished, and when he had finished he said to him, "Have you concluded all the praise of your Master? Why do we want all this? Even with these three that we do say [great, mighty, and terrible in the first benediction of the *Amidah*] had not Moses our master mentioned them in the Torah, and had not the Men of the Great Assembly come and inserted them in *the prayer* we should not have been able to mention them, and you say all these and still go on!"[4]

We must be very careful in our choice of words when we praise God. Indeed, Rabbah b. Bar Hanah said: "One who descants upon the praises of the Holy One, blessed be He, to excess is uprooted from the world."[5]

It is not God who needs to be praised by man, but man who needs to praise God. When man witnesses the magnificence of the world around him and is overwhelmed by a feeling of awe, he must give vent to this feeling by expressing praise to God the Creator of the universe. Consider this: By praising God man makes reference to a multiplicity of Divine attributes and acts. Firmly establishing in his mind the omnipotence and the omniscience of God, he is secure in his conviction that God is readily able to perform natural as well as supernatural acts in man's behalf. This serves as a fitting precursor to petition.

There is another way of looking at praise. Man cannot know God's essence. But, as we have already explained, there is an aspect of Divinity that man is capable of knowing, namely, God's ways in the world. This is the root of praise. Man sees God as Helper, Savior, and Shield, as He who supports those who fall, as Healer of the sick, as He who revives the dead, etc., and he praises God for these manifestations of providence. It is not at all inconceivable that by speaking of Divine righteousness and loving-kindness man will come to realize that it is worthwhile to

---

4. *Berakhot* 33b.
5. *Megillah* 18a.

adopt these Divine qualities, and acting upon this awareness he will become a better human being.[6]

One thing is certain. The notion that praise precedes petition in order for man to ingratiate himself in God's eyes before submitting his requests not only denigrates the concept of God but is sheer foolishness. Only a fool would attribute to God the frailties that, much to our dismay, define us as human beings.

Petition

Petition in Jewish prayer is not merely a series of requests; it is a statement of dependency. In light of this, Jewish tradition teaches that petition rather than praise is the most vital component of prayer. To declare before God that we are totally dependent upon Him for our physical, emotional, and intellectual needs is the ultimate gesture of humility. As such it is also the highest form of praise. Notwithstanding this, however, the notion of petition presents a serious philosophical dilemma. How can man petition God for that which God has obviously seen fit to deny him? Considering that the world was created and is governed by Divine wisdom and *what is . . . should be,* would it not be audacious for us to petition God to modify His plan and grant our personal requests?

The resolution of the dilemma lies in our understanding of God's relationship with the world and man in particular. Unlike the Deists who believe that God created the world and left it to chance, Judaism believes that God is continually concerned with the world and the preservation of its inhabitants. He has demonstrated His concern for man by revealing the Torah and demanding man's commitment and adherence to its norms. Of course, to demand adherence to the law is to imply that man has free will, that he can choose to obey and be rewarded or to disobey and be punished. God's motivation in giving

---

6. Cf. Shabbat 133b: *"This is my God and I will adorn Him.* Abba Saul interpreted, and I will be like Him: be like Him: just as He is gracious and compassionate so should you be gracious and compassionate."

man free will when He could have simply programmed him to be obedient is not for us to ponder. Let us just say that had this been the case, reward and punishment would be pointless. Be that as it may, considering the many ingredients that enter into the process of decision making—genetic predisposition and sociological influences to be specific—it is not at all surprising that many people, leaders and laymen alike, have made improper choices and horrendous decisions. Now while the decisions made by laymen only affect them and their families, those made by leaders impact upon the entire world.

We petition God that He grant us forgiveness and that He endow us with knowledge and understanding so that our future decisions in life be grounded in wisdom and limited to the confines of Jewish ethics. We petition Him to intervene in the historical process and right the wrongs that society has brought upon itself. We implore Him to bring peace to the world and reign over all mankind with justice and compassion. Finally, God's awareness of the imperfections with which He has endowed us, the shortcomings that define us as human beings, gives us the right to petition Him to help us overcome our inadequacies and create a better world.

The petitions were designated to be recited in the *Amidah* after three introductory benedictions of praise. Now here we must differentiate between critical and noncritical prayer. Obligatory prayer, i.e., the prayer services that we recite three times a day, by the very nature of its regularity is considered noncritical prayer. It is not a particular crisis that brings us to God in the regular prayer services; it is our obligation to confront God daily in acknowledgment of life. There is something interesting about the wording of the petitions in the *Amidah*. We request that God redeem Israel and call Him the redeemer though Israel has not yet been redeemed. We ask God to gather us from the four corners of the Earth and refer to Him as He who gathers the dispersed though He has not yet done so. We request that God rebuild Jerusalem and restore the throne of David and refer to Him as He who rebuilds Jerusalem though this has not yet been accomplished. The petitions of the *Amidah* are more than requests; they are a declaration of faith in God's never-ending beneficence and concern for the world.[7] As such the petitions of obligatory prayer are declarations rather than cries out of pain. They are written in plural form because they are petitions in behalf of the entire Jewish community. Knowledge, forgiveness, healing, redemption, etc., a total of thirteen petitions, are recited on weekdays, three times a day. Should one have requests of a personal nature, they may be included in whichever one of the thirteen petitions is relevant to that request.

Thanksgiving

In our discussion above we were concerned with the matter of propriety: whether we have the right to confront God with praise and petition. We looked for a precedent that would give us that right. Should we be so concerned with expressions of thanksgiving? Perhaps we should not. After all, thanksgiving is acknowledgment: we acknowledge the fact that all the good that we experience in life derives from God. What possible objection could there be to such a gesture? On the other hand, what possible benefit could God derive from man's expressions of thanksgiving? In point of fact, it is man who benefits from thanking God. It teaches him the meaning of gratitude, the importance of giving credit where credit is due, and it reminds him to apply these lessons to his fellow man. Be that as it may, there happens to be a precedent for thanksgiving found in the Bible. When Leah, Jacob's wife, gave birth to Judah, her fourth son, she declared, "This time I will thank the Lord."[8] This is, indeed, the first time an expression of thanks to God appears in the Bible.[9]

The most common expression of thanksgiving is the benediction. With the opening formula "Blessed are You O Lord our God King of the

---

7. Cf. Midrash, Psalms 31:8.
8. Genesis 29:35
9. Cf. Berakhot 7b where we find: "From the day that the Holy One blessed be He created His world there was no man that praised the Holy One blessed be He, until Leah came and praised Him For it is said: 'This time I will praise the Lord.'"

universe" we acknowledge and thank the Supreme Being for the multiplicity of good things that He has created in this world. As we derive benefit from the food we eat and the wonders of nature we thank God as well. Our sages teach us that it is this acknowledgment that gives us the right to benefit from the multiplicity of God's creations.

There are other reasons for thanksgiving. The Talmud states: "There are four classes of people who must offer thanksgiving: those who have crossed the sea, those who have traversed the wilderness, one who has recovered from an illness, and a prisoner who has been set free."[10] A special benediction was composed for this purpose. The designee is called to the Torah, and after he has completed the appropriate Torah blessingss he recites: "Blessed are You O Lord our God King of the Universe who does good to the undeserving, and who has also rendered all good to me." The congregation then responds: "He who has rendered to you all good, may He do only good to you for ever." Jewish law ordains that a good thing that derives from God that is shared by two people necessitates the following benediction of thanksgiving: "Blessed are You O Lord our God King of the universe who is good and dispenses good."[11]

The last three benedictions of the *Amidah* are designated "expressions of thanksgiving," although they contain both praise and petition as well. We thank God for the blessing of life and for returning our souls that are in His hand. We thank Him for the miracles he performs for us daily and for all the other benefits that He has wrought for us evening, morning, and noon. The second benediction concludes: "And everything that lives shall give thanks to You forever and shall praise Your name in truth, O God, our salvation and our help Selah. Blessed are You, O Lord, whose name is All-good, and unto whom it is becoming to give thanks." In the third benediction we petition God for peace and we thank Him for the Torah, loving-kindness, righteousness, blessing, mercy, life, and peace.

---

10. *Berakhot* 54b.
11. *Tur Shulhan Arukh Orah Hayyim* 222:1.

Kavanah

The term *kavanah* means "concentration." It is of the utmost importance that one who is engaged in prayer concentrate intently on the meaning of the words and the significance of the ideas. The Talmud adds: "When you pray, know before whom you pray,"[12] and "When a man prays he should direct his heart to Heaven."[13] Maimonides insisted: "Prayer without concentration is not prayer."[14] When one prays he must vacate his heart of all mundane thoughts in order to fill it with the consciousness of standing in God's Presence. He must think of God's awe-inspiring greatness and his own lowliness. Without this transformation, prayer is not a religious experience; it is merely the mechanical reading of a text. Nowadays, considering the harried life that most of us lead, it is difficult to insist on the ideal.[15] Nevertheless, one can certainly improve the experience of prayer by following these guidelines:

1. When at home, one should pray in the room that is the least distracting. Additionally, the sages advised that one should pray in the corner of the room facing the wall.
2. The synagogue should befit the mood of prayer. The decor should not be somber, for that would be depressing, but neither should it be ostentatious. Simplicity should be the key to synagogue design.
3. The *mehitzah* is a fundamental requirement in the synagogue. The obvious distraction when men and women sitting together is clearly detrimental to proper concentration. The family pew is a Christian concept; it is diametrically opposed to the Jewish posture of prayer.
4. Whoever leads the service must be knowledgeable in the meaning of the texts, the laws of the service, and the proper *nus-haot* (prayer chants) so that his rendition of the prayers be appropriate.
5. One must create the mood for prayer. Setting aside a few moments for Torah study or for meditation on the significance of

---

12. Berakhot 28b.
13. Ibid., 31a.
14. M. Maimonides, *Mishneh Torah: Laws of Prayer* 4:15.
15. Cf. *Shulhan Arukh Orah Hayyim* 101:1 in the gloss of *Rama*.

the encounter with God in prayer before beginning the service could do a great deal to heighten the experience.

The Talmud tells us something very interesting about the way to pray. "The pious men of old used to wait [meditate] for an hour and pray for an hour and then wait [meditate] again for an hour."[16] While it may be difficult for the average person to spend so much time in prayer, the threefold format, i.e., meditation, prayer, and meditation, would certainly be well worth implementing. To meditate on what one is about to do before one confronts God in prayer and on what one has just done after that confrontation would certainly do a great deal to make the experience more meaningful. Proper concentration is so important that Maimonides taught: "Finding that one's mind is confused and the heart preoccupied, one must not pray until one has regained calmness and composure."[17]

In the Talmud we read: "A man's prayer is not heard unless he makes his heart [soft] like flesh."[18] To fulfill this requirement, it is customary to put some coins in the *Kupat Tsedakah* ("charity box") before or during the service as an expression of our heartfelt compassion for the poor.

The Posture of Prayer

How do we relate to God in our supplications? A prime example of the recurring theme in Jewish prayer is found in *Ribon HaOlamim*, recited in the *Ne'ilah* service of Yom Kippur. This prayer was subsequently added to the *Shaharit* service. It reads as follows:

> Master of all times! It is not on the basis of our merits that we pour out our supplications before You, but on the basis of Your great compassion What are we? What is our life? What is our loving-kindness? What [is] our righteousness? What [is] our helpful-

---

16. *Berakhot* 32b.
17. M. Maimonides, op. cit.
18. *Sotah* 8a.

ness . . . Are not all the heroes as nothing before You, the men of renown as though they had never been, and the wise as if they were without knowledge, the intelligent as though they lacked understanding? For the multitude of their actions are worthless; the days of their lives are as nothing before You, and the pre-eminence of man over the beast is vanished, for all is nothingness.

But we are Your people, the sons of Your covenant, the sons of Abraham who loved You . . . the descendants of Isaac his only son . . . the community of Jacob Your firstborn. . . . Therefore we are duty bound to give thanks to You, to bless and hallow You and to offer thanksgiving to Your name.[19]

We stand before God in prayer with mixed emotions. On the one hand we humble ourselves and belittle our merits. On the other, we take pride in the accomplishments of our people. In the *Tahanun* prayer we confront God with the words, "Our Father, our King, favor us and answer us for we have no merits to show," and again, "Yours O my Lord, is tender righteousness, while ours is the shame that covers the face." But in the *Minhah Amidah* for Shabbat we say, "You are One and Your name is One, and who is like Your people Israel, a people unique on Earth." In the Mussaf *Amidah* of the Festivals and the High Holidays we vacillate between the two themes. On the one hand, we say, "You have chosen us from among all peoples; You have loved us and taken pleasure in us," and later "but as a result of our sins we were exiled from the land." This ambiguity is found in the Psalms as well. King David wrote: "What is man that You have been mindful of him, mortal man that You have taken note of him, that You have made him little less than Divine, and adorned him with glory and majesty; You have made him master over Your handiwork, laying the world at his feet."

We cannot dismiss the fact that most of us have not lived up to our intellectual and spiritual potential, that we have not set ethics and morality above personal gain. Neither as individuals nor as a nation can we come to God and boast of our accomplishments. In point of fact we know that we are remiss in our fulfillment of *mitzvot*. We admit our

---

19. *Tanna D've Eliyahu*, chapter 21.

shortcomings and our failures, and we present ourselves before God with the utmost of humility and regret. Note the words of the Yom Kippur prayer recited at the end of the *Amidah*: "O my God, before I was created, I was of no worth, and now that I have been created, I am as if I had not been created. Dust am I in life, how much more so in death. I am here before You like a vessel filled with shame and confusion."[20]

At the same time we know that, having been created in God's image, we are the most sublime of all His creations. Indeed, man alone has been endowed by the Creator with freedom of will. We are the children of Abraham, Isaac, and Jacob, the sons and daughters of prophets and sages. We can speak with pride of every generation, including our own, who gave their lives for *Kiddush Hashem* ("the sanctification of God's name"). Indeed we have *z'khut avot* ("merit of the fathers") that works in our behalf.

We bring both these themes to the encounter with God in prayer. We confront Him with feelings of guilt and with pride, not knowing which of the two will serve best to gain for us the fulfillment of our needs and ensure our survival. It has been said that man should keep two principles in mind throughout his life. The first is that the world was created for him; the second, that he is but dust and ashes. The prayer service does just that.

II. THE SERVICES

The three daily services are *Shaharit*, *Minhah*, and *Ma'ariv*.[21] On Shabbat, Rosh Hodesh, and the Festivals a fourth service, i.e., *Mussaf*, is added after *Shaharit*; and on Yom Kippur a fifth service, i.e., *Ne'ilah* is added after *Minhah*. Every service follows a pattern, a sequential arrangement of the prayers into sections. This pattern was designed by the sages to engender a true religious experience. Let us examine the services and discover the significance of this pattern.

---

20. *Yoma* 87b.
21. Morning, Afternoon, and Evening services.

Shaharit

Preliminary Recitations

The prayer recited upon awakening in the morning[22] addresses our first concern of the day: the experience of life. We thank God for returning our souls, thus enabling us to begin another day of living. As we mentioned earlier, every child is taught to recite this prayer by rote when he awakens in the morning, but let no one think that it is merely a child's prayer. The themes put forth in this prayer, i.e., the return to conscious living, the meaning of fear and awe of God and the personal benefit one derives from following the commandments, are of ultimate significance to every Jew. We praise God for having been granted life and for having been given the privilege of knowing and benefiting from Torah and *mitzvot*.

Subsequently, we recite two benedictions. The first focuses on the mechanics of physical existence: it expresses our thanksgiving to God for maintaining the efficient operation of the multiple systems in the human body. We know full well that should any of these systems break down man could not endure for very long. The second benediction focuses once again on the human soul. It expresses thanksgiving to God for creating it, for implanting it within the human body, and for preserving it. It acknowledges that just as there will come a time when man must relinquish his soul to God, so, too, will the time come when man's soul will be returned to him and with it the blessing of life. Two benedictions follow: the first is an expression for thanksgiving to God for having revealed the Torah to the nation of Israel, the second for commanding us to be involved in the study of the Torah.

The Sequential Benedictions

The synagogue service begins with the recitation of a series of benedictions that allude to the step-by-step process of awakening, dressing, and preparing for the day's activities. Composed in the fifth

---

22. In Hebrew it is referred to as *Modeh Ani*.

century B.C.E., by the Men of the Great Assembly, these benedictions are personal expressions of thanksgiving; they were meant to be recited sequentially in the privacy of one's home. For example, when one opened his eyes he would recite a benediction, when he stretched his limbs a second benediction, when he rose up in his bed a third, when he stepped down on the ground a fourth, and so on, each act was connected to an appropriate benediction. But the masses became confused and misappropriated the benedictions. For the sake of conformity, they were moved to the synagogue. No longer considered the individual's personal expressions of thanksgiving to God for having granted him the ability to wake up in the morning and function normally, the benedictions assumed a universal tone. One expressed his thanksgiving to God for having given mankind the ability to function as normal human beings. Thus man was initiated into his second concern: addressing God in terms of that which all men have in common.

The Ritual of Sacrifice

The second major division of *Shaharit* is korbanot, the laws of the sacrificial service once performed in the Holy Temple in Jerusalem. With the destruction of the Temple, the people were panic-stricken. How would they attain atonement for their sins? Read the biblical verses that are concerned with the sacrifices, said the prophet, and atonement will be forthcoming.[23] The ritual of sacrifice is complex and highly sophisticated in its symbolism. As those who witnessed it testified, it was marked by reverence and great splendor. Offerings of many sorts were brought in the Temple: some in behalf of the individual, others in behalf of the community of Israel, and still others in behalf of the nations of the world. One can only imagine the awesome effect that the ritual had on the individual who brought an offering in partial atonement for his sin. Watching the animal being sacrificed on the altar he must have said to himself, "There but for the grace of God

---

23. "Take words with you and return to the Lord. Say to Him: 'Forgive all guilt and accept what is good; instead of bulls we will pay [the offering on our lips'" (Hosea 14:3) and the commentary of Rashi.

go I!" Reading some of these laws with imagination might indeed capture some of the splendor of the Temple service.

The readings are followed by a selection from the *Sifra* that enumerates the principles of rabbinic exegesis, and the section concludes with the following prayer: "May it be Your will, O Lord our God and God of our fathers, that the Temple be speedily rebuilt in our days, and grant that our portion be in Your Torah. And there we will serve You with awe as in the days of old, and as in ancient years." Although this section of the morning service does mention sacrifices offered by the individual, its primary focus is on those offered in behalf of the Jewish community as a whole.

Kaddish D'Rabbanan

To separate the section on sacrifice from the section that follows, a special prayer of praise to God called *Kaddish D'Rabbanan* ("Rabbinic *Kaddish*") is recited."[24] The name derives from the fact that a special paragraph is inserted that prays for the peace and welfare of the teachers and disciples of the Torah so that they may continue to devote themselves to their noble calling. Since this section concluded with an excerpt from the *Sifra*, which was composed by the rabbis, this special *Kaddish* is appropriate. Designated by the sages as a *davar shebikedushah* ("a holy utterance"), the *Kaddish* may only be recited in the presence of a quorum of ten Jewish males.

The Verses of Song

The *Pesuke D'Zimrah* ("verses of song") to which the Talmud refers is a "service of praise" that originally consisted of Psalms 145-150. Later, readings from I Chronicles and the book of Nehemiah were added as

---

24. There are four types of *Kaddish*. The "Half *Kaddish*" divides sections of the service; the "Full *Kaddish*" is recited after the *Amidah* designates the completion of the service; the "Rabbinic *Kaddish*" is recited after having studied [read] a portion of the Oral Law; the "Mourners' *Kaddish*" as the name indicates is recited for thirty days by those who mourn relatives and for eleven months by those who mourn parents.

well as several additional psalms. The section concludes with Exodus 14:30, 15:1–18.[25] This service of praise is recited in the *Shaharit* on weekdays in preparation for the *Amidah*,[26] the "prayer" par excellence. Our sages tell us that by reciting this service of praise to God we uproot and remove our sins. Our prayers will be heard and they are more acceptable to God.[27] To mark it as a unit, this section is enclosed by benedictions. It opens with *Barukh She-omar* ("Blessed be He who spoke"), a group of benedictions that allude to God as the Creator of the world. The closing benediction *Yishtabah* ("May He be Praised") enumerates a number of praises and speaks of the pleasantness of praising God.

The following are but a few of the multiple themes found in *Pesuke D'Zimrah*:

1. The Lord is good; His loving kindness is everlasting, and His faithfulness is from generation to generation.
2. From sunrise until sunset the Lord's name is to be praised. Let them say among the nations that the Lord is King and shall be King forever and ever.
3. The Lord's greatness is unsearchable.
4. One generation shall laud the Lord's work to another and declare His mighty acts.
5. He gives food to the hungry; He sets the prisoners free; He opens the eyes of the blind; He raises those who are bowed down.
6. His understanding is infinite; He upholds the weak and brings the wicked down.
7. Praise God in His sanctuary; praise Him for His mighty acts. Let everything that has breath praise the Lord.

To separate the *Pesuke D'Zimrah* from the section that follows, the *Kaddish* is recited once again. What follows is a short responsive. The leader of the service recites the *Borekhu* ("Blessed be the Lord who is

---

25. A few other verses are appended: Psalm 22:29, Ovadiah 1:21, Zechariah 14:9.
26. See note 3.
27. Cf. Isaac Abuhav, *Menorat HaMaor* (Jerusalem: Mossad Harav Kook, 1951), p. 212.

blessed") and the congregation responds, "Blessed is the Lord who is blessed forever and ever." This recitation is also considered *davar she-bikedushah*. Consequently, it necessitates a *minyan*, i.e., a quorum of ten males above the age of thirteen.

Keriat Shema

The next section is called *Keriat Shema* ("Reading of the *Shema*"). To mark it as a unit, it is likewise enclosed by benedictions. In *Shaharit*, two benedictions precede it and two follow it. Both benedictions praise God for creating light: the first, *yotser* or ("forms light"), focuses on the physical light that serves to illuminate the world without which life could not exist; *the* second, *ahavah rabbah* ("great love"), focuses on the Torah, the spiritual light without which society cannot survive. The *Shema*[28] is the declaration of the unity of God; it is perhaps the most well-known verse in the Bible. Three biblical passages follow [29] The first mandates: love of God, the study of Torah by day and by night, teaching Torah to our children, and the laws *of tefillin* and *mezuzah*. The second speaks of the reward for following the *mitzvot* and the punishment for disobedience. The third is the source for the mitzvah of *tsitsit* ("fringes"), and also speaks of the redemption of Israel from Egypt. The concluding benediction *emet v'yatsiv* ("true and firm") praises God acknowledging His eternal Kingship and His involvement in the redemption of the Israelites from Egypt. It concludes with a plea that God once again redeem His people Israel The redemption theme is in conformity with the rabbinic ruling to juxtapose the prayer for redemption to the *Amidah*.[30] The *Amidah*, which we have already outlined in the preceding pages, is the prayer par excellence of the Jewish liturgy. In *Shaharit* and *Minhah*, it is recited by the congregation and repeated by the leader.

---

28. Deuteronomy 6:4—"Hear O Israel the Lord our God the Lord is One."
29. Deuteronomy 6:4–8, 11:13–22, and Numbers 15: 37–42.
30. Cf. *Berakhot* 4b.

Tahanun

Tahanun ("supplication for pardon") follows the *Amidah*. It is a petition to God that He pardon our sins. When reciting this supplication, the worshipper rests his brow on his arm as a sign of total humility before God. Note the plaintive words: "You who are merciful and gracious, I have sinned before You. O Lord full of mercy, have mercy upon me and receive my supplications." This is followed by Psalm 6:2–11. On Mondays and Thursdays Tahanun is preceded by seven somber elegies. It has been said of these prayers, "Consciousness of sin is the opening note, passing into lamentation because of persecution. In all of them, the love of God and His forgiveness are the hope and trust of the worshipper."[31] On these days, the weekly Torah reading follows *Tahanun*. The service continues with Psalm 145 and Psalm 20, a reading entitled *U'va L'tsiyon Goel* ("A Redeemer shall come to Zion"), which is an amalgam of biblical verses; and Alenu *L'shabeah* ("It is our duty to praise"), which is a proclamation of God as the Supreme King of the Universe. The *Shaharit* service is concluded with the Psalm of the day.

Minhah

Minhah, consisting only of Psalm 145, the *Amidah*, *Kaddish*, and *Alenu L'shabeah*, is the shortest service of the day. It is in place of the sacrifice that was brought in the Temple in the afternoon. *Shaharit* is recited in the morning before one's daily routine commences; *Maariv* is recited at night having completed one's daily routine. *Minhah* must be recited in the afternoon, however. When man is intimately involved in his daily routine he must take time out to recite the *Minhah* service. This is the reason for its brevity. Our sages taught that of the three services recited during the day, *Minhah* earns the greatest reward. One who finds time in a busy day to fulfill the *mitzvah* of prayer deserves recognition.

---

31. Joseph Hertz, *The Authorized Daily Prayer Book* (New York: Bloch, 1960), p. 168.

Maariv

The final service of the day is *Maariv or Arvit*. In order to fulfill the requirement of reciting *Keriat Shema* in the evening, the *Maariv* service is somewhat longer than *Minhah*. Recited after dark, when time is not of the essence, this does not present a problem. The service opens with *Borekhu*, after which the *Keriat Shema* and the *Amidah* are recited. Unlike in *Shaharit* and *Minhah*, the leader of the service does not repeat the *Amidah*. The *Keriat Shema* of *Maariv* is enclosed with four benedictions. As in *Shaharit*, the two that precede it speak of light, praising God for the physical light of the luminaries and the spiritual light of the Torah. The first benediction that follows *Keriat Shema*, however, differs from its corresponding benediction in *Shaharit*.

Night engages human emotions. Feelings of loneliness and trepidation beset man. He wonders about the future and looks to God for reassurance of His protection. In his comment on this benediction S. R. Hirsch writes: "We are reminded that our many deliverances in the past should be to us a source of trust in God through all the dark moments that the future may bring."[32] The second benediction, *Hashkivenu* ("Cause us to lie down"), is also very much in line with the feelings generated by night. We ask God that He cause us to lie down in peace and rise up in the morning in peace for He is our sole Protector. Lastly, we ask that God spread over us and all Israel the shelter of peace.

In the Gaonic period (eighth-tenth century C.E.) a long benediction was introduced entitled *Barukh Hashem L'olam* ("Blessed be the Lord forever") to replace the *Amidah*. Several reasons have been given for this innovation, the most popular of which is that it was instituted at a time when synagogues were located in fields outside the boundary of the towns and villages. It was dangerous to stay there long into the night so this shorter prayer that contained the name of God eighteen times corresponding to the eighteen benedictions in the *Amidah* was substituted, and the people were able to return home earlier.[33] Although the rationale for this innovation may no longer be relevant, the benediction

---

32. S. R. Hirsch, *The Hirsch Siddur* (New York: Feldheim, 1972), p. 262.
33. D. Abudraham, *Abudraham HaShalem* (Jerusalem: 1963), p. 141.

has remained in the liturgy. The verses proclaim God as our Guardian and Redeemer. They declare His love and His justice and petition Him for peace. Lastly, they pray for the recognition of God and His Unity by all peoples of the world.

On Shabbat and Festivals the order of the services is the same. The *Amidah* differs from the weekday *Amidah* in that the petitions are omitted and a special paragraph that deals with the occasion is substituted. Several Psalms are added in *Pesuke D'Zimrah,* and *Mussaf,* an additional service, follows *Shaharit.*

III. RELATING THROUGH *MITZVOT*

The greatest manifestation of Divine providence in behalf of the Jewish people is the revelation of the Torah. The primary purpose of the encounter with God at Mount Sinai was to reveal the *mitzvot* to Israel. As such revelation was an expression of Divine concern of the highest order. E. Berkovits writes: "As religion is inconceivable without revelation, neither is it possible without the law of God. The law is the bond that preserves the relationship of the Divine concern beyond the fundamental experience of the encounter itself . . . The law is the avenue of contact beyond the point of encounter."[34] We must recognize that Divine concern is Divine love. The revelation of the Torah, therefore, is a manifestation of Divine love. The point is made in the Talmud: "Beloved is Israel for the Holy One blessed be He, surrounded them with commandments."[35] The world considers the Torah to be the greatest book ever written. It recognizes the Torah as a primary source for the history and culture of ancient times. Be that as it may, to the Jewish people all this is secondary. First and foremost, the Torah is a book of *mitzvot;* a way of life revealed to man by none other than God Himself. As such, every time we perform a *mitzvah* we relate to God.

We must make a further point here. One of the 613 commands is to love God. In Deuteronomy 6:5 we read: "You shall love the Lord your

---

34. E. Berkovits, *God, Man and History* (New York: Jonathan David, 1959), p. 87.
35. *Menahot* 43b.

God with all your heart with all your soul and with all your might." But how does one express his love of God? To love God is to follow His commands. I. Epstein writes: "The love of God is an active love. Here the center of gravity is placed in the action of man. Man loves God best when he acts best. The love of God must be rooted in knowledge, and gains its full ripeness in action."[36] Ideally, every time we perform a *mitzvah* we are conscious of this fact. Considering that *mitzvot* apply to every facet of life from the moment we awaken in the morning till the moment we retire at night, whether at home or in business, on weekdays, on Shabbat and on holidays, our lives should be filled with "God awareness."

To illustrate this, let us look at a typical day in the life of an observant Jew. He awakens in the morning and he recites the *Modeh Ani* prayer thanking God for returning his soul and the gift of life. Presently, whether at home or in the synagogue, he begins his day by reciting the *Shaharit* service offering praise, petition, and thanksgiving to God. Having completed his prayers, he sits down to breakfast and recites the appropriate benedictions before and after eating. He then sets out to meet the world. Whether he is a laborer, a professional, or a business person, blue collar or white collar, he knows that in terms of his interpersonal relationships with his fellow man he must adhere to the *mitzvot*, the guidelines of the Torah. If he is a professional, he must deal honestly with his colleagues and clients. If he is in business, he must refrain from outright theft, chicanery, cheating, or in any way taking undue advantage of his competitors or customers. Lunchtime arrives, and he must not forget to recite the proper benedictions before and after his lunch. He must make time during his busy day for the *Minhah* service.

Seeing lofty mountains, beautiful trees, the new spring blossoms, or the rainbow after a rain, smelling the aroma of fragrant plants or spices, all of these things that beautify the world call for a proper benediction to acknowledge that they derive from God. Sitting down to dinner he once again recites benedictions before and after the meal. Before long it is night, time for the *Maariv* service. Torah law must guide even his

---

36. I. Epstein, *The Faith of Judaism* (London: Soncino Press, 1954), p. 68.

interaction with his wife and children, relatives and friends. And when he retires after an eventful day, he must confront God once more to recite the special prayers before retiring, among which are the beautiful words, "Let not my thoughts trouble me, nor evil dreams nor evil fancies, but let my rest be perfect before You. Lighten my eyes lest I sleep the sleep of death, for it is You who give light to the apple of the eye." Last, but most important, he must set aside time during the day to study Torah, the ultimate encounter with God.

Whether he is consciously aware of it or not, the observant Jew is continuously relating to God. E. Berkovits writes, "Every important event in the life of the Jew is brought under the dominance of the law. There seems to be no niche or nook into which the law has not penetrated . . . The Jew is indeed surrounded by *mitzvot* on all sides."[37] The goal, of course, is to make the Jew aware of the fact that each time he fulfills a *mitzvah* he is relating to God. Too many of us fulfill the *mitzvot* simply by force of habit. Focused on the fear of punishment rather than the beauty of fulfillment, we fail to set aside sufficient time to concentrate properly on the act. Consequently, fulfillment is never appreciated as a genuine religious experience. That is not to say that fulfillment of a *mitzvah* without proper concentration is valueless. Routinization has some distinct advantages even with regard to *mitzvot*. It teaches self-discipline, and builds a sense of confidence and security. Our sages taught: "A man should always occupy himself with Torah and good deeds, though it is not for their own sake, for out of [doing good] with an ulterior motive there comes [doing good] for its own sake."[38] It is easier to correct the flaws of an existing life style than to have to embark on a new life style altogether.

By relating to God, the observant Jew gives meaning, direction, and interest to his life. Whether in thought or in deed, he is preoccupied with *mitzvot* for the better part of the day. King David wrote, "I have put the Lord before me at all times" (Psalms 16:8). This is the nobility of *mitzvot*.

---

37. Ibid., p. 89.
38. *Pesahim* 50b.

INDEX

613 commandments, 183, 254

Aaron, 29, 121–124, 127–128, 130, 132–134, 142, 144, 146, 154, 156–158, 160, 170
   children of, 170
Abba, R., 161
Abel, 44–45
Abraham, 4–5, 9, 11–12, 49, 54–61, 63–84, 86–87, 89, 91, 106, 221
Abram, 14, 58, 63, 68 *See Also* Abraham
Abravanel, Isaac, 43
Adam, 13, 45–46, 51
Adam and Eve
   temptation of, 42–43
Alenu L'shabeah, 252
Amalek, 143–144
Amaziah, 224
Amidah, 240–242, 250–254
Amos, 224
Anthropomorphism
   in the Bible, 24–29, 48
Arvit, 253
Asher, 95
Avihu, 154
Avimelekh, 73, 76–77, 85–86
Aviram, 169

Babel, Tower of, 52–54
Bahya Ibn Pakuda, 196, 211
Balaam, 171–174, 188, 214, 220
Balak, 171, 173–174
Barukh Hashim L'olam, 253–254
Behavior
   human, 213
   of man, 23, 43
   proper, 23–24
Benjamin, 109–110
Berkovits, R. Dr. Eliezer, 11, 28, 187, 189, 254, 256
Betuel, 81, 83, 89
Bezalel, 164–165
Bilhah, 94
Borekhu, 253

Cain, 44–45
   descendents of, 47
Canaan, land of, 12, 55, 58, 60, 63–64, 67, 85, 104, 126
Circumcision, 67–70, 74
Creation
   of earth, 193
   of heaven and earth, 191
   of light and dark, 194
   of man, 39–42

Creation *(cont.)*
   story of, 39, 44, 156
   of universe, 197–198
   of woman, 41
   of the world, 192

Dan, 94
Datan, 169
David, 220, 245, 256
Death, 233
Deism, 40, 118
Dinah, 95, 102–103
Divine attributes, 4, 25–29, 37, 98, 145
   authority, 6
   awesomeness, 182
   compassion, 4, 8–10, 12, 18, 31–33, 36, 40–41, 44–45, 48–54, 58–66, 70–72, 74, 76, 80, 84–86, 90–91, 96, 99–100, 106–107, 109, 115–117, 119–122, 124, 127–128, 131, 139–140, 143, 149–150, 156–159, 166–167, 172–173, 175, 177–179, 182, 197, 200, 203–204, 206, 219, 233
   concern, 10
   creativity, 6–7, 47, 94, 165–166, 191
   erekh apayim, 33
   faithfulness, 10, 55–56, 182, 191
   faithfulness to thousandth generation, 180
   fatherliness, 18–21, 181
   firmness, 17
   forgiveness, 31, 35–36, 206
   graciousness, 32–33, 162
   hanun, 32–33
   holiness, 16
   immanence, 8, 11, 20, 40, 141, 204, 210–211, 236
   judge, 148–149, 154, 158
   judgment, 107, 110, 114, 131, 139–140, 144, 152–153, 168, 174, 178, 182
   justice, 4–5, 8, 12, 48, 50–51, 69–73, 75–77, 88, 90–97, 99, 101, 108, 115–117, 119, 121–122, 138, 147, 177, 179, 182, 184, 186, 189, 200, 233
   kindness, 34–35, 184
   kingship, 19–20
   law-giver, 148–149, 154, 158
   long-suffering, 33, 180, 188–189, 219
   love, 12
   loving-kindness, 5, 55, 67, 182, 206–207, 238
   and man's behavior, 23–24
   mercy, 9, 12, 15, 32, 72–73, 79, 96, 179
   might, 182
   morality, 18
   omnipotence, 4–6, 12, 15, 17, 55, 62, 89, 102–104, 112, 117, 120, 128, 131, 159, 184, 194, 212, 215, 238
   omniscience, 238
   patience, 33–34
   protection, 96, 101
   providence, 4, 12, 59, 61, 70, 88, 91, 94, 106, 108–109, 125, 130, 143, 146, 148–149, 158, 163, 166, 168, 174, 178, 180, 183, 203, 238
   rahum, 32
   rav emet, 34
   rav hesed, 34
   righteousness, 131, 238
   salvation, 5
   self-sufficiency, 14–15, 55, 89, 109, 117, 120
   strength, 17
   thirteen, 30–31
   transcendence, 8, 11, 20, 204, 210–211
   truthfulness, 34
   understanding, 65
   uniqueness, 16

Index

Divine compassion
  and God's love, 202
  and God's role as father, 203–204
  and goodness of God, 202
  and orphans and widows, 204–205
  and poverty, 207
  and prayer, 212
  and righteous people, 212
  and sin, 206
  and wealth, 205
Divine exclusivity, 163–165
Divine intervention, 59, 62, 125–126, 128–139
Divine judgment
  and hashgahah k'lalit, 198–199
  and hashgahah p'ratit, 199
  and righteous people, 200
  and wicked people, 200
Divine names, 3, 21, 56, 185
  Adon, 164
  Adney, 3, 11–12, 62, 71, 119–120, 122, 124, 153, 162, 181
  Adney E-lohim, 177
  Adney Havayah, 177, 181
  Av, 3, 18–20
  Ehyeh, 3, 11, 13–14, 116–117, 122
  Ehyeh Asher Ehyeh, 3, 12–13, 116–118, 122
  E-l, 3–5, 32, 66, 103, 111–112, 140, 164, 174, 178–180, 182, 200
  E-l Elyon, 5
  El Rahum, 179
  E-l Sha-dai, 55, 66–67, 89, 104, 117
  E-li, 139
  E-loha, 6–7
  E-lohe Yisrael, 4, 123, 164, 166
  E-lohim, 3, 5–9, 11–12, 39–42, 44–48, 50–52, 59, 64, 67–70, 72–79, 88, 90–104, 107–108, 110–112, 114, 116, 119, 121, 130–133, 136, 138, 144–156, 158, 161, 165–166, 168, 171–173, 177–179, 181–182, 192, 200

God, 3–4
HaTzur, 184
Havayah, 3, 7–12, 31–32, 39–53, 58–67, 69–74, 79–86, 88, 90–92, 94–97, 99–100, 106–107, 115–117, 119–150, 152–173, 175–183, 192, 200–201
Havayah E-l Elyon, 61
Havayah E-lohe Yisrael, 159
Havayah E-lohekha, 176
Havayah E-lohehem, 178
Kadosh, 3, 15–16
Lord, 3–4, 8–9
Melekh, 3, 18–20
Sha-dai, 3, 14–15, 109, 132, 174
Tsur, 3, 17
Divine promise, 10, 12, 56, 63–64, 66–70, 74, 77–78, 83, 100–101, 104, 134, 167–168
Divine providence, 39, 45, 50, 161, 189–191
  and barren women, 207
  and compassion, 185
  and creation of light and dark, 194
  and creation of the universe, 197
  and creation of the world, 192–193
  and divine judgment, 198–200
  and divine punishment, 194
  and food, 196
  hashgahah k'lalit, 185–186
  hashgahah p'ratit, 186
  and human behavior, 213
  and human intellect, 209–210
  and human perfection, 186, 199, 201–202
  and Israel, 216
  and miracles, 207–208
  and nature, 197
  and poverty, 207
  and predestination, 187–188
  and protection of the unaware, 208
  and rain, 193–195

Divine promise *(cont.)*
   and restoration of Jewish people to homeland, 215
   and righteous people, 199–201, 203, 208–209, 213
   and sacrifices, 213
   and the seas, 192–193
   and the stars, 195
   and the Torah, 254
   and water, 195
   and wicked people, 201, 213

Eldad, 220
Eliezer, 81–83, 145, 221
Eliezer, R., 135, 232
Eliezer, R., son of R. Jose, 232
Enokh, 46–47, 49
Enosh, 45
Ephraim, 108
Epstein, I., 224, 255
Esau, 85, 87–89, 96, 100–103
Eve, 44
Ezekiel, 220
   prophecy of, 230–233
   and valley of dry bones, 231–233

False gods, 152
Festivals, 153, 164
Flood, The, 50–52
Free will, 9, 31, 92, 187–188, 193, 239–240, 246
Fringes, law of the, 168

Gad, 95
Gershom, 114, 145
God
   of Abraham and Isaac, 99–100
   of Abraham, Isaac and Jacob, 115–116
   of all people, 7
   covenant with Israel, 163, 178, 180
   as creator, 191
   of evil, 132–133
   of good, 132–133
   of Israel, 4, 7, 154
   love of, 254–255
   misconceptions concerning, 25, 28
   and potentiality, 24
   and prayer, 211
   relating to man, 217
   relationship to man, 239
   reviling, 153
Golden calf, 29, 156–159, 161, 181
Graetz, Heinrich, 226

Hagar, 64–66, 75–76, 83, 94
Haggai, 225
Halevi, J., 14, 16, 209
Ham, 49
Hamor, 102
Hanina, R., 186, 238
Hashkivenu, 253
Heavens, 190, 192, 198
Hirsch, S. R., 16–17, 34–36, 43, 88–89, 93, 118, 120, 122, 125, 127, 140, 143–144, 147, 154, 156, 164, 169, 173, 191, 195–197, 202, 204–206, 253
Homer, 17
Human sacrifice, 167
Huna, R., 188

Idolatry, 36–37, 45, 57, 153, 156, 163–164, 177–178, 183
Iniquity, 35
   of fathers visited on children, 36–37
Isaac, 9, 55–56, 69, 74–76, 80–91, 94
   sacrifice of, 77–79
Isaiah, 76, 220, 226–227, 233
Ishmael, 66, 69, 75–76
Israel, 101, 104–105, 111–112 *See Also* Jacob
   children of, 113–114

Index

Israel
    as firstborn son, 122
    land of, 58
    nation of, 74, 95, 117, 214
    people of, 215
    place in the world, 215–216
Israelites
    battle against Amalek, 144
    battles with Edom, 171
    blessing of by Balaam, 174
    chosen people, 183, 214
    covenant with God, 163, 178, 180
    cursing of by Balaam, 172–174
    in the desert, 142–143, 169–170
    exodus from Egypt, 135–143, 145
    judges of, 147
    at Mara, 141–142
    reception of the Torah, 161
    at the Red Sea, 138–140
    redemption from Egypt, 5, 10, 13, 115–117, 119, 121, 123–128, 130–132, 134–135, 157, 169
    sacrifices of, 146–147
    at Sinai, 148–149, 151, 154–155, 157–159, 161
    stiffnecked people, 160, 162–163
Issachar, 95
Its'haki, R. Solomon *See* Rashi

Jacob, 4, 9, 55–56, 85, 87–100, 102–103, 105, 109–112, 214, 221, 229, 241
    renaming of, 101, 104
Jacob's ladder, 90–91
Japheth, 49
Jehoiachin, King, 230
Jeremiah, 222, 228–230
Jethro, 145–147
Jewish dietary laws, 165
Jewish people
    chosen by God, 214–215
    relation to God, 235–236
Johanan, R., 204

Jose, R., 237
Joseph, 95, 104–113
Joshua, 144, 221
Joshua, R., 135
Judah, 93, 109–110, 241
Judah, R., 165, 197, 232
Judah b. Bathyra, R., 232

Kaddish, 252
Kaddish D'Rabbanan, 249–250
Keriat Shema, 251, 253
Keturah, 83
Korah, rebellion of, 168–169

Laban, 82–83, 89, 93, 95–100, 229
Leah, 93–97, 229, 241
Lemech, 47
Levi, 93, 102–103
Levites, 159–160, 170
Lot, 60, 72

Ma'ariv, 246, 252–253, 255
Maimonides, 8, 13–14, 24, 27–28, 36, 57, 162, 186, 198, 201, 203, 213, 217–219, 221, 225, 243–244
Malachi, 226
Malchizedek, 4
Man
    creation of, 39–42
    relation to God, 235
Manashe, King, 229
Manasseh, 108
Manslaughter, 152
Marital laws, 166
Medad, 220
Messianic era, 227–228, 233
Methuselah, 46
Minhah, 246, 251–253
Miriam, 114
Mitzvot, 142, 223, 235–236, 254–256 *See Also* Commandments
Molekh, law of, 166–167

Monotheism, 4, 6, 24, 150
   ethical, 57, 77, 84, 179
Moses, 3, 9–10, 12–13, 15, 27, 29, 33, 117–118, 151, 154, 162–163, 168–171, 175–184, 217, 221–224, 237–238
   calling of by God, 115–116, 119–120
   and the exodus from Egypt, 135–145
   and Jethro, 145–147
   message to pharaoh, 121–125
   and miracles, 225
   rescue of from Nile, 114
   role in redemption of Israel, 126–134
   at Sinai, 148–149, 151, 154–155, 157–161
Moshe *See* Moses
Multiplicity, 4, 7
Mussaf, 246, 254

Nadav, 154
Naftali, 95
Nahmanides, 5, 30, 117, 163, 187
Names, 1–2
   divine, 3, 21, 56
Naming
   a child, 2
Nature, law of, 6, 15, 91
Ne'ilah, 246
Nehemiah, 198
Nehemiah, R., 232
Noah, 13, 46–47, 49–53, 55–57
Noahide commandments, 41

Peleg, 53
Peor, 173–174
Pesah, 164
Pesuke D'Zimrah, 249–250, 254
Pharaoh, 107–108, 113, 120–124, 126–137
Phikhol, 77
Plagues on Eqypt, 129, 132–134, 142
Potiphar, 105–106

Prayer, 211–215
   evening, 256
   and excess praise, 238
   and kavanah, 243–244
   and meditation, 244
   Modeh Ani, 255
   obligatory, 240–241
   and petition, 238–242
   posture of, 244–245
   and praise, 237–239, 242
   and relating to God, 236
   of Shaharit, 247–248
   and thanksgiving, 241–242
   themes of, 244–246
Prayer service, 236, 240
Prophecy, 217
   degrees of, 219–221
   and dreams, 221
   function of, 218
   and visions, 221
Prophet
   attributes of, 223
   in Israel, 226
   and Moses, 223
   nature of, 218–219, 222, 224–225
   and signs, 224

Rabbah b. Bar Hanah, 238
Rachel, 93–98, 109, 229
Rashi, 5, 9, 17, 33, 53, 55–57, 69, 76, 124, 140
Rav, 165, 197, 232
Reason, 78–79
Rebecca, 81–85, 87, 89, 93–94, 207
Redemption, 150
Repentance, 10, 31, 33, 36, 179, 189, 211, 229–230
Reuben, 93, 105–106, 109
Reuel, 114
Revelation, 78–80, 151
   of the Torah, 126, 148

Index

Saadya Gaon, 26
Sabbath, 150 *See Also* Shabbat
Samuel, 220, 232
Sarah, 54, 57–59, 64–70, 73–75, 80, 83, 94–95, 207
Seth, 45–47
    descendents of, 47
Sexuality
    illicit, 166
Shabbat, 155–156
Shaharit, 246, 250–255
    benedictions, 247–248
    prayer, 247
    and ritual of sacrifice, 248–249
Shakespeare, William, 1
Shavuot, 164
Shekhem, 102
Shem, 49, 57, 85
Shem Hameforash, 7
Shem HaMeyuhad, 7
Simeon, 93, 102–103, 109
Simlai, R., 237
Sin, 35
Social laws, 152
Sodom and Gomorrah, 70–72
Solomon, 182, 208, 210, 220
Soloveitchik, R. Dr. J. B., 13
Sukkot, 164

Tahanun, 252
Ten Commandments, 149, 151–152, 176
Terah, 56
Teshuvah, 10, 31, 188–189
Tetragrammaton, 8, 233
Tokhahah, 167
Torah
    acceptance of, 154, 161
    revelation of, 126, 148
Transgression, 35
Tsisit, 168

Uzziah, King, 226

War, 144
Woman
    creation of, 41

Yitzhak, R., 12
Yokheved, 114

Zechariah, 220, 225
Zilpah, 95
Zipporah, 114, 145

About the Author

Dr. Walter Orenstein is a graduate of Yeshiva University, from which institution he earned his B.R.E., M.A., and D.H.L. degrees. He is also an ordained rabbi. He was actively involved in Jewish studies at Yeshiva University for thirteen years, teaching in the James Striar School, Stern College, and the Teachers Institute of Women, where he also served as chairman of the faculty. In 1974 he was listed in "Outstanding Educators of America" and in 1983 he received the coveted "Senior Professor Award" from the students at Stern College. Dr. Orenstein has lectured widely in adult education programs in some of the foremost synagogues in New York. He is the author of *The Transformation of a Skeptic: A Jewish Perspective* (Aronson) and *Letters to my Daughter: A Father Writes about Torah and the Jewish Woman* (Aronson).